RENATO MIRACCO

OSCAR WILDE'S
ITALIAN DREAM 1875—1900

The Infamous St. Oscar of Oxford, Poet and Martyr
Undecided between the Cloister and the Café

Introduction
PHILIP KENNICOTT

Contents

As the cultural understanding of Oscar Wilde evolved over the past 120 years, from a disgraced aesthete with unsavory sexual habits to a beloved hero of the modern gay-rights movement, a great many details of his life fell by the wayside. The narrative of his downfall became simpler and more tragic, and the complexity of his character was burnished into something more palatable to popular audiences. In films such as Ken Hughes' 1960 *The Trials of Oscar Wilde*, and Brian Gilbert's 1997 *Wilde*, the drama focused on the years just before and during his downfall, the disastrous decision in 1895 to sue the Marquess of Queensberry for libel, the failure of his case and his two subsequent trials and imprisonment for gross indecency. As an Irish martyr to English priggishness, Wilde's story seems to end with his exile to France, following his 1897 release from prison. Richard Ellmann's 1987 biography of the writer refers to the last seasons of Wilde's life as *The Leftover Years*.

By focusing on Wilde's visits and sojourns in Italy (as well as trips to Algiers, Switzerland and Greece, and long stays in Paris and the south of France), *Oscar Wilde's Italian Dream* gives readers a much more nuanced sense of these "leftover years." It is true that by 1897, Wilde had published his last major work, the extended poem *The Ballad of Reading Gaol*, and he often professed himself written out, with nothing more to say and no burning need to focus again on literature. But as the letters, reminiscences, magazine and newspaper articles and other documents gathered together by Renato Miracco demonstrate, Wilde was far from a spent force after his incarceration. He supervised the publication of the ballad with minute care, a keen eye to its layout and presentation, an exacting ear for every syllable of the text and a canny sense of how it was to be marketed (spurred by his own desperate poverty through many of these months). In 1898, he wrote a long, smart and passionate letter on the subject of prisoners' rights to the *Daily Chronicle*, succinctly laying out the superfluous cruelties—hunger, insomnia, disease and isolation of prisoners from mental stimulation—which made English prisons not only inhumane, but socially counterproductive. He devoted himself to photography: "My photographs are now so good that in my moments of mental depression (alas! Not rare) I think that I was intended to be a photographer," he wrote to his friend Robbie Ross in the last year of his life. His conversational powers were diminished (by alcohol, depression and ultimately illness), but they could still be incandescent. "Oscar is very amusing as usual," Ross wrote in 1898, while noting that he was "very abstracted at times."
But Miracco's texts are not limited to these final years. He has gathered documents of Wilde's earliest encounters with Italy and southern Europe, when the young, and

already reckless Oxford student visited the wellsprings of the two dominant spiritual forces in his life: Catholic Italy (and especially Rome) and the larger, classical world of paganism. There was an 1875 trip to Italy with his classics tutor from Trinity College in Dublin, and another visit in 1877 which included a pilgrimage to the palace of Agamemnon and a private audience with Pope Pius IX. Although relatively brief, these trips had an outsized importance in Wilde's life, and the collation of his public persona. The impulse to Catholicism was strong throughout Wilde's life and he received a conditional baptism into the Catholic Church on his deathbed. His indecision on religious matters, maddening to his close Catholic friends and unnerving to the Anglican professors who had marked him out for a prominent career, became a template for his life. He confronted a dualistic world, Catholic and Protestant, respectable and reprobate, full of saints and sinners, yet he did not seek to resolve the contradictions. To the extent that his aestheticism can be accounted a coherent philosophy of life, it amounted to this: beauty and meaning are found in extremes, in the polar opposites of our existence, in purity and degradation. Paradox was the only way to express this idea, and articulate his resolute commitment to irresolution. Accepting paradox was the fundament of good taste, and the middle of life was drab: "The Catholic Church is for saints and sinners alone. For respectable people the Anglican Church will do."

So Italy, and the larger world outside of London, was essential to the formation of Wilde's identity, and its reformation in his last years. But these letters also reveal the most important fact of Wilde's character that is often elided in popular treatments of his life: it was always a work in progress. He had no fixed identity, he was given to borrowing, refining and repeating the *bon mots* and aesthetic discourses which led many to believe (including Wilde himself) that he brought genius to his talk and mere talent to his writing. During his 1875 visit to Italy, he wrote letters to both his father and mother, burnishing his anecdotes and observations, and demonstrating both a maddening confidence and inconsistency in his precocious judgments on art. "Titian's *Assumption* certainly the best picture in Italy," he wrote to his mother, only to add a few paragraphs later: "Giotto [. . .] is the first of all painters." He detected mediocrity in a new opera, was moved by a funeral procession, dismissed the cathedral of Milan ("an awful failure. Outside the design is monstrous and inartistic") and gloried with a tourist's simple enthusiasm in the sights of Venice ("Wonderful colour everywhere—windows hung with striped yellow awnings, domes and churches of white marble, campaniles of red brick, great gondolas filled with fruit and vegetables going to the Rialto where the market is").
Even in these earliest letters, and later ones from the 1877 visit, we see Wilde divided in himself, and using his powers of aesthetic observation and judgment to distract

the world (and likely his own keen powers of self-assessment) from those divisions. "He is an aesthetic to the last degree [. . .] and capable of talking a good deal of nonsense," wrote one of his traveling companions, adding, "but for all that a very sensible, well-informed, charming man." Italy and Greece, in particular, offered visitors such as Wilde a landscape which animated and sometimes exacerbated their social and personal conflicts. Latin and Greek formed the basis of a proper English gentleman's education, and the ancient world offered exemplars for the democratic and imperialist leanings inherent in English geopolitical ambition at the time. Yet Rome and Greece were the sources both of civilization—as it was defined in London—and decadence, models both to admire and spurn. A visitor from Great Britain could travel these lands with wide-eyed wonder and confident condescension, luxuriating in its riches, judging its content, and indulging its blandishments all at the same time.

And it offered an emerging subculture of self-identified Uranians, or gay men, a great deal of sexual liberty unavailable at home. Cities like Naples had a particularly unsavory reputation as gathering places for homosexual men, but there were many reasons to go to Naples that had nothing to do with sex. The grand tour of Italy had been a status marker in England for at least a century. "The name of Italy has for the educated world a kind of magic sound," wrote one visitor. But Naples and Sicily also attracted men such as the poet Theodore Wratislaw, who wrote a famous, early tribute to homoeroticism, a poem called "To Sicilian Boy," and the photographer the Baron von Gloeden, who took up residence in Taormina, and produced sensual and erotic photos of young men and boys, often naked, with classical trappings. The pursuit of something respectable and cherished—the classical ideal—brought some visitors into wonderfully dangerous proximity with something widely loathed: same-sex eroticism. The particular *milieu* of London, in which Wilde lived, loved and was ultimately disgraced, was in large part a creation of expatriates who had fled the North for the South from the North, who made it possible, for a while, for gay men to hide in plain sight so long as they spoke the language of 'Hellenism.'

No wonder, then, that during a period in which emerging nationalism confronted what we would call larger forces of globalism, same-sex desire became fraught with political implications. Friedrich Engels, who spent much of his life in England championing the greatest transnational political movement of the age, communism, saw homosexuality as a threat: "Pederasts are beginning to count themselves and are discovering that they are a power in the State. All they lacked was organization." They weren't just a perceived threat within the state, they were emerging as a subculture that crossed perilous lines of class, religion and national affiliation. There is, perhaps,

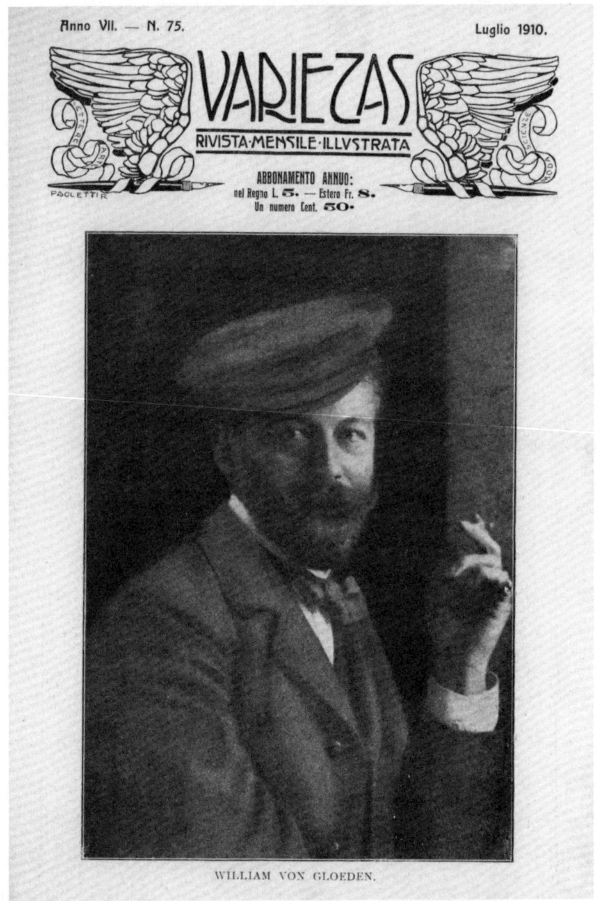

WILLIAM VON GLOEDEN.

a thread that connects the emergence, across national boundaries, of self-identified Uranian men and lesbian women in 19th-century Europe to the fears that animate today's debates over nationalism, pan-European identity and even Brexit.

Those debates would not likely have interested Wilde as political or sociological phenomena. But one senses in his letters, and writings, that sexuality was closely bound up with his crises of identity, as an Irishman, as a cosmopolitan artist, as a European, and as an Anglican with powerful Catholic leanings. And it was particularly difficult when it came to his class identity, as a product of a highly educated, middle-class Irish family, a son of Oxford, and a man deeply self-conscious about his status as a gentleman. The central and seminal crisis of Wilde's character was his deep reluctance to leave behind his hard-won respectability. He could push to the very limits of flamboyance and provocation, but his moral code—articulated with an outsider's preciosity—was always that of "a gentleman." Even in the lowest moments of his life, abandoned by his lover Lord Alfred Douglas, and desperately poor, he appealed to Douglas for money that had been promised him on the basis of "honour," and was horrified that Douglas responded, "lots of gentlemen don't pay their debts of honour." It is in those moments when Wilde's inner recognition of his sexual desires is at the greatest conflict with his inability to step outside of gentlemanly respectability that he becomes most tragic, articulate, and absurd. In the famous "the love that dare not speak its name" response during his first criminal trial, Wilde cites Michelangelo and Plato, twin poles of his dualistic relation to Christian and classical world, and he rises to the zenith of his eloquence: "It is beautiful, it is fine, it is the noblest form of affection. There is nothing unnatural about it. It is intellectual and it repeatedly exists between an elder and a younger man, when the elder man has intellect, and the younger man has all the joy, hope and glamour of life before him." The speech is true in every particular, and a masterful example of Wilde's gentlemanly obfuscation.

Wilde could not abandon his self-definition as a gentleman, but he could have his status as gentleman torn away. His trial and ignominy gave him something he could not have given himself: a keener sense of his own values, and the ability to embrace identities that would have been untenable during his London years. As he considered publications in which he might debut the ballad, he wrote, "*Reynolds* is an organ that appeals directly to the criminal classes, so my audience is gathered together for me." He playfully and ruefully acknowledged that he had now affiliated himself with the lowest rungs of the social world: "I am now simply an ordinary pauper of a rather low order." But he grasped at an identity as a homosexual man that transcended the aestheticism of his past and was analogized to national identity: "A patriot put in prison for loving his country loves his country, and a poet in prison for loving boys loves boys." His time out of London—his exile—brought with it a proliferating sense of multiple national identities. One day, in April 1900, he "found that the Vatican Gardens were open to the Bohemian and the Portuguese pilgrims. I at once spoke both languages fluently, explained that my English dress was a form of penance, and entered that waste, desolate park."

He also sensed himself not just as a target for international opprobrium, but for international scrutiny. "I am also a pathological problem in the eyes of German scientists" and, "in their works I am tabulated, and come under the law of averages!" Wilde's distress at this objectification was palpable. He was no longer the man who was constantly improvising and refining the identity of the celebrated author Oscar Wilde; he was a subject for study and analysis, a legal and social problem, an international vagabond, and a poet who could no longer publish under his own name.

Late in life, he said of another poet who suffered disgrace and imprisonment after falling disastrously in love with a young man: "The century will have two vagabonds, Paul Verlaine and me." It's a curious choice of word, vagabond. Verlaine traveled and spent years outside of France, yet returned to Paris and died there. It's not the literal meaning of the word Wilde is after, but a larger sense of deracination, or perhaps even post-national identity. Cast out of London, shorn of his respectability and reduced to penury, Wilde wasn't just an international scandal, he was face to face with the multiplicity of identities that he had, for some time, managed to suppress under the cloak of his provocative aestheticism.

It wouldn't be easy bringing order to this chaos, and in the final years of Wilde's life, one senses him surfing, almost passively, on the currents of his fractured self. Sometimes he reasserted the old confidence of his impeccable taste, as if the old habit of standing in judgment of beautiful things could bring new coherence to his life. "I became again Pre-Raphaelite, and loathed the ordinary Impressionists," he wrote to Ross, after visiting Palermo. The Borghese Gardens were "too lovely for words," the Byzantine mosaics in Palermo "the marvel of marvels." He also indulged recriminations against Douglas, brooded over perceived slights from even his closest friends, anxiously awaited the world's verdict on his last poem, and wheedled friends incessantly for money. In a letter to Ross, he declared himself torn between royalist and papal affiliations, lamenting that he reflexively doffed his hat when the Italian king passed by: "It was only when the King had passed that I remembered I was Papista."

That anecdote of conflicted identity leads directly to another. In 1900, he found himself in an Italian café, surrounded by students who had recognized the infamous Oscar Wilde. "To their great delight I always denied my identity. On being asked my name, I said every man has only one name. They asked me what name that was. 'Io' was my answer. This was regarded as a wonderful reply, containing in it all philosophy." He was bemused that his interlocutors thought the response profound. But perhaps a man who had spent his life using humor and paradox to hide his fundamental irresolution about his identity, his affiliations, his religious inclinations and sexuality, had accidentally hit upon a truth. His gift for paradox and obscurantism struck home. He thought he was being his old self, flippant and amusing, but they found it meaningful. At the end of a short, brilliant, complicated and tragic life, he had for once gathered up what Thoreau called "the parcel of vain strivings tied" and given them a momentary flash of coherence. He was no longer Oscar Wilde, but he had successfully named himself, asserted an identity, and he did it on foreign soil in a foreign tongue.

Philip Kennicott

In 1981 Gaetano Colonnese, a wise and diligent Neapolitan publisher, suggested to me that I write the chronicle of Oscar Wilde's Neapolitan stay. I lived between Paris and London at the time and found myself roaming betwixt the Bibliothèque Nationale de France and the British Museum in search of documents and articles. The book came out, in various editions, with the title *Verso il Sole - Chronicle of the Neapolitan Stay of Oscar Wilde*, and fourteen radio episodes were also produced for RAI (Italian Radio and Television). But the "Wilde thought," during all these years, writing more than seventy volumes between catalogs and books, continued to be strangely present in my various work experiences as curator for the Metropolitan Museum, as cultural attaché to the embassy of Washington DC, or lecturer for the universities of South America. There was something I couldn't grasp, and the voice of Wilde came back to me asking at the end of his verdict: "And I? May I say anything, Your Excellency?" At that time his trial was an incredible scandal that went beyond all that was real because it was emblematic of a society that wanted to 'punish' any proclaimed diversity. In twenty years from 1875 to 1895 his was certainly scandalous: it was intolerable because he was a public figure, a man who 'lived' as a homosexual and did not 'hide' his being such. Certainly, his personality, more than his works, have opened the way to a new way of thinking as well as to a kind of literature with a homosexual theme that goes beyond the confines in which it was circumscribed, and begins to reclaim a well-deserved space of its own. Starting with Xavier Mayne who published his book *The Intersexes* in Naples in 1909, and the book *Imre* (set in the Balkans, which tells the tale of a love story between a civilian and a soldier), and with Arnaldo De Lisle, pseudonym for Giuseppe Rocco, faithful friend of Wilde's, who published *L'uomo Femmina* in 1899. This underground literature would deserve, in the future, more careful consideration! Often in this last period, Wilde considers his life to be a continuous search that adheres more and more to reality and even words acquire another meaning for him: just think of the letter to Frank Harris of June 13, 1897 when he says:

Words, now, to me signify things, actualities, real emotions, realized thoughts.

Or when he says:

I wrote when I didn't know about life. Now that I know the meaning of life, I have nothing more to write. Life cannot be written, life can only be lived."

Or, when he declared to his friend Anna, in tears, a few months before dying, "I found my soul. I was happy in prison because I found my soul." "At the very beginning, the homosexual component of Wilde's aestheticism resides in the desperate attempt to escape the alternative of wearing a bourgeois mask or to interpret the part of the scandal by resolving, in that way dissolving himself, in his own existence in an aesthetic reality of the reality that becomes a work of art."[1] Which coincides with what Wilde advocates before prison—"revealing art and hiding the artist is the purpose of art." But slowly, in Wilde, the pairing of art and sin takes the upper hand: partly because it is in this direction that Oscar glimpses a different form of knowledge. He feels that society is changing, that he can "dare" make his character a "more complex work of art." Beginning with opposing Bosie's father's provocation and refusing to flee to France after the verdict as he had previously told André Gide in Algiers. It is in fact in Naples, among masterpieces of marble and flesh, as he himself will say, that he finishes *The Ballad of Reading Gaol*, which is his most complete, most modern literary expression, together with *De Profundis* and the letters of his final period, of the inner passage that has taken place, subtending the intimate search "to achieve the perfection of my temperament and my soul" (September 23, 1897). Wilde desperately seeks a new identity, well aware that his soul is no longer suited to his old shell: Sebastian Melmoth, his pseudonym after prison, will be an anarchist who, laughing it off, will squander his brilliance in words, or rather will make of this a rule of life, deliberately flaunting those weaknesses that made the "pursuit of perfection" bearable: "alcohol and boys." But he also has the need to find a new spirituality. He wants, as he wrote to Robert Ross on May 31, 1897, to establish a relationship with religion, hoping that religion would give him an identity, although he is well aware that

> The Artist must live the complete life, must accept it as it comes and stands like an angel before him, with his drawn and two-edged sword. I have had great success. I have had great failure. I have learned the value of each; and I know that failure means more, always must mean, more than success. Why then should I complain? I have at last come to the complete life which every artist must experience in order to join beauty in trust. (Oscar Wilde, 1899, in conversation with Laurence Housman)

Renato Miracco

---

[1] Hans Mayer, *Außenseiter* (Frankfurt am Main: Suhrkamp, 1975).

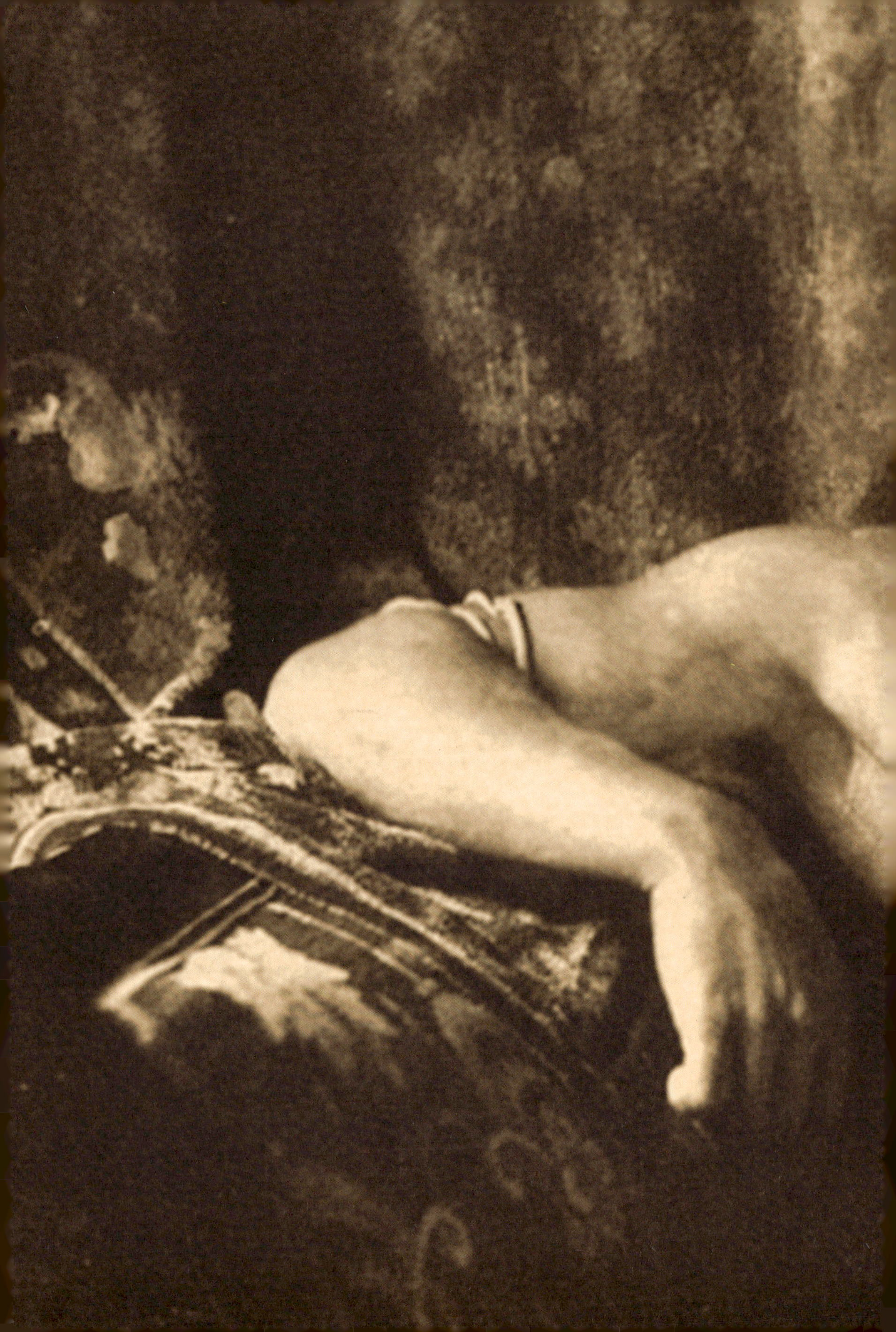

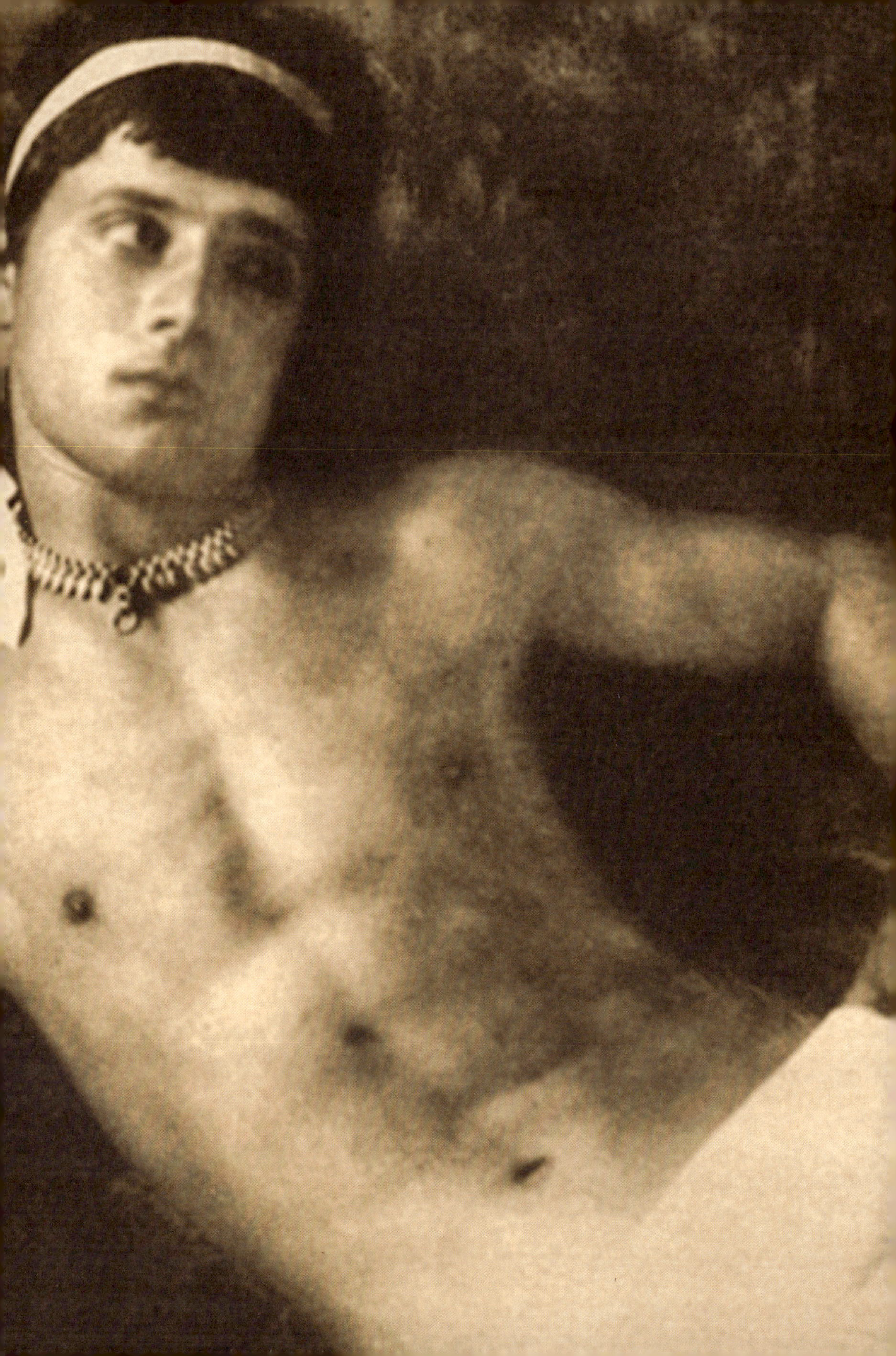

We cannot continue our story if we don't mention two of the co-protagonists: Robert Ross and Alfred Douglas.

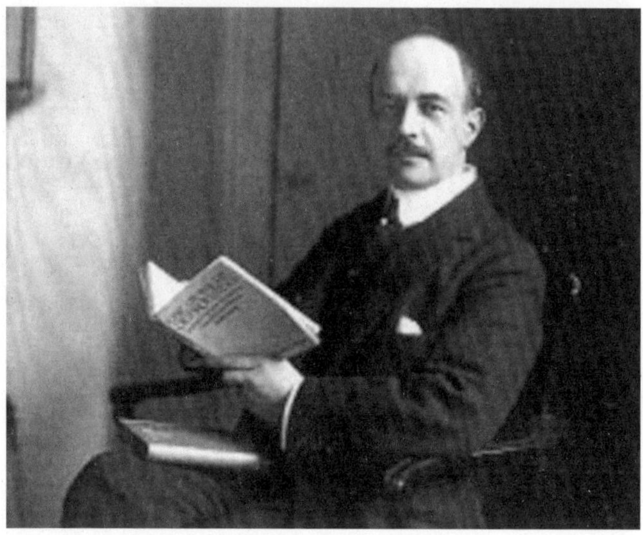

Robert Baldwin Ross (May 25 1869–October 5 1918) was a Canadian journalist, art critic and art dealer, best known for his relationship with Oscar Wilde, to whom he was a devoted friend, lover and literary executor. He was openly gay, a fact that didn't go over very well in Victorian England, busy at the time with passing bigoted laws against homosexuality. The exact circumstances as to where and how the two met are unknown. Frank Harris tells that one day Oscar told him that he had met Robert in a public lavatory often used as a venue for gay prostitution. Certainly, Robbie was sexually precocious, and he loved older men and had an acceptance of himself and his sexuality.

His devoted friendship and love was recognized by Oscar in some of his letters:

> I shall now live as the Infamous St Oscar of Oxford, Poet and Martyr. My niche is just below that of the Blessed St Robert of Phillimore, Lover and Martyr—a saint known in *Hagiographia* for his extraordinary power, not in resisting, but in supplying temptations to others.
> Letter to R.B. Ross, March 18 1898.

---

[2] Alfred Douglas, *Autobiography of Alfred Douglas* (London: Martin Secker, 1929).

And another:

> When I was brought down from my prison to the Court of Bankruptcy between two policemen, Robbie waited in the long dreary corridor, that before the whole crowd, whom an action so sweet and simple hushed into silence, he might gravely raise his hat to me as handcuffed and with bowed head I passed by him. Men have gone to heaven for smaller things than that. It was in this spirit, and with this mode of love that the saints knelt down to wash the feet of the poor, or stooped to kiss the leper on the cheek.

Lord Alfred Douglas (October 22 1870–March 20 1945), nicknamed Bosie—a derivative of "boysie," as in boy— the third son of the 9th Marquess of Queensberry and his first wife, Sibyl Montgomery, was a British author, poet, translator and political commentator, better known as the friend and lover of Oscar Wilde.

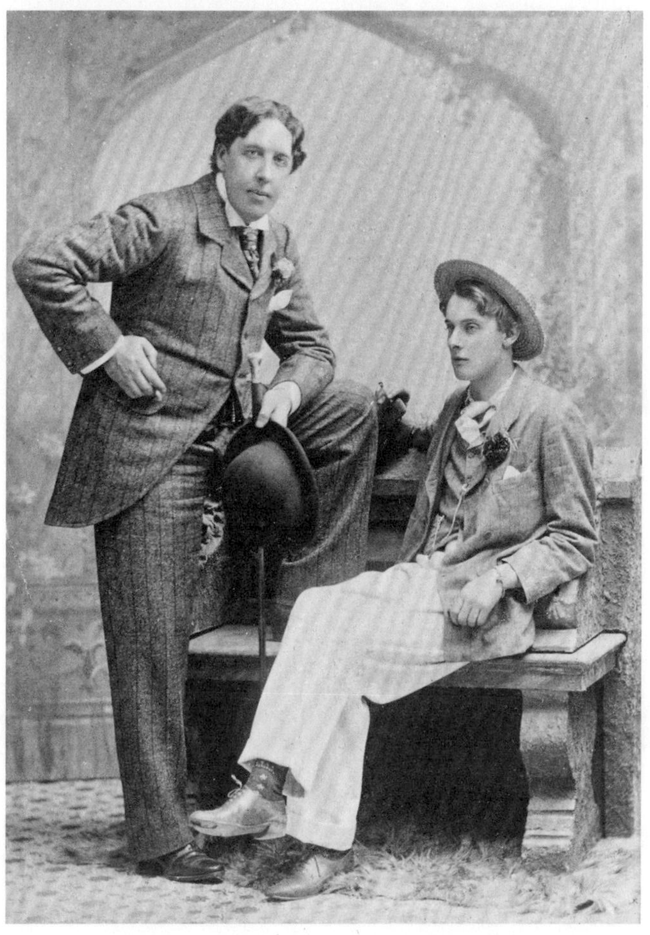

In June 1891, Bosie was introduced to Oscar Wilde by his cousin Lionel Johnson; Johnson had, for a short time in 1890, been Oscar's lover. Bosie was open about his sexuality in his youth, and wrote as follows regarding his experiences at University (Magdalen College at Oxford, the so-called "Temple of Eros"):

> I remember thinking that my parents must be quite mad to send me to such an awful place [. . .]. However, after the first shock I got used to the conditions, adapted myself to the standard of morality—or rather immorality—and enjoyed the whole thing immensely [. . .]. The practice of Greek love is so general that it is only those who are physically unattractive that are reduced to living without love."[2]

At some point in June the love of Oscar and Bosie was consummated in Tite Street while Constance was away. "Wilde treated me—confessed Bosie to Frank Harris—as an older boy treats a younger one at school and he added what was new to me [. . .] he sucked me!"

Although Bosie was initially open about his sexual experiences, in later years (following Oscar's infamous trial) he denied his multiple and well-known homosexual stories.

Sonnet on Approaching Italy
by Oscar Wilde (1881)

I reached the Alps: the soul within me burned,
Italia, my Italia, at thy name:
And when from out the mountain's heart I came
And saw the land for which my life had yearned,
I laughed as one who some great price had earned:
And musing on the marvel of thy fame
I watched the day, till marked with wounds of flame
The turquoise sky to burnished gold was turned.
The pine-trees waved as waves a woman's hair,
And in the orchards every twining spray
Was breaking into flakes of blossoming foam:
But when I knew that far away at Rome
In evil bonds a second Peter lay,
I wept to see the land so very fair.   *TURIN*

At the very beginning of the 19th century, Britain's outlook on Italy and Greece was that they were 'exceptional': foreign countries where the grace of a superior civilization was acquired—rather than imparted. "A man who has not been to Italy is always conscious of an inferiority, from his not having seen what it is expected a man should see."[3] Let us recall that in the Victorian era, Britain's superior classes were traveling classes, and constantly traveled abroad. Their lives were a constant bustle of arrivals and departures; their *portmanteaux* and hatboxes were plastered with foreign labels, and many of the letters that they wrote and received bore exotic postmarks. "The only remarkable thing people can tell of their doings these days is that they have stayed at home" declared George Eliot in 1869.[4] The names of places in the South acted like an incantation on the emotions of cultivated Victorians.

I was looking on the Mediterranean, it was the first time those hunted waters had met my gaze. I pondered on the name—the Mediterranean—as if the very letters had folded in their little characters the secret of my joy.[5]

---

[3] James Johnson, *Change of Air, or the Pursuit of Health* (London, 1837).
[4] Gordon Haight, *The Letters of George Eliot* (New Haven: Yale University Press, 1978).
[5] John Edward Bowden, *The Life and Letters of Frederick W. Faber* (London, 1869).

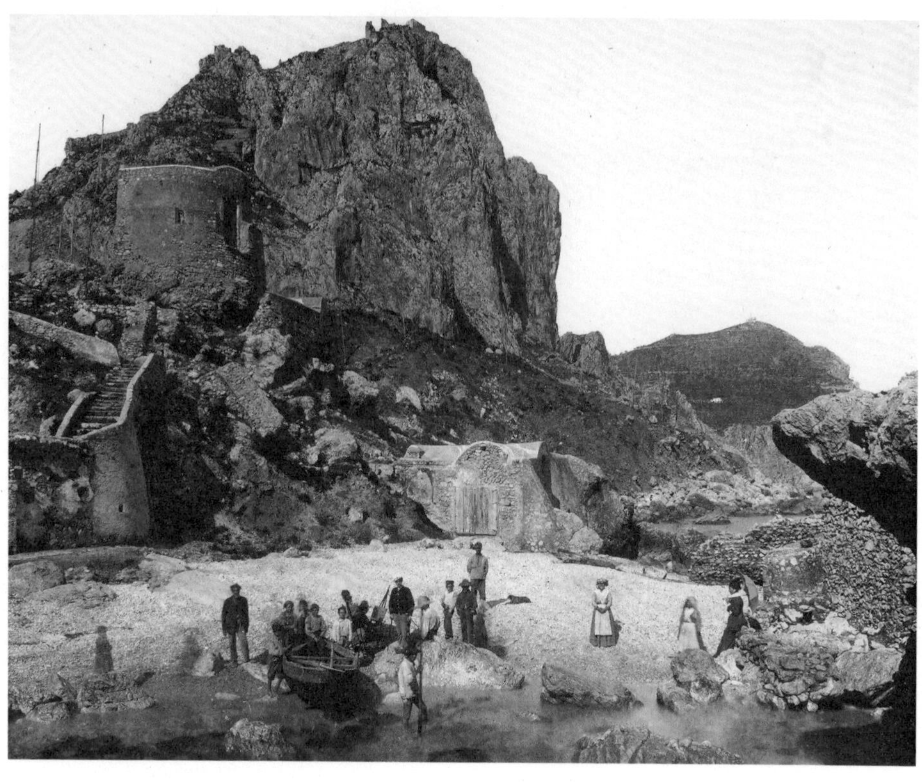

The name of Italy has for the educated world a kind of magic sound.[6]

It is difficult to think of a Victorian sculptor, writer, poet, historian or critic of any note who did not make at least one trip to the Mediterranean. Another strong element of appeal was the inexpensive cost of living available in the South where, as Elizabeth Browning used to write, with 300 pounds a year one could live "much like the Grand Duchess." And, judging from Wilde's letters, we can see that this was truly the case! (see his letter when he says "I want to live with 10 francs a day [boy compris!]"). But the man who did most to mobilize the British bourgeoisie was Thomas Cook, the Leicester Baptist and temperance evangelist who became a major figure in Victorian organized travel. An important aspect of Cook's talent for organization was its psychological effect. Cook's Select Parties, Popular Holiday Tours, through-tickets, hotel coupons, exchange bureaux, and uniformed agents, couriers and interpreters in foreign parts lowered resistance to Southern travel. "By 1870 Rome boasted a Hotel de Londres, a Hotel de l'Angleterre, a Hotel des Iles Britanniques, a Hotel Brighton and a Hotel Victoria. In addition, the cluster of

---

[6] Mabel Sharman Crawford, *Life in Tuscany* (London, 1859).

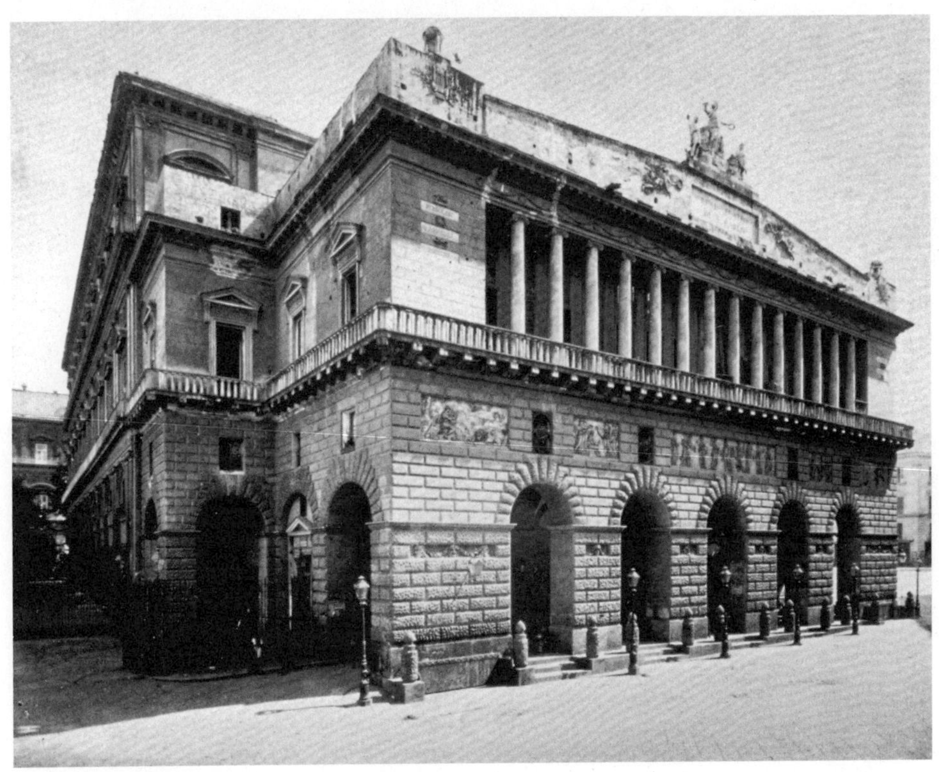

lodging houses in and about the Via Condotti was known as the *ghetto inglese*. Naples also boasted a Hotel Grande Bretagne, a Hotel Bristol, a Hotel Britannique, a Hotel de Londres, and a Hotel Victoria where maids wore the complete traditional apron and caps of English parlors in plenary correctness." Another reason of such popularity was that the Mediterranean was used extensively by Victorian climate-therapists, first and foremost because it was comparatively warm and dry in winter.

Until 1870, when Oscar Wilde first came to Italy, the Victorians followed a very specific course from the classic Grand Tour: autumn in Florence, Christmas and New Year in Rome, to Naples for the rest of winter and then back to Rome for Holy Week and Easter. We have to consider that nothing in Italy was so enticing as the religion of Papal Rome, which British Protestants were particularly taken with, leading them to spend all Christmas and Easter festivities in the Eternal City. But there were other reasons that could push some travelers into the South and they were reasons that one could whisper only between close and trusted friends. In fact, during the 19th century, a number of poets camouflaged their homosexuality in reference to male friendship. Many are minor writers, but even the titles of their poems give an indication of their references to Greece and Rome. It is sufficient here to quote the *Heraclitus* by W.J. Cory and his "Ionica" collection of 1858, the *Hermaphroditus* by Algernon Charles Swinburne of 1866, or the *Antinous* by Charles Kains-Jackson of 1861. At the time, verses were published only in literary journals with a limited circulation, or in the more famous *The Artist and Journal of Home Culture*. All these poets were called "Uranian" by Timothy d'Arch Smith in his 1970 book.[7] One of the most popular places in the 19th century, Naples had become the foremost gay Italian city: a warm and wicked place which was, to quote Macmillan's *Guide to the Western Mediterranean*, "a delightful winter residence for those fond of pleasure and gaiety." The San Carlo Opera, the theaters, concerts and Anglo-American hospitality ensured that a few weeks' stay in this lively capital was a good cure for *ennui* .To show how fond the British were of Italy, London's Covent Garden was also renamed Royal Italian Opera. Other comments, not openly specified in guidebooks, attracted homosexual predators such as Lord Ronald Gower[8] and Oscar Wilde who wrote in 1897: "it is not for pleasure that I come here, though pleasure, I am glad to say, walks all round. " We may say that some "homosexual literati" projected their sexual fantasies on the South or on the Sicilian 'other,' and looked for the reincarnation of the Hellenic ideals in the contemporary youths. Sicily was a space for Hellenic transgressions in more than one sense: as a travel destination for the actualization of illicit desires, and as a strategic cultural space from which to invoke the legitimization of the ancient tradition of "Greek love." In 1893 poet Theodore Wratislaw published a sonnet celebrating the superiority of male over female eroticism in the aesthetic magazine *The Artist*. Wratislaw's poem is remembered in gay cultural history as it marked the emergence of an openly homosexual theme—that of modern "queer" desire—for the first time in the public world of British culture and society.[9] Italy and Greece offered the possibility of eluding inhibitions and at the same time finding a reference cultural background. Here it was possible to appreciate both the ancient culture and that of the Renaissance, which were an inspiration for the creation of artistic and literary works. Italy was the venue for artistic discovery and, at times, one's own self–discovery. Half a century after the death of Winckelmann, forty years after Goethe's visit, August von Platen, another German and well-known homosexual influenced by both of the above, added his undeniable contribution to

---

[7] Timothy d'Arch Smith, *Love in Earnest: Some Notes on the Lives and Writings of English Uranian Poets from 1889 to 1930* (London: Routledge & Kegan Paul, 1970).

[8] Author's NoteLord Ronald Charles Sutherland-Leveson-Gower (August 2 1845–March 9 1916), known as Ronald Gower, was a Scottish Liberal politician, sculptor and writer from the Leveson-Gower family. He was well known among the homosexual community of the time. Oscar Wilde's story *The Portrait of Mr. W. H.* has been interpreted as a comment on Gower's social circle, and Gower is generally identified as the model for Lord Henry Wotton in *The Picture of Dorian Gray*. In 1890 he was implicated in the Cleveland Street Scandal. See also Robert Aldrich, *The Seduction of the Mediterranean: Writing, Art, and Homosexual Fantasy* (London: Routledge, 1993); and Richard Dellamora, *Masculine Desire: the Sexual Politics of Victorian Aestheticism* (Chapel Hill, N.C.: University of North Carolina Press, 1990).

[9] Stefania Arcara, *Hellenic Transgressions, Homosexual Politics: Wilde, Symonds and Sicily* (Catania: Cavallotto, 1998).

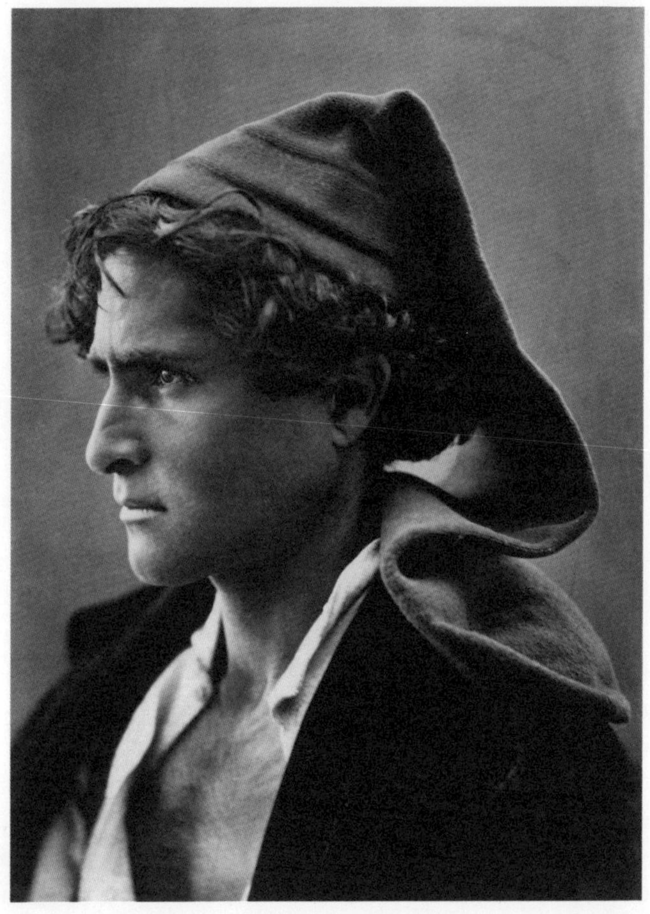

the collective imagination that already existed in Italy.[10] He was particularly taken with Neapolitans: "One sees here many handsome faces and extremely interesting physiques. In Naples a handsome, cheerful and adorable young man made a deep impression on me, an impression such as I have never experienced in Italy, although the Italians are so much more handsome than the Germans and although here in Naples love between men is so common that one cannot choose to refuse the most daring demands."[11] These 'confessions' provided clues as to how and where a homosexual such as himself could find soul and (perhaps) bedmates, and were at the base of an exciting homosexual fantasy at the time when Oscar Wilde decided to move to Naples.

[10] See also Aldrich, *The Seduction of the Mediterranean*.
[11] August von Platen, *Tagebücher*, ed. Rudiger Gorner (Zurich: Manesse-Verlag, 1990).

I am so clever that sometimes I don't understand a single word of what I am saying.
Oscar Wilde

In 1874, at the age of nineteen, Wilde crowned his academic success by winning a demyship (scholarship) to Magdalen College, Oxford. During his first summer holidays as an adult he went to Italy, as evidenced by the numerous letters with which my research began.

***

Letter to Sir William Wilde, June 15 1875 (Florence):

Went in the morning to see San Lorenzo, built in the usual Florentine way, cruciform: a long aisle supported by Grecian pillars: a gorgeous dome in the centre and three small aisles leading off it. Behind it are the two Chapels of the Medici. The first, the Burial Chapel, is magnificent; of enormous height, octagonal in shape. Walls built entirely of gorgeous blocks of marble, all inlaid with various devices and of different colours, polished like a looking-glass. Six great sarcophagi of granite and porphyry stand in six niches: on top of each of them a cushion of inlaid mosaic bearing a gold crown. Above the sarcophagi are statues in gilded bronze of the Medici; on the dome, of course, frescoes and gilded carving. The other chapel is very small, built simply of white marble. Two mausoleums in it to two great Medici; one bearing Michael Angelo's statues of Night and Morning and the other those of Evening and Dawn. [. . .] Then to the Etruscan Museum, which is in the suppressed monastery of San Onofrio and most interesting. You come first to a big tomb, transplanted from Arezzo; cyclopean stonework, doorway with sloping jambs and oblong lintel, roof slightly conical, walls covered with wonderfully beautiful frescoes, representing first the soul in the shape of a young man naked, led by a beautifully winged angel or genius to the two-horsed chariot which is to convey them to Elysium—and then represents the banquet which awaits him. This same idea of the resurrection of the soul and a state of happiness after death pervades the whole system of Etruscan art. There were also wonderful sarcophagi which I have roughly drawn for you. On the top the figure of the dead man or woman holding a plate containing the obol for paying the ferryman over Styx. Also extraordinary jars with heads and arms—funeral of course—I have drawn them. The sarcophagi, of which there are over a hundred and fifty to be seen, are about two and a half feet long and about three feet high. The sides of the sarcophagi are sculptured with the achievements and adventures of the dead man, mostly in bas-relief which are sometimes coloured. There were some with frescoes instead of sculpture, beautifully done. [. . .] In the evening I dined at a restaurant on top of San Miniato, air delightfully clear and cool after the thunderstorm. Coming back I met just opposite the Pitti Palace a wonderful funeral; a long procession of monks bearing torches, all in white and wearing a long linen veil over their faces—only their eyes can be seen. They bore two coffins and looked like those awful monks your see in pictures of the Inquisition. [. . .] Yours ever truly affectionately Oscar O'F. WI. Wilde

***

Letter to Lady Wilde, June 23 1875 (Milan, Albergo della Francia):

So busy travelling and sight-seeing for last five days that I have had no time to write. Diary. Left Florence with much regret on Saturday night; passed through the Apennines, beautiful Alpine scenery; train runs on side of mountains half-way up, above us pine-forests and crags, below us the valley, villages and swollen rivers. Supper at Bologna; about 5.30 in the morning came near Venice. Immediately on leaving the mountains a broad flat tableland (there are no hills in Italy—mountains or flat plains) cultivated like a rich garden [. . .]. Finally, through long narrow canals we arrived at our hotel, which was in the great Piazza San Marco—the only place in Venice except the Rialto anyone walks in. Plan of it [Rough sketch]. The Church of San Marco is most gorgeous; a splendid Byzantine church, covered with gilding and mosaics, inside and out. The floor of inlaid marbles, of colour and design indescribable, and through the sinking of the piles undulates in big sweeping waves. Splendid gates of bronze, everything glorious. Next to it the Doge's Palace, which is beyond praise. Inside, giant council chambers; the walls painted with frescoes by Titian of the great battles of the Venetians; the ceiling crossed by gilded beams and rich in gilded carving; rooms fit for the noble-looking grave senators whose pictures are on the walls by Titian or Tintoretto. [. . .] Here we spent the morning; afterwards took a gondola and visited some of the islands off Venice; on one an Armenian monastery where Byron used to live. Returned home in the flood of a great sunset. Venice as a city just risen from the sea; a long line of crowded churches and palaces; everywhere white or gilded domes and tall campaniles; no opening in the whole city except at the Piazza San Marco. A great pink sunset with a long line of purple thunderclouds behind the city. After dinner went to the theatre and saw a good circus. Luckily a wonderful moon. We landed from our gondola coming from the theatre at the Lion of St Mark. The scene was so romantic that it seemed to be an "artistic" scene from an opera. We sat on the base of the pillar; on one side of us the Doge's Palace, on the other the King's Palace, behind us the Campanile. The water-steps crowded with black gondolas, and a great flood of light coming right up to us across the water. Every moment a black silent gondola would glide across this great stream of light and be lost in the darkness.

***

Letter to Lady Wilde, June 24–25 (Milan):

I believe you left me last looking at the moon from the Piazza San Marco. With difficulty we tore ourselves away to the hotel. Next morning, we went up the Grand Canal in a gondola [. . .]. Wonderful colour everywhere—windows hung with striped yellow awnings, domes and churches of white marble, campaniles of red brick, great gondolas filled with fruit and vegetables going to the Rialto where the market is. Stopped to see the picture galley which as usual, was in a suppressed monastery. Titian and Tintoretto in great force. Titian's *Assumption* certainly the best picture in Italy. Went to a lot of churches, all however in extravagant "baroque" style—very rich in worked metal and polished marble and mosaic but as a rule inartistic. In the picture gallery besides the Titians there are two great pictures; one a beautiful Madonna by Bellini, the other a picture of Dives and Lazarus by Bonifazio containing the only *lovely* woman's face I have seen in Italy. [. . .] After marriage the Italian women degenerate awfully, but the boys and girls are beautiful. Amongst married women the general types are "Titiens" and an ugly sallow likeness of "Trebelli Bettini."[12] [. . .] Arrived at Padua at two o'clock. In the middle of a rich vineyard stands the Baptistery, the great work of Giotto; the walls covered entirely with frescoes by him; one wall the life of Mary, the other the

---

[12] Author's Note: Thérèse Tietjens or Titiens (1831–1877) and Zélie Trebelli (1838–1892), who married Alexander Bettini, and Italian tenor, were prima donnas of ample proportions who had regularly sung in Dublin with J.H. Mapleson's Italian Opera Company in the 1860s and 1870s.

life of Christ; the ceiling blue with gold stars and medallion pictures; the west wall a great picture of Heaven and Hell suggested to him by Dante [. . .]. Arrived at Milan in a shower of rain; went in the evening to the theatre and saw a good ballet. This morning the Cathedral. Outside most elaborate in pinnacles and statues awfully out of proportion with the rest of the building. Inside most impressive through its huge size and giant pillars supporting the roof; some good old stained glass and a lot of hideous modern windows. These moderns don't see that the use of a window in a church is to show a beautiful massing together and blending of colour; a good old window has the rich pattern of a Turkey carpet. The figures are quite subordinate and only serve to show the sentiment of the designer. The modern fresco style of window has *suâ naturâ* to compete with painting and of course looks monstrous and theatrical. The Cathedral is an awful failure. Outside the design is monstrous and inartistic. The overelaborated details stuck high up where no one can see them; everything is vile in it; it is, however, imposing and gigantic as a failure, through its great size and elaborate execution. [. . .] Milan is a second Paris. Wonderful arcades and galleries; all the town white stone and gilding. Dined excellently at the Biffi Restaurant and had some wine of Asti, like good cider or sweet champagne. [. . .] I write this at Arona on the Lago Maggiore, a beautiful spot. Yours Oscar

***

Letter to Reginald Harding, March 22 1877 (Oxford, Magdalen College)

My dear Kitten, I start for Rome on Sunday; Mahaffy comes as far as Genoa with me: and I hope to see the golden dome of St Peter's and the Eternal City by Tuesday night. This is an era in my life; a crisis. I wish I could look into the seeds of time and see what is coming. I shall not forget you in Rome, and will burn a candle for you at the Shrine of Our Lady. Write to me like a good boy, Hôtel d'Angleterre, Rome. Yours ever Oscar

***

Wilde went on to Greece with the others, and they all visited Rome on their way home. He had been formally censured by the Board of Trinity for abandoning his teaching obligations in favor of a previous journey to Greece.

Referring to the Italian stays, later, Wilde composed a series of sonnets (*San Miniato*, 1878; *Sonnet on Approaching Italy*, 1881; and *Scoglietto*, 1881).

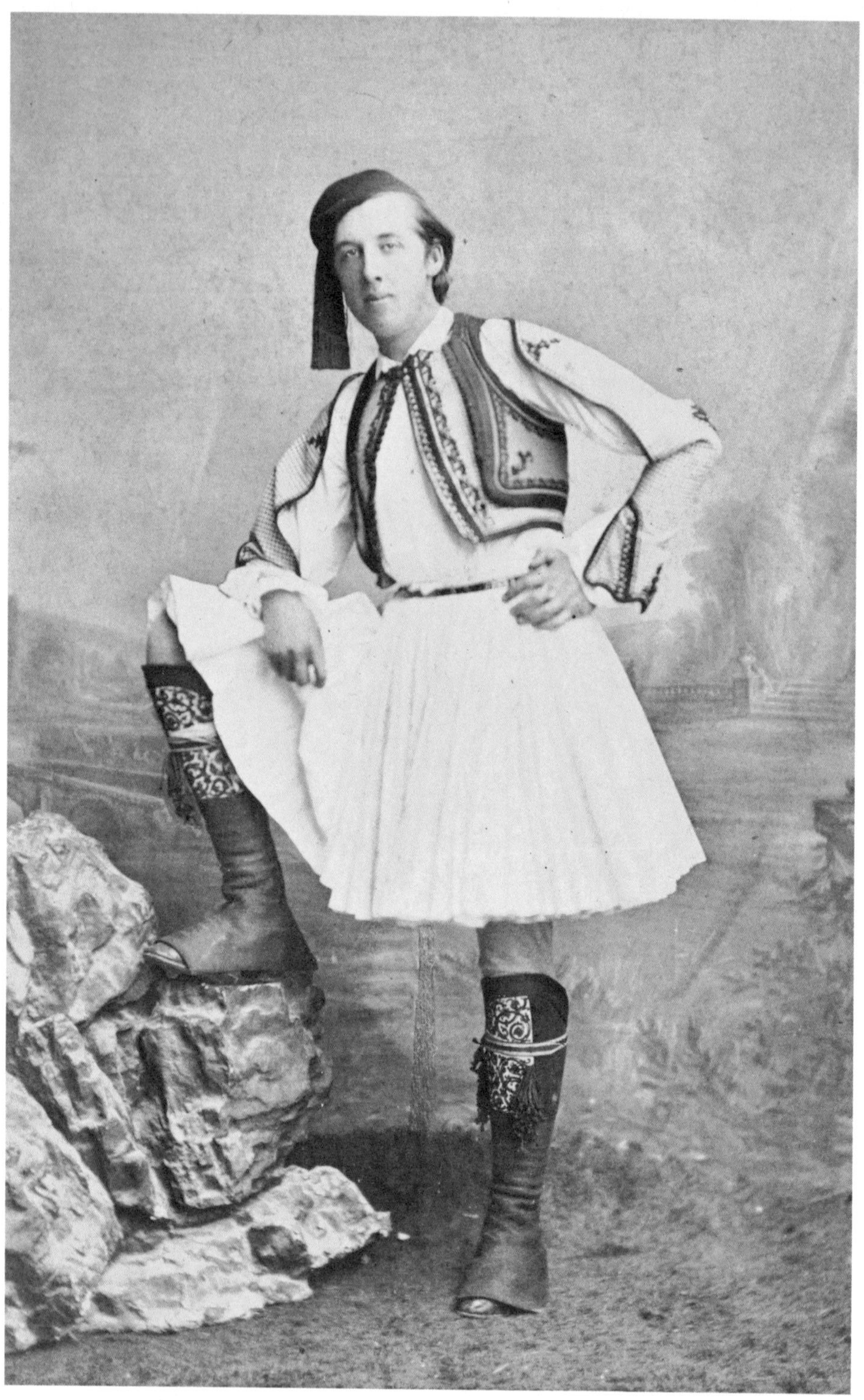

Be yourself; everyone else is already taken.
Oscar Wilde

By the time he arrived in Oxford, Oscar had begun to experience vague feelings and attraction towards young men. His first coming out was with his friend and biographer Frank Harris, to whom he admitted that he had some "sentimental friendships with boys" one of whom in particular struck him:

There was one boy [. . .] we were great friends, we used to take long walks together [. . .]. And I talked to him interminably [. . .]. One day I was leaving the Portora Royal School and my friend came to the railway station [. . .] to say good bye and before I knew what he was doing he had caught my face in his hot hands and kissed me on the lips [. . .]. The next moment he had slipped out of the door and was gone [. . .]. This is love [. . .] for a long while I sat unable to think, all shaken with wonder and remorse.[13]

In his first year at Oxford, he had a number of emotional—but not sexual—experiences. When he first arrived there, Oscar could only invoke the concept of Greek love to define his feelings for men. He was in fact familiar with this concept as he had helped his friend and mentor Mahaffy to write *Social life in Greece*, a book which was the first to note the existence of that kind of love, although Mahaffy had used these words to describe it: "These things are so repugnant and disgusting that all mention of them is usually omitted in treating of Greek culture." Whilst in Oxford, Oscar referred to "spooning" to describe the attachment between a fellow undergraduate at Magdalen and a younger boy. At the same time, during the summer of 1875, Oscar flirted with at least two young women one of whom, Florence Balcombe, he described to his friend Reginald Kitten Harding as having "the most beautiful face I ever saw!!" But during the whole "two sweet years" of their courtship," Oscar was sexually involved in a relationship with Frank Miles, with whom he moved to Salisbury Street. Oscar and Frank would host "Tea and Beauties parties" and attempt to enter high London society in consonance with Wilde's own motto: "feed people, amuse people or shock people."

---

[13] Frank Harris, *Oscar Wilde* (London: Constable, 1938); see also George Thomas Atkinson, "Oscar Wilde at Oxford," *Conhill Magazine*, no. 3905 (1929).

Frank and Oscar used all three tactics simultaneously. Whistler, Burne-Jones, Walter Sickert, the Prince of Wales and Lillie Langtry were among those who came. Together the two kept, according to Oscar, an "untidy and romantic house." Miles occupied the top floor, Oscar the second, and a young schoolboy named Harry Mariller was allowed to use the ground floor as a space in which to keep his books and study. Oscar brightened his floor with green rugs, Burne-Jones drawings and lilies everywhere.

Lillie Langtry, who was to become his dearest friend, recalled the first meeting with Oscar in those days in the studio of Frank Miles and how astonished she was at his strange appearance:

> His face was large, and so colourless that a few pale freckles of good size were oddly conspicuous. He had a well-shaped mouth, with somewhat coarse lips and greenish-hued teeth. To me he was always grotesque in appearance, although I have seen him described by a French writer as "beautiful" and "Apollo-like." He had an incredible stage presence. With one of the most alluring voices, round and soft and full of variety and expression.[14]

Anxious to be recognized as one of the aesthetes of the time, Wilde was ready to do almost anything to further his career as a poet and a writer. In later years, Oscar himself would describe his double life: on the one hand he flirted with pretty girls and made love to beautiful young women, while on the other he had "affairs" with young men. In his own words, the former was "a cloak to hide his secret." Oscar met Frank Miles in the spring of 1876. Frank was two years older and lived in London, where he was pursuing a career as a portrait painter of society ladies. According to Frank Harris, Miles was "a very pleasant, handsome young fellow who made a sympathetic impression on everyone." In June 1876, Frank took Oscar to meet his friend and patron, sculptor Lord Ronald Gower, who was also his guide to London's sexual underworld. Wilde would later base *Dorian Gray*'s Lord Henry Wotton, "the corrupting prophet of sin" on Gower. Oscar's relationship with Frank was not to be monogamous. In December 1876 Oscar occasionally visited Lord Gower with another man named Arthur May. Later he dated Walter Pater, a writer on Renaissance studies. According to O'Sullivan, Pater was timid and afraid that Oscar would compromise him.[15] Anyway, marriage had been always on Oscar Wilde's mind and he had proposed to at least two young women in the two years since he had left university: Charlotte Montefiore and Violet

---

[14] Lillie Langtry, "The Oscar I Knew." In *Oscar Wilde. Interviews & Recollections*, ed. E.H. Mikhail (London: Macmillan, 1979).

[15] Vincent O'Sullivan, *Some Letters to A. J. Symons* (Edinburgh: Tragara Press, 1975).

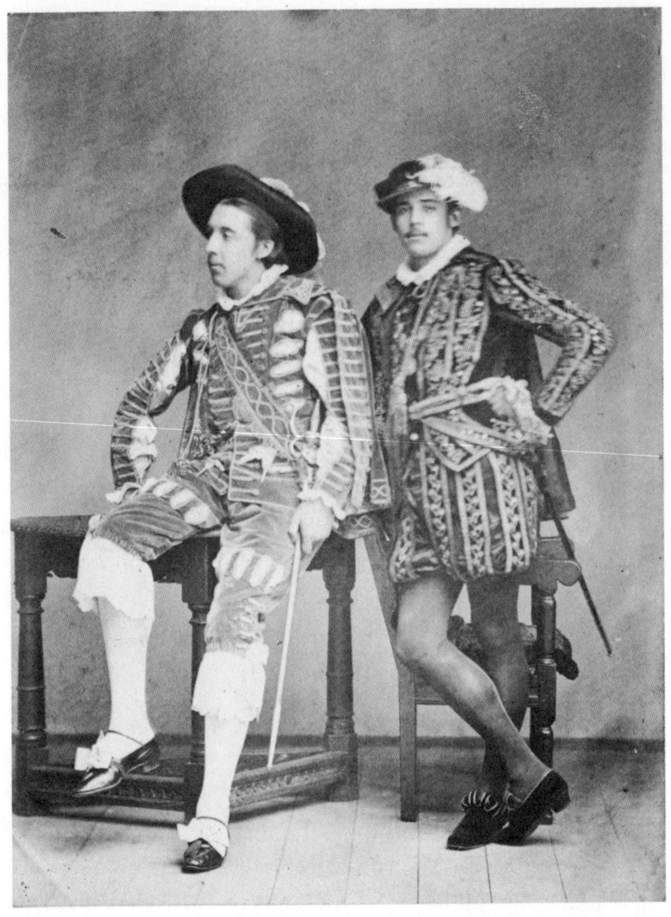

Hunt, daughter of the painter Alfred Hunt. She and her mother, the famous novelist Margaret Raine Hunt, were invited to tea with Oscar and Frank Miles at Salisbury Street. But her father was not to agree to their marriage. Rumors surrounding Wilde, and the front page of the *Punch* caricaturizing him as effeminate, were not good omens for the happiness of his daughter. In the early summer of 1881 Oscar met the woman who was to become his wife, Constance Mary Lloyd, at the time twenty-three years old. Oscar had met her older brother Otho four years earlier in Dublin. Constance knew much about Oscar from her brother, who described the poet and the professor of Aesthetics as one of the most prominent writers of the future. In a way, she was very pleased that a man of such an importance should show interest in her. And Oscar was so impressed by her that in talking to his mother, he said: "By the way, Mama, I think of marrying that girl!" Oscar introduced his future wife in glowing terms: "I am going to be married to a beautiful young girl called Constance, a grave, slight, violet-eyed little Artemis, with great coils of heavy brown hair which make her flower-like head droop like a flower, and wonderful ivory hands which draw music from the piano so sweet that the birds stop singing to listen to her." Both seemed very ready to fall in love. By the time Constance and Oscar became engaged, two and half years after they were first introduced, they hardly knew each other. Oscar had spent an entire year in America and in his own private life he referred to her as a person who "scarcely ever speaks, and I am always wondering what her thoughts are like." He also met Walt Whitman, the famous American poet, and "had a Jolly Good Time." In a letter to his friend Ives, Oscar said: "I have the kiss of Walt Whitman still on my lips."[16]

In turn, Constance did not have details of Oscar's life, except of his devotion to Florrie Balcombe, and his proposals to Charlotte Montefiore and Violet Hunt. And on the other hand, Oscar in all likelihood did not talk openly to her about his visit to women prostitutes in Oxford, London, America and Paris, and certainly not of the male brothels he knew very well, but he may have discreetly alluded to his previous experiences with the fair sex, sparking the following response from his bride-to-be: "When I have you for my husband, I will hold you fast with chains of love and devotion so that you shall never leave me, or love anyone else."[17]

Later, W.H. Auden would write that Oscar's marriage to Constance was "certainly the most immoral and perhaps the only really heartless act of Wilde's life."[18] Oscar was well aware that he was attracted to men, and had sex with them, but never considered anything resembling a relationship with them. Many men, then and now, considered the homoerotic desires as a "disease" that could be cured with a healthy and prolific heterosexual life—starting with female prostitutes. Fortunately, the wedding night sex had worked out well, as a happy Oscar told to Robert Sherard the morning after, and after their honeymoon in Paris and Dieppe the couple returned to London. Constance told her brother that she was very happy and "enjoying my liberty enormously!" Clearly Constance saw her marriage as a liberation from her aunt Emily after the death of her dear granpapa Lloyd. But soon Oscar realized that the marriage was not enough because Constance became a woman, not a surrogate of a slim boy: "my wife was a beautiful girl, white and slim as a lily [. . .] within a year or so she became heavy, shapeless, deformed [. . .] it was dreadful. I tried to be kind to her, forced myself to touch and kiss her [. . .] but I used to wash my mouth and open the window to cleanse my lips in the pure air."[19] His biographer Jonathan Fryer

---

[16] See "Letters of George Ives," in Jon Stokes, *Oscar Wilde: Myths, Miracles and Imitations* (Oxford: Cambridge University Press, 1996).

[17] Louis Joplin, *Twenty Years in My Life, 1867–1887* (London: John Lane/Dodd Mead, 1925). See also Emer O'Sullivan, *The Fall of the House of Wilde* (London: Bloomsbury Publishing, 2016).

[18] Wystan Hugh Auden, *Forewords and After Words in Improbable Life*, sel. by Edward Mendelson (London: Methuen, 1957).

[19] Harris, *Oscar Wilde*.

says that: "Oscar's passion for his wife seems to have survived her first pregnancy, and the birth of their son Cyril in June 1885. But when, in early 1886, Constance became pregnant again with Vyvyan, Oscar observed her increasingly bloated body with little short of revulsion. His idolization of her as the physical manifestation of feminine grace was over. Instead, how much more aesthetically pleasing were the narrow-waisted working-class boys he saw in the streets; how much more appealing the puckish, cheeky Robbie Ross."[20]

In less than a year he returned to "the criminal classes that have always had a wonderful attraction" for him[21] and became closer to the Uranian movement, in particular to John Addington Symonds, its founder, and to Charles Sayle, one of its poets, who wrote in his poems: "There is no Sin, nor any need of cure / for we are Nature's children, and She sure / it is, is wholly pure and sanctified."[22]

That being said, he fully realized that "In mad and coloured loves there is much danger [. . .]. There is the danger of losing them no less than the danger of keeping them"[23] as he commented, especially in reference to affairs such as the one with Harry Marillier and Douglas Ainslie who accused him at the trial.
According to André Raffalovich [24] who heard him hold forth, he was fascinated by the story of James I and his favorite, Robert Carr, Earl of Somerset, who, on the eve of his trial for the murder of Sir Thomas Overbury, threatened to reveal publicly that "the King had slept with him," and the precautions taken at the trial to prevent any embarrassing revelations of the kind.

In this context Wilde studied the lives of Plato and Michelangelo, and conducted an ingenious piece of research into the origins of Shakespeare's sonnets to "Mr. W. H.," whom he claimed to be a boy actor named Willie Hughes whom the dramatist admired.

---

[20] Jonathan Fryer, *Robbie Ross, Oscar Wilde's Devoted Friend* (New York: Carroll & Graf, 2000).
[21] Robert Harborough Sherard, *The Life of Oscar Wilde* (London: T.W. Laurie, 1911).
[22] "Charles Sayle," in d'Arch Smith, *Love in Earnest.*
[23] Neil McKenna, *The Secret Life of Oscar Wilde* (New York: Basic Books, 2005).
[24] Marc-André Raffalovich (September 11 1864–14 February 1934) was a French poet and writer on homosexuality, best known today for his patronage of the arts and for his lifelong relationship with the poet John Gray, the man who inspired *The Portrait of Dorian Gray*. Oscar Wilde reviewed one of his books anonymously in the *Pall Mall Gazette*: "To say of these poems that they are unhealthy and bring with them the heavy odours of the hothouse is to point out neither their defect nor their merit, but their quality merely."

I represent all the sins you have never had the courage to commit.
Oscar Wilde

The exact dates of the visit to Algiers are not known, but seems to be around the rehearsals of *The Importance of Being Earnest*. In a letter to Ada Leverson written around January 16, 1895 Wilde said: "I fly to Algiers with Bosie tomorrow." On January 22 Constance Wilde wrote to her brother: "Did I tell you that Oscar has gone for a fortnight to Algiers?" On January 27 André Gide ran into Wilde and Douglas in Blidah, a town thirty miles from Algiers much frequented by Englishmen in search of boys. He was about to sign the register when, to his consternation, he saw the names of Wilde and Douglas already on it. The memory of their uncomfortable meeting in Florence was only seven months old, and to be at the same hotel seemed to him too compromising. His own homosexual life had begun, but surreptitiously. He took his bags and started to go back to the station, only to decide that he was behaving ridiculously. He went back, registered, and soon after met Wilde and Douglas. Gide and Wilde spent several days in Algiers together. As he went through the streets, Wilde was followed by a group of petty thieves. Wilde confided to Gide that Queensberry was tormenting him.

> "But if you go back, what will happen? Do you realize the risk?" said Gide. Wilde responded. "That one can never know. My friends advise me to be prudent. Prudent! How could I be that? It would mean going backward. I must go as far as possible. I cannot go any further. Something must happen. . . something else. . ."
> Gide concluded that Wilde had what Henry James calls "the imagination of disaster." Nothing less than total ruin would do."[25]

Wilde's influence was so strong, so unsettling, that Gide destroyed several pages of his *Journal* for November and December of 1891 and referring to Wilde he wrote: "he is always trying to instill into you a sanction for evil." Later, in a book Gide wrote about Oscar Wilde, he stated as follows:[26]

---

[25] William Martin Murphy, *Lily Yeats's Scrapbook* (1889).
[26] André Gide, "Oscar Wilde. In memoriam," in *Oscar Wilde. Interviews and Recollections*, ed. E.H. Mikhail (London: Macmillan, 1979).

He seems to apply all his care, all his courage to the task of exaggerating his fate, and making it worse for himself. He went about his pleasure as one goes about one's duty. "It is my duty," he said, "to amuse myself frightfully." Nietzsche did not surprise me so much later, because I had heard Wilde say: "Not happiness! Anything but happiness! But pleasure, yes; pleasure, joy! One must always want what is most tragic."

"I hope," he said, "that I have thoroughly demoralized this town." I thought of Flaubert's reply, when he had been asked what glory he had most worthy: "La gloire de demoralisateur."

He leaned towards me and added: "Do you wish to know the great drama of my life? I have given my genius to my life, and to my work only my talent."

Oscar left the little town for London on February 3, while Douglas stayed at Biskra until February 18.

From late 1892, Wilde saw his life divide more emphatically between a clandestine, illegal aspect and an overt, declarable side. The more he consorted with rough but ready boys in deliberate self-abandonment, the more he cultivated a public image of disinterestedness and self-possession. The relationship between Wilde and Douglas was intense and romantic, but with many ups and downs. Douglas was fascinated by young boys who for a little cash and a good dinner were happy to prostitute themselves. He was the guide for Wilde in this world, and one could say that there was a kind of competition between them. Through Maurice Schwabe, a nephew of the solicitor general, whom Douglas brought into his circle, he met Alfred Taylor, the errant son of a cocoa manufacturer. Taylor introduced him to a series of boys, the first important one being Sidney Mavor. He continued to see Mavor for the next year and a half. Schwabe also introduced Wilde to Freddy Atkins in October 1892; he was already an accomplished blackmailer.

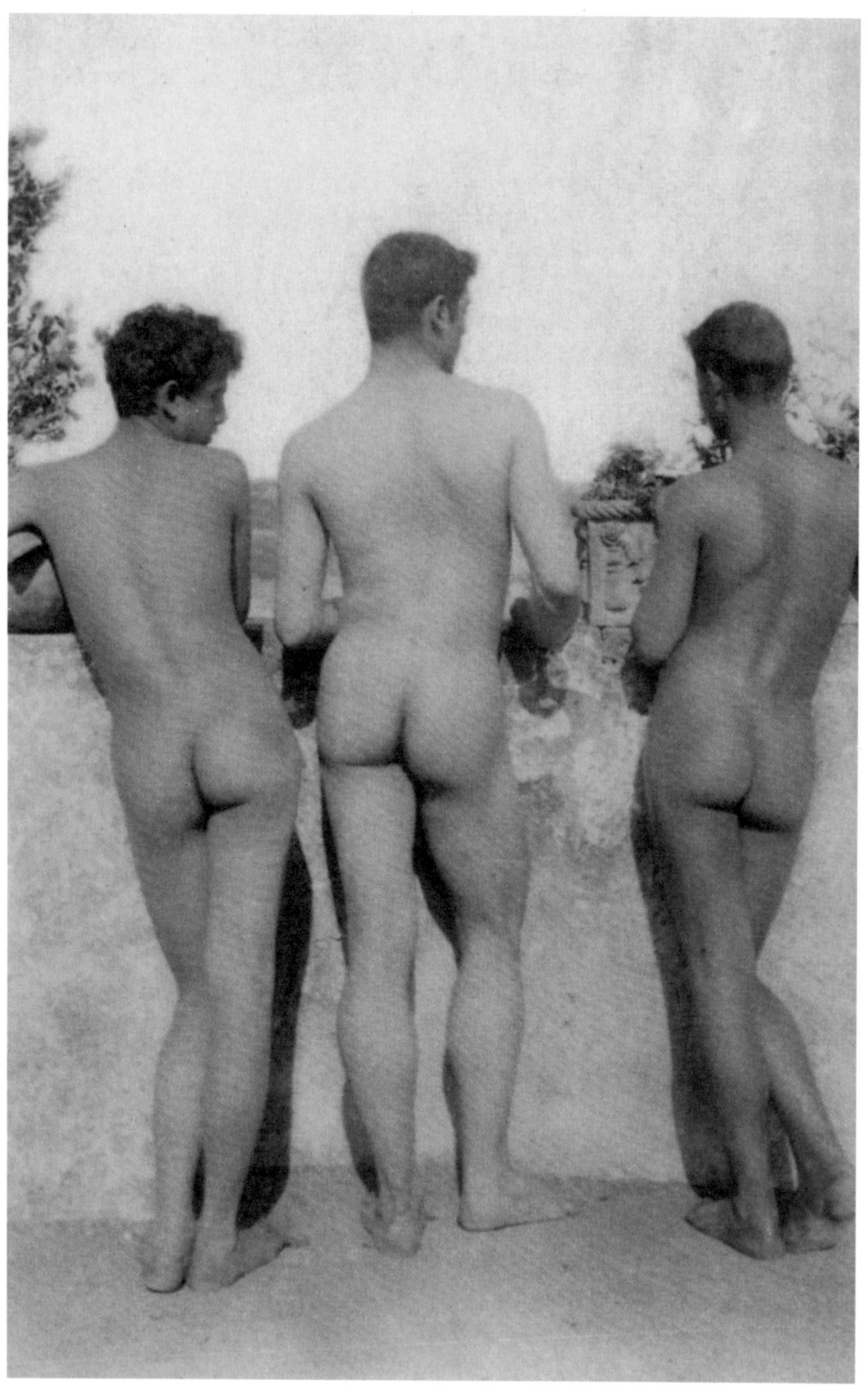

Because our world has music, and we dance;
Because our world has colour, and they gaze;
Because our speech is turned, and schooled our glance,
And we have roseleaf nights and roseleaf days,
And we have leisure, work to do and rest;
Because they see us laughing when we meet,
And hear our words and voices, see us dressed
With skill, and pass us and our flowers smell sweet;
They think that we know friendship, passion, love!
Our peacock, Pride! And Art our nightingale!
And Pleasure's hand upon our dogskin glove!
And if they see our faces burn or pale,
It is the sunlight, think They, or the gas.
– Our lives are wired like our gardenias.[27]

Sources and definitions

We cannot understand the reaction of the English-speaking world against Wilde, the accusation that was made against him and the consequent imprisonment, if we do not know the social context in which all this took place, as well as the laws that governed homosexuality in Europe in these years. Let us start by saying that in the first half of the nineteenth century there was a remarkable change in the public perception of the homosexual figure compared to that of the eighteenth century. From that of an effeminate succubus of society to a cultured man who in some way influences the society in which he lives.[28] One of the richest sources of information on gay history examines the arrest and punishment of homosexuals: laws, court records and criminal statistics. This is quite tricky because by grouping homosexuals—men and women—in the same category as mad or violent people, the records present a confused and inaccurate picture of the nineteenth century: the "sodomites," in fact, were categorized in the same sexual "zoo" as exhibitionists, pedophiles and sexual murderers. The fact that

---

[27] Marc-André Raffalovich, "The World Well Lost IV," in *In Fancy Dress* (London, 1886).

[28] For the cultural uses of the image of sodomites in the 18th century, see Randolph Trumbach, "The Birth of the Queen: Sodomy and the Emergence of Gender Equality in Modern Culture, 1660–1750," in *Hidden from History: Reclaiming the Gay and Lesbian Past*, eds. George Chauncey, Martha Vicinus, and Martin Duberman (New York: New American Library, 1989); Graham Robb, *Strangers: Homosexual Love in the Nineteenth Century* (London: Picador, 2003); Matt Cook, *London and the Culture of Homosexuality, 1885–1994* (Cambridge UK: Cambridge University Press, 2003).

sodomy was punishable by death in England and Wales until 1861 suggests that many people lived their sex lives in the shadows.[29] Later, when the notion of homosexuality became less abhorrent, homosexuals were seen more as "perverts" or "social deviants" than as dangerous sinners.[30] It was also believed that only men partook of homosexual acts. In the words of Queen Victoria: "Ladies would never engage in such despicable acts. . ." However, although not openly persecuted under the law as gay men were, lesbians also had to suffer a lot of hardships. Suffice it to say that the last execution for sodomy in France took place in 1783 and the last one in continental Europe, in the Netherlands, in 1803. But in England, executions continued until 1835. To draw a comparison we may examine what was happening in continental Europe at the turn of the nineteenth century: with the Code Napoléon, the principle that sexual activity was licit between consenting adults became a familiar concept in France by 1804. Indeed, while it is true that the penal code promulgated by Napoleon in 1804 did not make homosexual relations a criminal offence, this was no innovation in France. The French Revolution (1789–1799) had already decriminalized homosexuality. The Low Countries adopted this French perspective, but the American and British position on homosexuality did not change. However, in the United States the French influence was felt in Louisiana, where there was also a clear French linguistic influence.

The first scholars to create a rudimentary vocabulary to define homosexuality were sexologists in Europe towards the end of the nineteenth century.[31] The term "homosexuality" was first used in 1869 by Karl-Maria Kertbeny. Since then, the nature of homosexuality has been debated by sexologists all over the world.[32] In 1886, a famous sexologist, Havelock Ellis, wrote *Sexual Inversion*, which claims that homosexuals were created by a combination of biology and upbringing. He also wrote that people who were not homosexual by nature could become so if they let themselves be influenced by the "inverts." The book argued that "inversion" was an inborn condition and should not be treated as a crime. Twenty years later, on October 31, 1898, the secretary of the Legitimation League (a London-based organization dedicated to securing the legal rights of illegitimate children), George Bedborough, was fined £100 for selling Henry Havelock Ellis's and John Addington Symonds's book *Sexual Inversion*.

---

[29] Robb, *Strangers*.

[30] Cook, *London and the Culture of Homosexuality*.

[31] Uranism, a nineteenth-century synonym of homosexuality, was coined in 1864 by homosexual militant Karl Heinrich Ulrichs (1825–1895) from the German "*Urningthum*." This in turn was based on the name of "Aphrodite Urania" (i.e. "celestial, heavenly" from the Greek name of the sky, "*Ouranos*," indicated by Plato in his *Symposium* as the goddess who protects those loves not destined to procreation. The difference between this term and "homosexuality" (coined in 1869 by another militant homosexual, Karl-Maria Kertbeny) reflects a difference in points of view on the nature of people who loved people of their own sex.

[32] Cook, *London and the Culture of Homosexuality*.

"Its publication," wrote George Bernard Shaw in the league's journal *The Adult*, "was more urgently needed in England than any other recent treatise [. . .]. Until it appeared there was no authoritative scientific book on its subject within the reach of Englishmen and Englishwomen who cannot read French or German."[33]

In Italy gay relationships were decriminalized only with the introduction of the Napoleonic Code, but, once the Empire fell and the historical phase of the "Restoration" was implemented, the Catholic Church, the Kingdom of Sardinia and the Austria-Hungarian Empire (which occupied part of the north of the country) willingly reintroduced laws to punish the crime of "unnatural lust." In Rome, gays could incur the "Regulations" of Pope Gregory XVI (1832), which condemned them essentially to life imprisonment; in Milan and Venice, then part of the Austrian territories of Lombardy-Veneto, paragraph 129 might imprison them for several years, while in Turin, Genoa and Cagliari, Article 425 of the Penal Code of the Kingdom of Sardinia stated "Any act of lust against nature, if it is committed with violence, in the ways and in the circumstances provided for in articles 489 and 490, will be punished with imprisonment of no less than seven years, extendable to time forced labor: if there has been no violence, but there be a scandal or a lawsuit, it will be punished with imprisonment, with possible extension to forced labour for ten years, as the case may be." The scholar Giovanni Dall'Orto writes:

> With the Unification of Italy (1861–1870) it was planned to extend the Penal Code of the Kingdom of Sardinia to all the annexed territories, but, having arrived in the South, some articles were repealed and among them were those relating to the punishment of homosexual relationships. This is a symptom of the discomfort with which the bigoted Sardinian legislative provisions on homosexuality were received in the rest of Italy. It is also an implicit recognition of the devastating effects that a repressive law would have had on the customs of southern Italy, where a phase of homosexual behavior was implicitly taken for granted in the life of each individual. In short, it was a first silent admission of the diversity between the two 'cultures' of homosexuality: the Mediterranean and the Nordic. Elsewhere things did not proceed in a uniform way either, since article 425 was almost never applied in Tuscany, a region where a relationship "against

---

[33] See George Bernard Shaw, "The Prosecution of Mr. Bedborough," *The Adult*, 2, 8 (September 1898): 230–1, and Jeffrey Weeks, *Coming Out: Homosexual Politics from the Nineteenth Century to the Present* (London: Quartet Books, 1990), 60. For Ellis' own account of the trial, see Henry Havelock Ellis, *A Note on the Bedborough Trial* (New York: privately printed, 1925).

nature" was not pursued before the arrival of the monarchy and where the police and the judiciary were able to turn a blind eye to homosexual practice, as long as it did not involve other crimes such as rape, abuse of minors or coercion.[34]

Even though homosexuality was more accepted towards the end of the nineteenth century, it was still considered a crime, and this would continue to be the case throughout the entire century.[35] The same mixture of tolerance and indifference was apparent in reactions to the Aesthetic Movement of the 1870s and 1880s. The aesthetes' 'flowery' excesses (see Wilde's sunflower) were mocked so affectionately that it is easy to assume that their audience was quite unaware of sexual subtexts until Oscar Wilde's trial.

Homosexual life and male prostitution

> *I met them in Soho Square. He took his hat off respectfully.*
> *"Go ahead, and I'll follow," said I.*
> *We crossed Oxford Street, to a long street, out of which turning up a paved court, he opened with a latch key a door, and up we all went to a first floor over a shop, and into a well furnished sitting room, and a bedroom.*
> *"Are you fond of a bit of brown", – he asked. – I did not understand and he explained. – "We always say a bit of brown among ourselves" – he questioned me – had I been up a man. – "No" – There was no pleasure like it. – "Shall I suck it?" – "You?" – "Yes!" – "Do you do so?" – "Lord yes. I have had it so thick in my mouth, that I've had to pick it out of my mouth with a toothpick." [. . .] "Do let me sod you" said he all at once quite affectionately. "I should so like to do it to you and take your virginity.[36]*

The London homosexual subculture continued in the nineteenth century with many interesting cases, each of which provides a new point of view and helps set the scene for the gay backdrop against which Wilde's affairs flourished.

---

[34] Giovanni dell'Orto, *Tutta un'altra storia. L'omosessualita; dall'antichità al secondo Dopoguerra* (Milan: Il Saggiatore, 2015).
[35] Rictor Norton, *Mother Clap's Molly House: The Gay Subculture in England 1700–1830* (London: GMP, 1992).
[36] Matt Cook, "A Pickup in 1870," in *London and the Culture of Homosexuality, 1885–1994.* Vol. 6, *My Secret Life* (Cambridge UK: Cambridge University Press, 2003).

The evidence suggests a busy, crowded homosexual life in the city, bustling with constant activity, chatter and noise. Rictor Norton notes that the area around Seven Dials was a productive cruising ground for William Beckford.[37] In 1810 and in 1825 John Muirhead, a member of the Society for the Suppression of Vice, was arrested after picking up an apprentice outside a print shop in Sackville Street, just off Piccadilly. In 1822 Percy Jocelyn, the bishop of Clogher, was caught with a guardsman in the White Lion Tavern in Haymarket. An ensuing condemnatory pamphlet asserted that "there were various houses in the metropolis used by such wretches for their nefarious purposes, especially in the neighbourhood of St Mary-le-bone."[38] Three years later, twenty-five men were arrested in an upstairs room at the Barley Mow in the Strand, seven of whom were subsequently convicted of indecent assault.[39] A raid on the Bull in Bulletin Court, just off the Strand, in 1830, revealed the use of an upstairs room by men who picked up soldiers in Horse Guards Parade.[40] *The Ledger*, a newspaper founded in 1760 in Berkshire and then published in London, in 1836 carries the following account of a gentleman who cut his own throat, driven to desperation by the most dastardly and ignoble treatment of a brutal mob at Brighton: "An inquest was held at Brighton on Tuesday on the body of Mr. Stanley Stokes, a proctor, of Doctor's Commons, who cut his throat in East Street in that town on Saturday night. Saunders, the landlord of the New Ship Hotel, on Saturday night had laid plans to interrupt him, and accompanied by a crowd of fellows, after charging him with an indecent assault on a boy's person, they simultaneously mobbed him, smeared his face with tar, gave him severe blows to the head with sticks etc., until he fell down. While undergoing the persecution, the unhappy man, in the open street, drew a penknife from his pocket, and inflicted a severe wound in his throat."

Also in 1836, James Stanhope was exposed as a homosexual in a libel suit, and hanged himself. A Mr. Bennet, accused in the *Age* newspaper of "improper intimacy" with a valet from Brussels named Valle, killed himself on June 16, 1836.[41] Other cases of

---

[37] The son of the wealthiest man in England, William Beckford (1760–1844) became the subject of newspaper gossip over his friendship with William Courtney, later 9th Earl of Devon, in the 1780s. He subsequently lived largely outside London society at his estate at Fonthill, near Exeter, but Norton shows that he nevertheless continued to explore the homosexual possibilities London offered.

[38] Cook, *London and the Culture of Homosexuality*. See also Luis Crompton, *Byron and Greek Love: Homophobia in 19th-century England* (Berkeley: University of, California Press, 1985). See also a recent book by Naomi Wolf, *Outrages: Sex, Censorship of the Criminalization of Love*, published in London in 2019, which is very illuminating.

[39] Cook, *London and the Culture of Homosexuality*.

[40] Cook, Ibid. See also Norton, *Mother Clap's Molly House*.

[41] Neil Bartlett, *Who Was That Man?: A Present for Mr. Oscar Wilde* (London: Serpent's Tail, 1988).

prostitution around this time involved soldiers at the Knightsbridge Barracks, and a canon of St. Paul's, who was found *in flagrante* in a wharf off Upper Thames Street, just south of the cathedral.[42] Many of these cases were greeted with considerable public anger. Jocelyn and his guardsman lover had to be protected from angry crowds, whilst the men arrested at the Bull faced a mob of 500, who pelted them with mud.

They were not the only ones. The Public Records Office file from which these details are all taken contains the calling cards of several homosexual prostitutes; illustrated papers of the time carried pictures of a stereotyped, and widely recognizable, effeminate male homosexual; evidence at the trial described a circle of at least twenty young men who were in the habit of cruising the West End together, either in drag or at least in full slap. Some of the more effeminate witnesses even left the stand to the sound of appreciative laughter. Mr. Thomas Gibbings, who had hosted drag balls at Maxell's Hotel, and whose voice and manner were decidedly effeminate, appeared to regard the modern pastime of going in drag as perfectly harmless; and was applauded for saying so.[43] All of this shows us that there was a flourishing trade in male prostitution in London from the 1860s onwards. Private soldiers, particularly guardsmen stationed in the capital, were also willing to supplement their meagre pay by obliging 'gentlemen' in this way. Night-house tarts, expensive courtesans, sailors' whores, dolly mops, synthetic virgins; these were only some of the many types of prostitutes available to moneyed Victorians. And it would be impossible to give a complete account of all of them, but almost any kind of taste and vice was catered to. The one common denominator: finding a place in which to practise it.[44]

The most celebrated venue in the 1850s and 1860s was the Café Royal in Princess Street off Leicester Square, better known as Kate Hamilton's. Its entrance was down a long passage and carefully guarded—probably not from fear of the law but to prevent the premises being cluttered with unprofitable customers and inferior prostitutes. Mrs. Hamilton, who presided, was a mountain of a woman, hideously ugly but with one of those mysterious talents for promoting 'atmosphere.' Throughout the night she would swig champagne, now and then shaking with laughter like a giant blancmange.[45]

An interesting book from this point of view is *Sins of the Cities of the Plain*, a pornographic novel published in 1881, which explores the sexual possibilities that London offered to a select number of readers. What the text usefully explains

---

[42] Norton, *Mother Clapp's Molly House.*
[43] Jonathan Goldberg, *Reclaiming Sodom* (New York: Routledge, 1994).
[44] Kellow Chesney, *The Victorian Underworld* (Middlesex: Penguin, 1972) and Fergus Linnane, *London's Underworld: Three Centuries of Vice and Crime* (London: Hodder and Stoughton, 1965).
[45] Linnane, *London's Underworld.* See also Chesney, *The Victorian Underworld.*

40

is how prevailing class, gender and racial power dynamics were replicated in the conceptualization of homosexual behavior of the time. It also outlines a fictionalized homoerotic geography of London which drew on people. Two hundred and fifty copies of *Sins of the Cities of the Plain* were privately published in 1881 by William Lazenby who had offices in Leicester Square. Peter Mendes believes that it was a collaborative work by the publisher of erotica James Campbell Reddie[46] and the painter Simeon Solomon who, unemployed after being accused of having sex with a man in a Marylebone public toilet in 1873, was in desperate need of money.[47] The story, presented in the form of a series of confessional essays, tells the tales of Jack Saul (a male prostitute who went by the name of Mary-Ann)[48] which he sold to one of his clients, Mr. Chambon for approximately £20 per session. Jack Saul, a person who really existed, was the most famous male prostitute in Victorian London. Born in a Dublin slum, he became embroiled in two of the major scandals of the era, and was the central character in an "infamous" work of pornography. Jack was good-looking, stood five foot five and a half inches, with fair hair and a fresh complexion, and the developing look of a young Adonis, if a somewhat effeminate one.

Secret societies, bookshops and specialized magazines in London.

The books that the world calls immoral are the books that show the world its own shame.
Oscar Wilde

Bookshops around Soho enjoyed a certain notoriety. Around 1850 a French bookseller named Charles Hirsch[49] came over from Paris to London and opened a bookshop called the Librairie Française in Coventry Street, to sell French publications. Among his first customers was Oscar Wilde, who used to buy the works of the leading French authors of the day, such as Zola and Maupassant. After a while, when he got to know the bookseller better and had taken him into his confidence, Wilde would order "certain licentious works of a special genre" which he euphemistically described as "Socratic" and which the bookseller was able to obtain, albeit not without difficulty. Most of these works were in French, like *Monsieur Venus* by "Rachilde."

---

[46] James Campbell Reddie (November 26 1807–July 4 1878) was a 19th-century collector and author of pornography who, writing as "James Campbell," worked for publisher William Dugdale.

[47] Peter Mendes, *Clandestine Erotic Fiction in England 1800-1930* (New York: Ashgate, 1993).

[48] Glenn Chandler, *The Sins of Jack Saul* (London: Grosvenor House, 2016).

[49] Charles Hirsch. He was, maybe, involved in the writing of *Teleny, or The Reverse of the Medal*, an early work of homosexual pornography, and described Oscar Wilde's involvement in its compilation. He also published in Paris and translated pornographic works from French into English and vice versa. He published a translation of *Teleny* into French in 1934.

Charles Hirsch claimed to have sold "Socratic" material, including *The Sins of the City of the Plain*, to Wilde and his friends from the bookshop he ran between 1890 and 1900. It was also from here that the growing manuscript of the homoerotic pornographic novel *Teleny* was available for borrowing during the course of 1890. Another character we must now consider is Leonard Smithers, who ultimately published *Teleny* (or *The Reverse of the Medal*)[50] in 1893 and also championed and published the work of both Wilde and illustrator Aubrey Beardsley. He had offices at 3 Soho Square, whilst his business partner, pornographer Harry Nicholls, had bookshops first in Wardour Street and then, from 1894, in the same building as Smithers.

It was against this background that by 1897 George Cecil Ives[51] created and founded the Order of Chaeronea, a secret society for homosexuals named after the location of the battle where the Sacred Band of Thebes, an elite unit of the Theban army consisting of 150 pairs of male lovers, was annihilated in 338 BCE. Members included Charles Kains Jackson,[52] Samuel Elsworth Cottam, Montague Summers and John Gambril Nicholson. That same year, Ives visited Edward Carpenter at Millthorpe. This marked the beginning of their friendship. The affiliation and the ritual that cemented it constituted a protective and quasi-Masonic bond based specifically on sexual preferences. But one had to be careful: public reaction to revelations of homosexual networks was always rather hysterical. Friedrich Engels for example, was fascinated by the idea of a homosexual state within the state. But when Karl Ulrichs, the German writer who championed gay rights, sent Marx one of his books

---

[50] *Teleny, or, The Reverse of the Medal*, is a pornographic novel, first published in London in 1893. The authorship of the work is unknown. There is a general consensus that it was a collective effort, but it has often been attributed to Oscar Wilde. Set in *fin-de-siècle* Paris, its concerns are the magnetic attraction and passionate though ultimately tragic affair between a young Frenchman named Camille de Grieux and the Hungarian pianist René Teleny. The novel is one of the earliest pieces of English-language pornography that focuses explicitly and near-exclusively on homosexuality (following *The Sins of the Cities of the Plain*, published in 1881). Wilde's authorship, while unproven, is claimed by erotic bookseller and pornographer Charles Hirsch (see the previous note); his supposition is that the book was authored in "round robin" style by a small group of Wilde's intimate associates. Neither Wilde's authorship nor editorship has ever been ascertained. By 1893, the manuscript had made its way into the hands of Leonard Smithers, who since 1892 had been in business with Harry Sidney Nichols, Smithers serving primarily as an "entrepreneurial" liaison between "authors, publishers and distributors." Smithers and Nichols were aligned with William Lazenby, Edward Avery and Charles Carrington, in a small and tightly interwoven group of late Victorian publishers heavily involved in the production and distribution of pornography in London and Paris. In the 1890s Smithers worked extensively with Wilde and his circle, as we will see in another part of the book.
[51] George Cecil Ives (October 1 1867–June 4 1950). Ives was the illegitimate son of an English army officer and a Spanish baroness. He was raised by his paternal grandmother, Emma Ives. They lived between Bentworth in Hampshire and the South of France. Ives met Oscar Wilde at the Authors' Club in London in 1892. Ives was already working for what he called "the Cause": the end of the oppression of homosexuals. He hoped that Wilde would join "the Cause," but was disappointed. In 1893, Lord Alfred Douglas, with whom he had a brief affair, introduced Ives to several Oxford poets whom Ives also tried to recruit.
[52] Charles Philip Castle Kains Jackson (1857–1933) was an English poet closely associated with the Uranian school. In addition to a career as a lawyer, he served as editor for the periodical *The Artist and Journal of Home Culture*, which became something of an official periodical for the movement.

in 1869, Engels had a vision of "pederasty" as a rival to international socialism: "pederasts are beginning to count themselves and are discovering that they are a power in the state. All they lack is organization."[53] It is here worth briefly recalling that it was Ives who, together with Edward Carpenter, Magnus Hirschfeld, Laurence Housman and others, founded the British Society for the Study of Sex Psychology in 1914. Ives was the archivist for the Society, whose papers are now held by the Harry Ransom Center at the University of Texas at Austin. He was also in touch with other progressive psychologists such as Henry Havelock Ellis and the Italian Professor Cesare Lombroso in Turin.

Between 1888 and 1894 *The Artist and Journal of Home Culture* became another point of reference: the journal itself served what Laurel Brake describes as "a community of self-identifying 'gay' readers and writers," published homoerotic verse and features, often in the Hellenic vein, as well as an explicit call for the legitimization of homosexual relations, especially under the editorship of Charles Kains Jackson. The journal managed to carry "homosexual material and keep the homo reader on board without offending his male and female heterosexual readers."[54] It did this partly through the evocation of ancient Greece, which could serve both homophile and national culture. Virtually every edition during Jackson's tenure included poetry which evoked the fantasy of youths with the idealized bodies of Greek statues bathing naked, and often there were also articles and reviews which reinforced such Hellenic and pastoral themes and images.[55]

The final issue of *The Artist* with Jackson as editor (April 1894) contained multiple images of male homosexuality. These included Lord Alfred Douglas's love poem for a sixteen-year-old boy, "Prince Charming," a bathing ballad by John Gambril Nicholson and a review of the decadent artist Aubrey Beardsley by Theodore Wratislaw—whose poem "To a Sicilian Boy" had been published in *The Artist* the previous year.[56] Another highly significant book, at that time, was *My Secret Life*, by "Walter." It is the memoir of a gentleman describing the author's sexual development and experiences in Victorian England, beginning around 1888. It was first published in a private edition of eleven volumes, at the expense of the author. The first edition was probably printed by Auguste Brancart, in an impression of only twenty-five copies. In the twentieth century, *My Secret Life* was "pirated" and reprinted in a number of abridged versions that were frequently suppressed for obscenity. The most

---

[53] Friedrich Engels, *Der Ursprung der Familie, des Privateigenthums und des Staats* (Zurich, 1884).

[54] Laurel Brake, *Print in Transition, 1850-1910: Studies in Media and Book History* (London: Palgrave, 2001).

[55] "The New Chivalry," *The Artist and Journal of Home Culture* 14/15 (April 1893).

[56] Lord Alfred Douglas, "Prince Charming"; John Gambril Nicholson, "On the River's Bank"; Theodore Wratislaw, "The Salomé of Aubrey Beardsley," *The Artist* 14/15 (April 1894).

commonly suggested author is Henry Spencer Ashbee (1834–1900). He was a book collector, writer and bibliographer and, judging from the three volumes he published under his pseudonym of Pisanus Fraxi, he was the leading expert on erotic books in his day. The question remains concerning to what extent the book is a record of true experiences (whether of Ashbee or of another writer).

We cannot fail to mention another very important figure of that time, Edward Carpenter (1844–1929),[57] who played an important role in the campaign for gay rights in Britain. He was an English socialist poet, philosopher, anthologist, writer and a close friend of Rabindranath Tagore and Walt Whitman. He was instrumental in the foundation of the Labour Party.

In the 1890s, Carpenter first started trying to publish on the topic of homosexuality. His first attempt was his pamphlet *Homogenic Love and Its Place in a Free Society*. However, following the public outrage caused by the Oscar Wilde trial in 1895, the pamphlet was not reprinted but only published and circulated privately. In 1908, Carpenter finally publicly published on the topic of homosexuality with his book *The Intermediate Sex*, which became the first generally available book in English that portrayed homosexuality in a positive light.

---

[57] He went to Cambridge in 1864, eventually became a fellow of Trinity Hall and was ordained into the Anglican Church. In 1868 he received a copy of Walt Whitman's poems *Leaves of Grass*, which had a profound influence on Carpenter, and started him on a path to socialism. Carpenter resigned from his fellowship in the Anglican Church to pursue a different life. In 1891, he met George Merrill, a working-class man twenty-two years his junior, and the two men struck up a relationship, eventually cohabiting in 1898.

A gentleman is one who never hurts anyone's feelings unintentionally.
Oscar Wilde

Before the three trials of Oscar Wilde there were three homosexual scandals that drew public attention to the "gay issue."

The first one,[58] around 1870, involved a member of Parliament, thirty-year old Lord Arthur Clinton, third son of the fifth Duke of Newcastle. Living in the same lodgings as Lord Arthur were two young men, Ernest Boulton, aged twenty-two, the son of a London stockbroker, and his inseparable companion, Frederick William Park, aged twenty-three, whose father was a master in the Court of Common Pleas. Boulton and Park were both transvestite homosexuals, who liked to play female parts in amateur theatre and frequently appeared in public dressed as women, rouged and painted, in low-cut dresses. Boulton, familiarly known as "Stella," was an effeminate-looking youth, extremely musical and with a fine soprano voice. From an early age Boulton's mother had encouraged his fondness for dressing as a girl and calling himself Stella. Starting around 1868, when they were approximately twenty, they both began to cross-dress in public: Fanny and Stella became, we know, a frequent sight around the West End. Stella and Fanny worked as male prostitutes too, providing services for a considerable number of gentlemen. Around 1868, Boulton struck up a relationship with Lord Arthur Clinton, in whose company Fanny and Stella were often seen. A servant in the lodgings deposed that she thought that Boulton was Lord Arthur's wife, and certainly his lordship did nothing to dispel the idea. Lord Arthur paid for his lodgings, his hairdresser (who visited the house daily), and commissioned a stationer to produce visiting cards in the name of "Lady Arthur Clinton" and a seal with the name "Stella" that Boulton could use. In a scene from *Sins of the Cities of the Plain*, Jack Saul recounts attending a sodomites' ball, where the 'women' were men dressed in drag. Fanny, Stella, and Lord Arthur were notable guests. Saul spent the evening with the trio, and in the morning, they breakfasted "all dressed as ladies." Fanny and Stella's arrest, which made national headlines, took place on the evening of April 28, 1870. The police had been following them for some time and when, in the company of a man, they were seen by a police detective leaving a house near Regent Square, the policeman followed them to the Strand Theater and observed them meet two gentlemen and enter a private box inside the theater (the theaters

---

[58] For more details see Morris Kaplan, *Sodom on the Thames: Sex Love and Scandal in Wilde Times* (Ithaca: Cornell University Press, 2005).

were known as hotbeds of vice, and were common haunting grounds of prostitutes, both male and female). The four were taken to a police station and subjected to an intrusive psychical examination to try to gain evidence that they had engaged in anal sex. No such evidence was found. Nonetheless, they were kept overnight and in the morning brought before a magistrate at Bow Street Court. Boulton and Park were still dressed as Fanny and Stella, and news of their appearance quickly spread through the streets. Soon a crowd had gathered outside to look at the men dressed as women. A search of their apartments produced love letters from John Stafford Fiske, the United States consul in Edinburgh. But the tragedy was just around the corner: when Clinton received his subpoena on June 18 to testify he could not bear the blow. The following day he was found dead. He was thirty years old. The official cause was recorded as scarlet fever, but he almost certainly committed suicide. A third theory, supported by the writer Mc Kenna hypothesizes that Clinton escaped abroad thanks to being a godson of the then prime minister William Gladstone and that he subsequently lived in exile.[59] However, although there could be no doubt that all the defendants were homosexuals, the prosecution was unable to prove that any of them had infringed the law. Fanny and Stella were recognized not as eccentrics, but as alien, the representatives of another world! London was not the home of such a creature: the crime did not exist!

The second scandal concerned the Marquess of Queensberry, Bosie's father. In 1892 his eldest son Francis Archibald Douglas (Viscount Drumlanrig) was appointed assistant private secretary to Lord Rosebery, then foreign minister in Gladstone's government. Rosebery had a particular liking for amiable young men with good looks, and took a considerable fancy to young Francis, and in the following year persuaded the prime minister to make him a lord-in-waiting, a junior ministerial post which involved answering for the government on occasion from the front bench in the House of Lords. One October afternoon in 1894, Francis was the victim of a shocking tragedy. A guest at a shooting party in Somerset, he died after receiving a gunshot wound. On the face of it, it looked like an accident—a fact confirmed by the verdict of "accidental death" subsequently brought in by a coroner's jury at the inquest. Nevertheless, there were rumors at the time that Francis was implicated in a homosexual affair with Rosebery and had committed suicide rather than face a public scandal. Given the circumstances, everything was silenced.

The third scandal[60] occurred in July 1889. Police Constable Luke Hanks was investigating a theft from the London Central Telegraph Office. During the

---

[59] Note McKenna, *The Secret Life of Oscar Wilde*.
[60] See Montgomery Harford Hyde, *The Cleveland Street Scandal* (London: W.H. Allen, 1976).

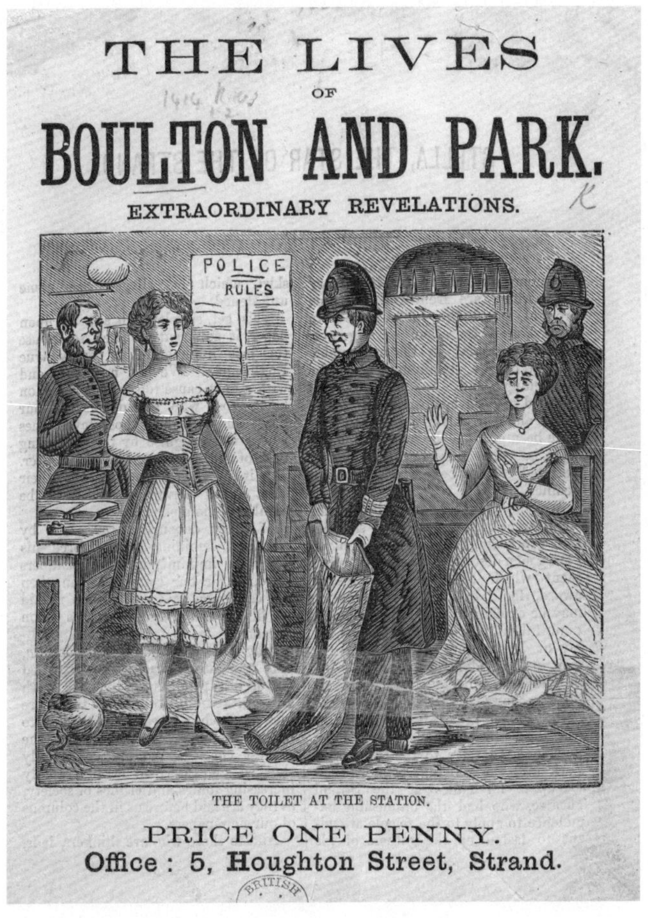

investigation, a fifteen-year-old telegraph boy named Charles Thomas Swinscow was discovered to be in possession of fourteen shillings, equivalent to several weeks of his wages. At the time, messenger boys were not permitted to carry any personal cash in the course of their duties, to prevent their own money being mixed with that of the customers. Suspecting the boy's involvement in the theft, Swinscow was taken in for questioning as part of the police operation. When asked how he came to have such a large sum of money in his possession, Swinscow panicked and confessed he'd been recruited by Charles Hammond to work at a house in Cleveland Street, where, for the sum of four shillings a time, he would permit the brothel's clients to "have a go between my legs" and "put their persons into me." After hesitating, Swinscow admitted that he earned the money working as a prostitute for Charles Hammond, who operated a male brothel at 19 Cleveland Street. According to Swinscow, he was introduced to Hammond by a General Post Office clerk, eighteen-year-old Henry Newlove. In addition, he named two seventeen-year-old telegraph boys who also worked for Hammond: George Alma Wright and Charles Ernest Thickbroom. The Cleveland Street story was the third scandal which the government was accused of covering up to protect the names of aristocrats and other prominent patrons. It was rumored that Prince Albert Victor, the eldest son of the Prince of Wales and second-in-line to the British throne had visited, though this has never been substantiated. Oscar Wilde alluded to the scandal in *The Picture of Dorian Gray*, first published in 1890. Reviews of the novel were hostile; in a clear reference to the Cleveland Street scandal, one reviewer called it suitable for "none but outlawed noblemen and perverted telegraph boys." On the advice of the publisher, Wilde's 1891 revision of the novel omitted certain key passages, which were considered too homoerotic. While many aristocrats were allegedly part of the list of clients the police discovered, those names were never revealed. But for months, the tale of the London sodomite brothel lit up the headlines of newspapers around the world. Prince Albert Victor went for a four-month tour of British India to avoid the press. In late 1882 Wilde went to a dinner. Before dinner the guests put their hands through a curtain so that the palmist Cheiro could read their palms without knowing who they were. When Wilde held out his hand, Cheiro found the markings on each so different to the other that he explained how in palmistry the left hand denotes hereditary tendencies and the right hand individual developments. The left hand in front of him, he said, promised a brilliant success; the right, impending ruin. "The left hand is the hand of a king, but the right that of a king who will send himself into exile." Wilde, a superstitious man (he had refused to join the skeptics of the Thirteen Club), asked "At what date?" — "A few years from now, and about your fortieth year." (He was then thirty-eight.) Without another word Wilde left the party.

The one disgraceful, unpardonable, and to all time contemptible action of my life was to allow myself to appeal to society for help and protection.
Oscar Wilde

On February 28 1895, Wilde went to his club. Upon arrival, the porter handed him a small envelope bearing the name of the Marquess of Queensberry with a note inside which read "For Oscar Wilde posing as somdomite" [*sic*].

What happened next is history and at the end Wilde was sent to prison for indecency after three trials. Both the defendant and prosecution conspired to maintain the innocence of Bosie, although his complicity in Wilde's life was clearly evident to the audience, to the judge and to all the journalists in the courtroom. A very particular version of the truth was presented to the court.[61]

> "Do you find him guilty or not guilty of an act of gross indecency?"
> "Guilty!"
> "And I? May I say nothing, my Lord?" said Oscar.

He was not allowed to say one word.

After that, the Crown issued a warrant for Wilde's arrest. Rather than flee to France, Wilde decided to remain and stand trial. After Wilde's sentence, many English homosexuals were alarmed by the scandal and deemed it prudent to leave the country for a time. Wilde's friend and biographer Frank Harris later described the immediate result of his arrest:

> Every train to Dover was crowded, every steamer to Calais thronged with members of the aristocratic and leisured classes, who seemed to prefer Paris, or even Nice out of season, to a city like London, where the police might act with such unexpected vigour. The truth was that the cultured aesthetes [. . .] had been thunderstruck by the facts which the Queensberry trial had laid bare. For the first time they learned that such houses as Taylor's were under police supervision, and that creatures like Wood and Parker were

---

[61] Merlin Holland, *The Real Trial of Oscar Wilde: the First Uncensored Transcript of the Trial of Oscar Wilde vs. John Douglas, Marquess of Queensberry* (London: Fourth Estate, 2003).

classified and watched. They had imagined that in "the home of liberty" such practices passed unnoticed. It came as a shock to their preconceived ideas that the police in London knew a great many things which they were not supposed to concern themselves with, and this unwelcome glare of light drove the vicious forth in wild haste. Never was Paris so crowded with members of the English governing classes; here was to be seen a famous ex-minister; there the fine face of the president of a Royal society; at one table at the Café de la Paix, a millionaire recently ennobled and celebrated for his exquisite taste in art; opposite him a famous general. It was even said that a celebrated English actor took a return ticket to Paris for three or four days just to be in the fashion. The majority of the migrants stayed abroad for some time. The wind of terror which had swept them across the Channel opposed their return, and they scattered over the Continent from Naples to Monte Carlo and from Palermo to Seville under all sorts of pretexts.[62]

After Wilde's conviction, *Reynolds's* was one of the very few papers to sympathize with the writer, refusing "to gloat over the ruin of the unhappy man." Its lead editorial announced the broader theme of "male prostitution": "Every person with any feeling will feel sorry that a man of such eminent parts as Oscar Wilde could have so far degraded himself and outraged the ordinary instincts of humanity, as to seek an outlet for his passion in male prostitution."

---

[62] Harris, *Oscar Wide*.

When the gods wish to punish us they answer our prayers.
Oscar Wilde

As we know, Oscar spent two years in prison.

Was prisoner 1122 (Harry Bushnell) Oscar's lover? There is no evidence of this and there is no evidence of an erotic interest, but there was an obviously friendly interest in the "little dark-eyed friend" mentioned by Wilde in a letter after his prison release.

Wilde sent Bushnell some money when he had been freed from prison, but alas, Bushnell was soon back in prison again.

"The friendship was born for a strange episode," said Peter Stoneley, a professor of English literature at Reading University, who has been poring through the old prison records now stored at the Berkshire Record Office. "The only thing we know is that one of the basic rules of the Prison was that the prisoners who committed infractions [. . .] should be locked up in the dark cells for no more than three days, but Oscar Wilde was actually kept there for two weeks, as punishment for talking to another prisoner (Harry Bushnell) in the chapel."

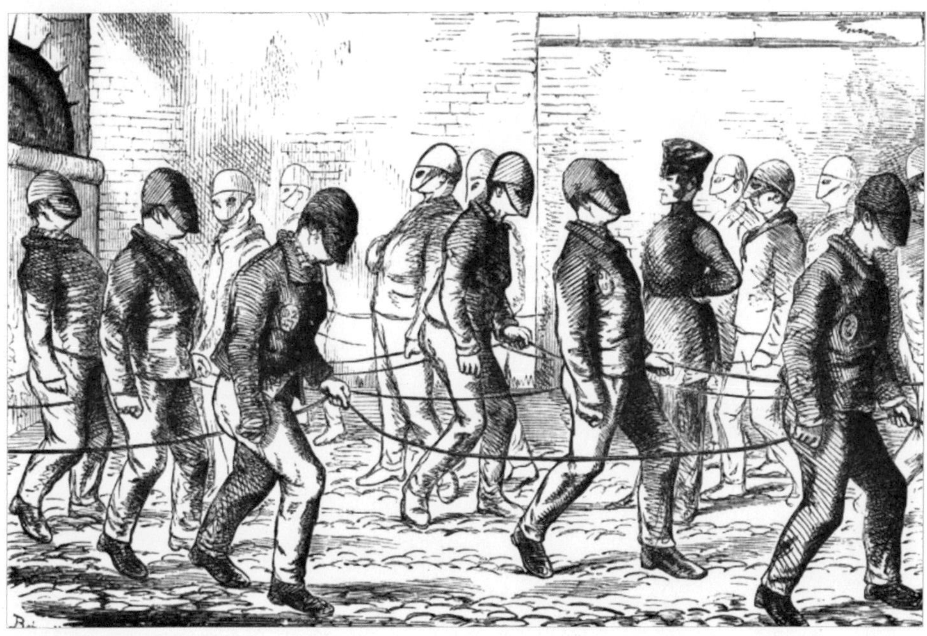

Emily O'Neil, who has written the guide of Reading Gaol for the National Trust, states as follows: "Wilde was certainly the only middle-class, university-educated man in the prison. It's striking that in his photographs Bushnell's hands are filthy while Wilde's were soft. The prisoners themselves told Wilde it was worse for him than for them, and they were probably right."

Love, or Passion with the mask of Love; is my only consolation.
Oscar Wilde

Wilde left Reading on the evening of May 18, 1897. Before he left, the prison governor handed him back his manuscript of *De Profundis*, a long combined poem and letter that Wilde had written, a page a day, during his imprisonment. Only two reporters were at the gates to see him leave. Wearing the same clothes (and now addressed as "Mr. Wilde" rather than his prisoner number C.3.3) he was driven in a cab to Twyford station for transfer to Pentonville Prison for the night. Taking the London train, the group left it at Westbourne Park and traveled by cab to Pentonville Prison. At 6.15 next morning he was fetched in a cab by More Adey and Stewart Headlam. They managed to avoid the press and drove straight to Headlam's house at 31 Upper Bedford Place, Bloomsbury, where Wilde changed and had breakfast.

Ada Leverson and her husband were among the first to greet him. But on May 19, 1896 Oscar Wilde ceased to exist. His place was taken by Mr. Sebastian Melmoth. Reggie Turner gave him a dressing coat and a set of suitcases stamped with the initials S. M. The name Sebastian was inspired by the same name as the saint who died transfixed by arrows (perhaps the legacy of a homosexual fantasy?) and Melmoth by *Melmoth the Wanderer*, a gothic horror novel by Charles Maturin. One of the first things that Wilde did was to write a long and contrite letter to his wife asking to see her and the boys. The letter, since lost, was described by Constance as one of the most beautiful he had ever written her. He also wrote to the editor of the *Daily Chronicle*, Henry Massingham, about the ill-treatment of children in prison which he had witnessed, about the dismissal of his own warder, Thomas Martin, for taking pity on the children and giving them biscuits, and about the case of a mentally disturbed prisoner by the name of Prince, who was being flogged regularly every day.

His letter was published on May 28 under the heading "The case of warder Martin, some cruelties of prison life."

It was during his time in Bernavel in France where Oscar took refuge, that Ernest Dowson, poet and friend, dragged him into a local "closed house." This enterprise was conducted without discretion: "several friends were waiting at the door. Oscar comes out proclaiming the famous phrase: 'My dear, after so many years, I had forgotten what women know. . . Cold ram!'"

Interview with Oscar Wilde after prison by Gédéon Spillet, November 22 1897 (Paris, *Gil Blas*)

The following scene takes place at Dieppe where the English novelist spent the last five days of autumn before embarking for the resort of Naples where, I believe, he has decided to spend the winter [. . .]. Oscar Wilde expresses himself with ease in a modern, highly-coloured French to which his slight British accent adds a certain charm of its own. [. . .] When he laughs—and he laughs often, rather like a contented ogre—you can see his long, broad, splayed teeth and the gold that fills the gap between them. Wilde is very much the fatalist, and wears a ring set with an emerald on the little finger of each hand. These precious stones are engraved with cabbalistic symbols, and come from an Egyptian pyramid. He claims that the emerald on his left hand is the real cause of all of this happiness, and that the one on his right hand is the cause of all his unhappiness. To my observation—which was logical enough, I think—that he should have taken off the evil ring, he replied with a changed voice: "To live in happiness, you must know some unhappiness in life."
Besides, green is Oscar Wilde's favorite colour. For him it is all important, and the symbol of Hell. He has his own very personal interpretation of what Hell is. He says that Heaven is made for decent people, for the upright members in the middle class, and, generally speaking, for all the ordinary people who are unaware of their new freedom of Will. God is good. He is merciful, far too merciful. It is easy enough to ring the bell at St Peter's door, but Satan demands far more of his followers. With him a certain ceremony is required. "To enter Paradise you only have to knock once at the door, but you must not three times to get into Hell. Believe me, love the green, loves Hell. The colour green and Hell are both made for thieves and artists." [. . .] He speaks readily enough of those two lost years, and of the remarks made about his fellow-prisoners whose mood he tried very hard to define. He doesn't seem to have suffered much physically, but he must have suffered great tortures of mind and soul. He had to pass through all the phases and anguish of the "*nuit de fâmes*" Huysmans talks about concerning St John of the Cross. When I asked him to describe all the hardships he suffered in prison, he replied with a sudden tremor in his voice, "Excuse me, I never speak of that."
Seeing him so gay, so lucid, so quick to deliver a retort, one forgets in the end the terrible ordeal he has undergone [. . .].
He describes the theatre he dreams of, the plays he wants to write, and

the unsurpassed worship he pays "the princess of beautiful gestures and postures," Sarah Bernhardt, on whom he is counting to bring to life one of his heroines. Next he relates to me in a lively fashion the scenario of a satiric play in three scenes which he planned to write but has given up, at least for the present.

Let him speak for himself:

"The Gospel often speaks of the sick in Christ cured; but nowhere in the holy books is there mention of what became of them. It's a missing piece in the story which a short story writer's or playwright's imagination ought to try to fill.

Here's my idea.

In the first scene we see a young man with a garland of roses on his head. He is getting drunk on wine. Christ happens to be passing by and He upbraids him for his drunkenness. The young man recognizes him, and after doing homage to Him says, "Master, I am the cripple whom you cured."

Christ comes in the second scene to a place where another man is indulging in debauchery with three courtesans. He upbraids him for his vice. The man recognizes Him, and prostrating himself says, "Master, I am the leper whom you cured."

Then Christ, very sad, goes to the desert (scene 3). Seeing a young man crying, Christ says to him softly, "Why do you weep?" And the young man, recognizing him, answers "Master, I was dead and you brought me back to life!"

But, adds Oscar Wilde as he ends his tale, "I don't think I'll carry out the idea for one must respect Christ in His majesty."

***

Letter to Robert Ross, May 28 1897 (Berneval-sur-Mer, Hôtel de la Plage)

My dear Robbie,

This is my first day alone, and of course a very unhappy one. I begin to realize my terrible position of isolation, and I have been rebellious and bitter of heart all day. Is it not sad? I thought I was accepting everything so well and so simply, and I have had moods of rage passing over my nature, like gusts of bitter wind or storm spoiling the sweet corn, or blasting the young shoots. I found a little chapel, full of the most fantastic saints, so ugly and Gothic, and painted quite gaudily—some of them with smiles carved to a rictus almost, like primitive things—but they all seemed to me to be idols. I laughed with amusement when I saw them.

Fortunately, there was a lovely crucifix in a side-chapel—not a Jansenist one, but with wide-stretched arms of gold. I was pleased at that, and wandered then by the cliffs where I fell asleep on the warm course brown sea-grass. I had hardly any sleep last night.

Bosie's revolting letter was in the room, and foolishly I had read it again and left it by my bedside. My dream was that my mother was speaking to me with some sternness, and that she was in trouble. I quite see that whenever I am in danger she will in some way warn me. I have a real terror now of that unfortunate ungrateful young man with his unimaginative selfishness and his entire lack of all sensitiveness to what in others is good or kind or trying to be so. I feel him as an evil influence, poor fellow. To be with him would be to return to the hell from which I do think I have been released. I hope never to see him again. [. . .]

Dear sweet Robbie, [. . .] you are helping me to save my soul alive, not in the theological sense, but in the plain meaning of the words, for my soul was really dead in the slough of coarse pleasures, my life was unworthy of an artist: you can heal me and help me. No other friend have I now in this beautiful world. I want no other. [. . .] You are made to help me. I weep with sorrow when I think how much I need help, but I weep with joy when I think I have you to give it to me. [. . .] It is not for nothing that I named you in prison St Robert of Phillimore.[63] Love can canonize people. The saints are those who have been most loved. [. . .] When I came out of prison *you* met me with garments, with spices, with wise counsel. You met me with love. Not others did it, but you. [. . .] I enclose a lot of letters. Please put money orders in them and send them off. [. . .] They are my debts of honour, and I must pay them, Jackson £1; Bushell £ 2.10; Groves, £3.10. [. . .]

With all love and affection, yours OSCAR

***

Letter to Robert Ross, May 29–30 1897 (Berneval-sur-Mer, Hôtel de la Plage)

My dear Robbie,
Your letter is quite admirable, but, dear boy, don't you see how right I was to write to the *Chronicle*? All good impulses are right. Had I listened to some of my friends I would never have written. I am sending

---

[63] Author's Note: This was a Saint invented by Oscar since Ross lived in Phillimore Garden.

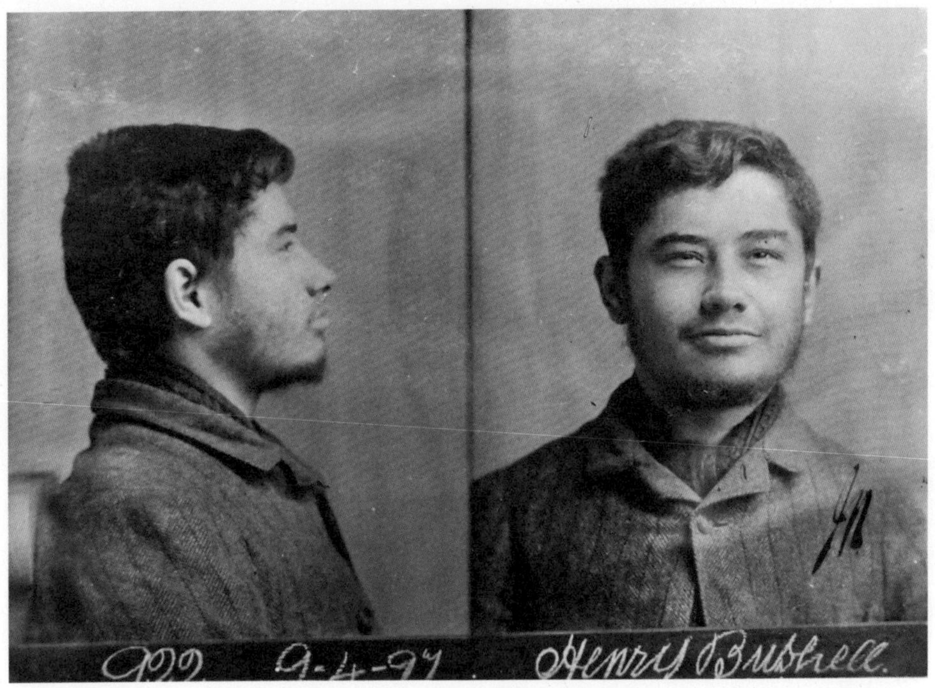

a postscript to Massingham of some importance: if he publishes it, send it to me.[64] I have also asked him if he wishes my prison experiences, and if he would share in a syndicate. I think now, as the length of my letter is so great, that I could do *three* articles on Prison Life. Of course much will be psychological and introspective: and one will be on Christ as the Precursor of the Romantic Movement in Life, that lovely subject which was revealed to me when I found myself in the company of the same sort of people Christ liked, outcasts and beggars.[65] I am terrified about Bosie. More writes to me that he has been practically interviewed about me! It is awful. More, desiring to spare me pain, I suppose, did not send me the paper, so I have had a wretched night.

Bosie can almost ruin me. I earnestly beg that some entreaty be made to him not to do so a second time. His letters to me are infamous. I have heard from my wife. She sends me photographs of the boys—such lovely little fellows in Eton collars—but makes no promise to allow me to see them: she says she will see me, twice a year, but I want my boys. It is terrible punishment, dear Robbie, and oh! How well I deserve it. But

---

[64] Author's Note: Massingham was the chief of the *The Daily Chronicle*.
[65] Author's Note: The only further prose writing by Wilde about his prison experiences was a second letter to *the Daily Chronicle* in March 1898.

it makes me feel disgraced and evil, and I don't want to feel that. Let me have the *Chronicle* regularly. Also write often. It is very good for me to be alone. I am working. Dear Robbie, ever yours Oscar

***

But, in the meanwhile, the tragic and inevitable rapprochement between Oscar and Bosie follows:

Letter to Lord Alfred Douglas, June 4 1897 (Berneval-sur-Mer, Hôtel de la Plage)

My dear Boy, I have just got your letter, but Ernest Dowson, Dal Young, and Conder are here, so I cannot read it, except the last three lines. I love the last words of anything: the end in art is the beginning. Don't think I don't love you. Of course I love you more than anyone else. What if left to us is the knowledge that we love each other, and every day I think of you, and I know you are a poet, and that makes you doubly dear and wonderful. [. . .] Ever, dear boy, with fondest love. OSCAR

***

Letter to Robert Ross, June 5(?) 1987 (Berneval-sur-Mer, Hôtel de la Plage)

Bosie telegraphs daily. This is an exaggeration, [. . .] Ever yours Oscar

***

Letter to Frank Harris, June 13 1897 (Berneval-sur-Mer, Hôtel de la Plage)

My dear Frank, [. . .]
I have been thinking of a story to be called "The Silence of Frank Harris". [. . .] I am told that you are hurt with me because my letter of thanks to you was non sufficiently elaborated in expression. I told you I was grateful to you for your kindness to me. Words, *now*, to me signify *things*, actualities, real emotions, realized thoughts. I learn in prison to be grateful. I used to think gratitude a burden. Now I know that it is something that makes life lighter as well as lovelier for one. I am grateful for a thousand things, from my good friends down to the sun and the sea. But I cannot say more than that I am grateful. I cannot make phrases about it. For *me* to use such a word shows an enormous development in my nature. Two years ago, I did not know the feeling the words denotes. Now I know it, and I am thankful that

I have learnt that much, at any rate, by having been in prison. [. . .]
Violin-variations don't interest me. I am grateful to you.
[. . .] your sincere friend and admirer Oscar Wilde.

***

Letter to Lord Alfred Douglas, June 16 1897 (Berneval-sur-Mer)

[. . .] *I have asked you to come here on Saturday*. I have a bathing costume
for you, but you had better get one in Paris. Also bring me a lot of books,
and cigarettes. I cannot get good cigarettes here or at Dieppe. The weather
is very hot, so you will want a straw hat and flannels. [. . .] I hope to be in
my chalet by Saturday: so you will stay with me there. [. . .] On Sunday I
go to the Mass, in a dark blue suit. You must not have your letters sent on
under your own name. It might do me serious harm. I still suggest—for
the third time—Jonquil du Villon, but any name you like will do. [. . .]
Bring also some perfumes and nice things from the sellers of the dust of
roses. Also bring yourself. Ever yours Oscar.

***

Letter to Lord Alfred Douglas, August 31 1897 (Dieppe, Café Suisse)

My own Darling Boy,
I got your telegram half an hour ago, and just send you a line to say that
I feel that my only hope of again doing beautiful work in art is being
with you. It was not so in old days, but now it is different, and you can
really recreate in me that energy and sense of joyous power on which art
depends. Everyone is furious with me for going back to you, but they
don't understand us. I feel that it is only with you that I can do anything
at all. Do remake my ruined life for me, and then our friendship and
love will have a different meaning to be world. I wish that when we met
at Rouen[66] we had not parted at all. There are such wide abysses now of
space and land between us. But we love each other. Good night, dear,
Ever yours, Oscar

***

---

[66] Author's Note: This fateful meeting seems to have taken place on August 28–29. In his *Autobiography* Douglas
wrote: "Poor Oscar cried when I met him at the station. We walked about all day arm in arm, or hand in hand,
and were perfectly happy."

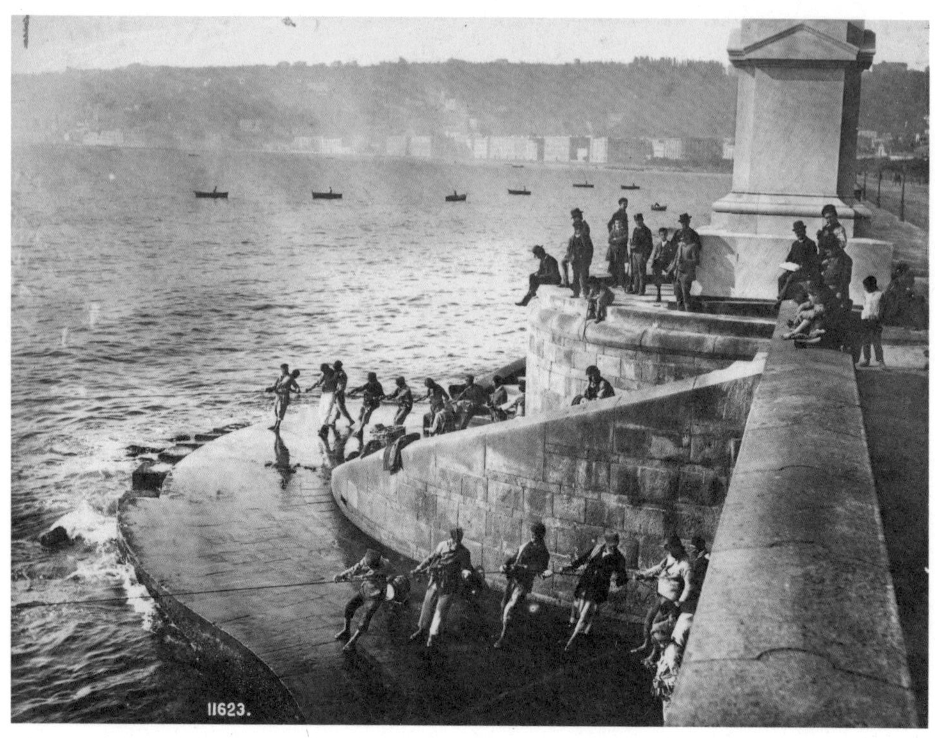

Letter to Leonard Smithers, September 14 1897 (Dieppe, Café des Tribuneaux)

My dear Smithers, It has been a great blow not seeing you again. I hope your leg is better. I leave here for Paris tomorrow—address Sebastian[67] Melmoth, Hôtel d'Espagne, Rue Taitbout, Paris—and from there I want to get on to Naples, in three days. At Naples I intend to finish my poem, and begin my play. [. . .] Could you advance me £20 on my poem? [. . .] I want to get away to Italy, but must have money. Sincerely yours Oscar Wilde

---

[67] Author's Note: Wilde occasionally wrote "Sebastien," but more often "Sebastian."

60

Keep love in your heart. A life without it is like a sunless garden when the flowers are dead.
Oscar Wilde

From Vincent O'Sullivan, *Aspects of Wilde* (London, 1936):

One day at the end of that summer, after he had come to Paris, I received a letter from him. He asked if I were in Paris, and if I were would I come to see him.

The next day I went about twelve o'clock to the address given—an hotel in the rue du Helder, just off the Boulevard. He was expecting a friend of his named Roland Strong.[68] After waiting about a quarter of an hour, seeing that Strong did not turn up, he left a letter for him and we went out to lunch. [. . .] Towards the end of the meal he said that he was rather troubled—as well as I remember, he said he was "passing through a crisis." It seemed that some friends of his family in England wanted him to go into a mountain village and write plays. This, it may be said in passing, was a most stupid suggestion which took no account of the havoc wrought on his brain and nerves by his trial and imprisonment. What he required was to forget, to be stimulated, distracted from his black thoughts. How could he find that in a mountain village? It would have continued the penal cell. He himself was inclined to go to Italy. [. . .] Finally he declared: "I shall go to Italy tonight. Or rather, I would go, but I am in an absurd position, I have no money." Upon leaving the restaurant we drove to the Banque de Paris et des Pays-Bas in the rue d'Antin where I had an account. He stayed in the cab and I brought him out the sum he wanted. It is one of the few things I look back on with satisfaction. It is not every day that one has the chance of relieving the anxiety of a genius and a hero. I think he left Paris the same evening; certainly very soon. When I saw him next it was a good while after, and in Italy.

***

Before he left Berneval, Oscar announced his intention to spend the winter in southern Italy. "I cannot stay in the North of Europe: the climate kills me," he told his

---

[68] Roland Strong (1865–1924), Paris correspondent of *The New York Times*, *The Observer* and *The Morning Post*. Author of the successful book *Where and How to Dine in Paris* (1900). He shared with Oscar the some lover, Maurice Gilbert, who was until the end a close friend of Oscar.

old friend Carlos Blacker, who lived in Switzerland: "I don't mind being alone when there is sunlight and *joie de vivre* all about me, but my last fortnight at Berneval has been black and dreadful, and quite suicidal. I have never been so unhappy." Blacker was skeptical. He suspected that Oscar's motives in going to Italy were primarily sexual and wrote to him, accusing him of "returning to his vomit." "You are really wrong in your views on the question of my going there," Oscar replied indignantly. "It is not perversity but unhappiness that makes me turn my steps to the South."[69]

In reality the decision to return to live together was in the minds of both Wilde and Lord Alfred Douglas, who was very emotional and not very rational.

It is true that Douglas asked Wilde an interval of six weeks before seeing him again. Bosie's plan, in fact, was to spend a few weeks with his mother in Aix-les-Bains to take care of his rheumatism and then a few weeks in Venice. The stage in Aix, in particular, as he himself recalls in his autobiography, helped him to complete what he considered his most beautiful ballad, *The Ballad of St. Vitus*, which had as its subject not a reconciliation with Wilde but with his father Lord Queensberry.

---

[69] McKenna, *The Secret Life of Oscar Wilde*.

THE FASCINATION OF PARTENOPE

We are all in the gutter but some of us are looking at the stars.
Oscar Wilde

In the previous pages, we have seen why tourists—mainly English and German—were drawn to the South to live the Italian Dream. At the time, Naples was one of the leading European cultural centers and close to the Greek, Roman and Egyptian heritage. Neapolitan culture—perceived as archaic, working-class, traditional, capable of great tolerance and openness, at once encompassing and conciliatory, able to preserve ambivalences and contradictions and to realize impossible integrations—was a sort of 'free port' where one could breathe, a freedom that Wilde yearned for. There was also that taste of magic, where dream and reality could coincide: it was the place where "The Souls of the Dead" could speak (see Oscar's confession to O'Sullivan), where streets were lit by *aedicule* (small shrines) with the Souls in Purgatory, where churches had whole walls adorned with votive offerings, and where the difference between sexes, albeit well-defined, also had delicate and malleable border areas. In 1586, a treatise by Giovanni Battista Della Porta whose partial translation was very popular at the time, *De Humana Physiognomia*, stated: "In Naples and Sicily there are many effeminate men who are neither men nor women, who shy away from men and who willingly converse with women."

The Neapolitan *femminielli*,[70] now and then, were not mere transvestites, as some have tried to classify them, nor effeminate homosexuals. They were considered to be a different genre that had to do with the Divine and with those sacred Greek initiation rites which always accompanied wedding ceremonies and funerals.[71] In his Roman History of 1857, T. Morrison confused *femminielli* with eunuchs and claimed of them as follows: "It is known that the ancients used to wither and numb their testicles with long applications of hemlock sauce to the scrotum: an operation that in Naples is entrusted to barbers and you can read signs such as 'here we castrate boys for cheap,' outside their shops, to make sure, among other things, that as they sang the Lord's praises in falsetto, with voices like those of children, they would convince God of their innocence."

A world, therefore, yet to be discovered and that deeply intrigued our writer.

---

[70] See Robert Jessie Stoller, *Sex and Gender. The Development of Masculinity and Femininity* (New York: Science House, 1968); William Simon, *Postmodern Sexualities* (New York: Harper and Row, 1968); Eugenio Zito and Paolo Valerio, "I femminielli napoletani: un genere al (di) confine," in *Sesso e genere*, eds. Roberto Vitelli and Paolo Valerio (Naples: Liguori, 2012).
[71] T. Morrison, *Storia Romana* (1857).

Letter to Robert Ross, September 21 1897 (Naples, Hôtel Royal des Étrangers)

My dearest Robbie,
Your letter has reached me here.
My going back to Bosie was psychologically inevitable: and, setting aside the interior life of the soul with its passion for self-realization at all costs, the world forced it to me.
I cannot live without the atmosphere of Love: I must love and be loved, whatever price I pay for it. I could have lived all my life with you, but you have other claims on you—claims you are too sweet a fellow to disregard—and all you could give me was a week of companionship. Reggie gave me three days, and Rowland[72] a sextette of suns, but for the last month at Berneval I was so lonely that I was on the brink of killing myself. The world shuts its gateway against me, and the door of Love lies open.
When people speak against me for going back to Bosie, tell them that he offered me love, and that in my loneliness and disgrace I, after three months' struggle against a hideous Philistine world, turned naturally to him. Of course, I shall often be unhappy, but still I love him: the mere fact that he wrecked my life makes me love him. "Je t'aime parce que tu m'as perdu" is the phrase that ends one of the stories in *Le Puits de Sainte Claire*— Anatole France's book—and it is terrible symbolic truth.[73]
We hope to get a little villa or apartment somewhere, and I hope to do work with him. I think I shall be able to do so. I think he will be kind to me; I only ask that. So do let people know that my only hope of life or literary activity was in going back to the young man whom I loved before with such tragic issue to my name. No more today.
Ever yours
Oscar

***

Postcard to Robert Ross, September 22 1897 (Naples)

A lovely day: we are going to Posilippo.[74] I am quite happy. Hope you got

---

[72] Author's Note: John Rowlands Fothergill (1876–1957) was a friend of Ross. His copy of *The Ballad of Reading Gaol* was inscribed by Wilde as follows: "To Rowland Fothergill, the Architect of the Moon, with the compliments of the author O.W." Fothergill later spent twelve years as an archaeologist, helping his American friend Edward Perry Warren (1864–1928) to form the collection of classical antiquities in the Boston Museum of Fine Arts.
[73] Author's Note: *L'Humaine Tragédie*. The book was published in 1895.
[74] Author's Note: Posilippo, as Wilde used to write, was instead correctly spelled Posillipo, which at the time was a community outside of Naples.

my letter of yesterday, and that you will tell people what I asked you to tell them. Please write soon, and tell me all the news. S. M.

But what was Wilde's appearance when he arrived in Naples?

Tall, hairless, a big paunch, blood red cheeks, ironic eye, protruding teeth, a child's playful mouth, the soft lips of milk, ready to suck yet. . . The arch of the eyebrows and lips are deceitful, the nonchalance affected. He never stops smoking half cigarettes from Egypt which are imbued with opium, not even while he eats. He is a dreadful absinthe drinker.[75]

***

Letter to Carlos Blacker, September 22 1897 (Naples, Hôtel Royal des Étrangers)

My dear Carlos,

Your letter was forwarded to me here from Paris. I will go and see Constance in October.

I know that all you have written to me about my coming here comes from the sympathy and loyalty of your great generous heart, and I am sorry that my being here gives you pain. It gives pain to most of my friends: but I cannot help it: I must remake my maimed life on my own lines. Had Constance allowed me to see my boys, my life would, I think, have been quite different. But this she would not know. I don't in any way venture to blame her for her action, but every action has its consequence. I waited three months. At the expiration of the long, lonely time, I had to take my life into my own hands.

I intend to winter here. Perhaps live here. Much depends of course on my ability to write again.

You must not, dear Carlos, pass harsh judgments on me, whatever you may hear. It is not for pleasure that I come here, though pleasure, I am glad to say, walks all round. I come here to try to realize the perfection of my temperament and my soul. We have all to choose our own methods. I have chosen mine. My friends in England are greatly distressed. Still, they are good friends to me: and will remain so, most of them at any rate. You must remain so too.

Ever yours

Oscar

---

[75] From a local newspaper in Naples at the time.

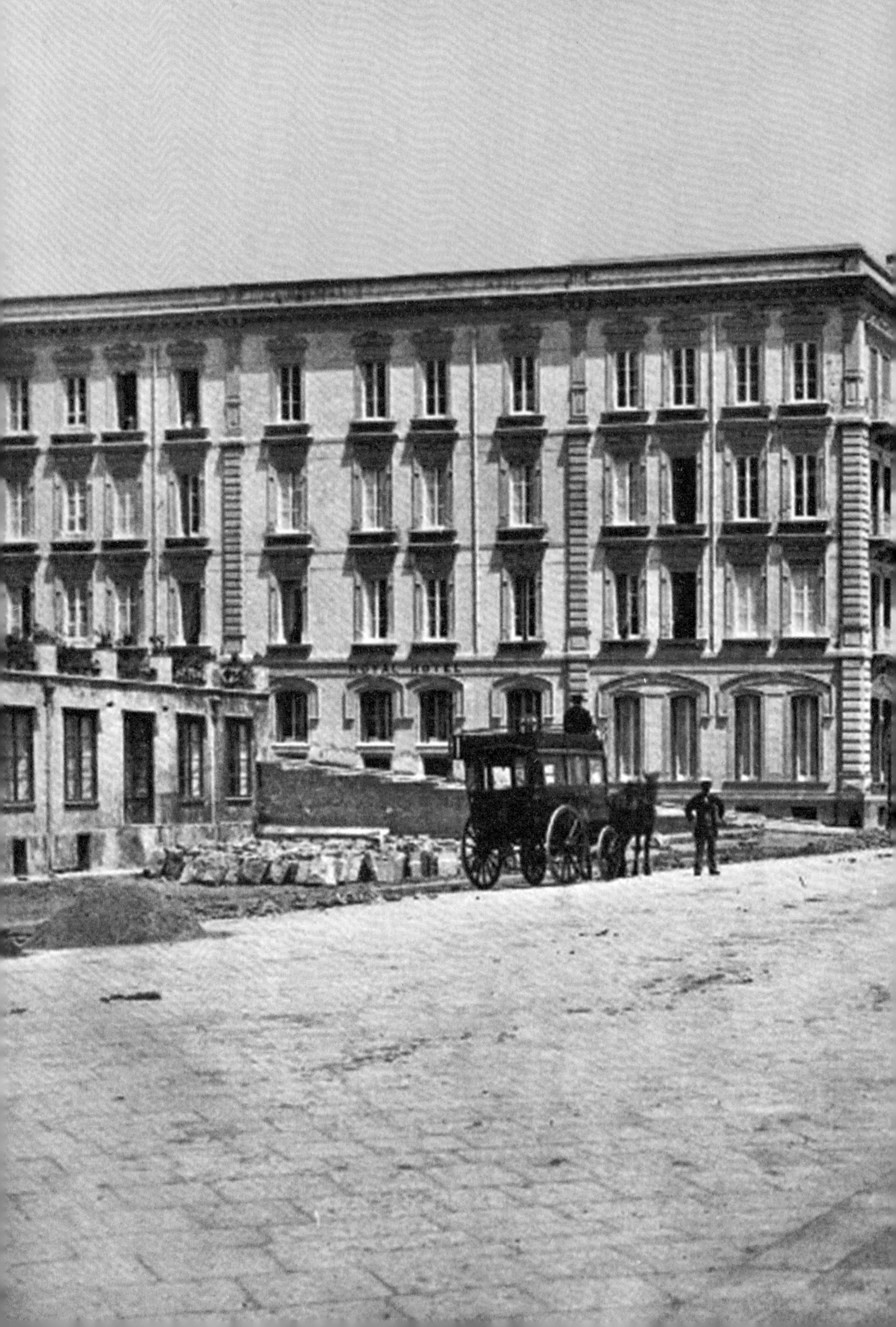

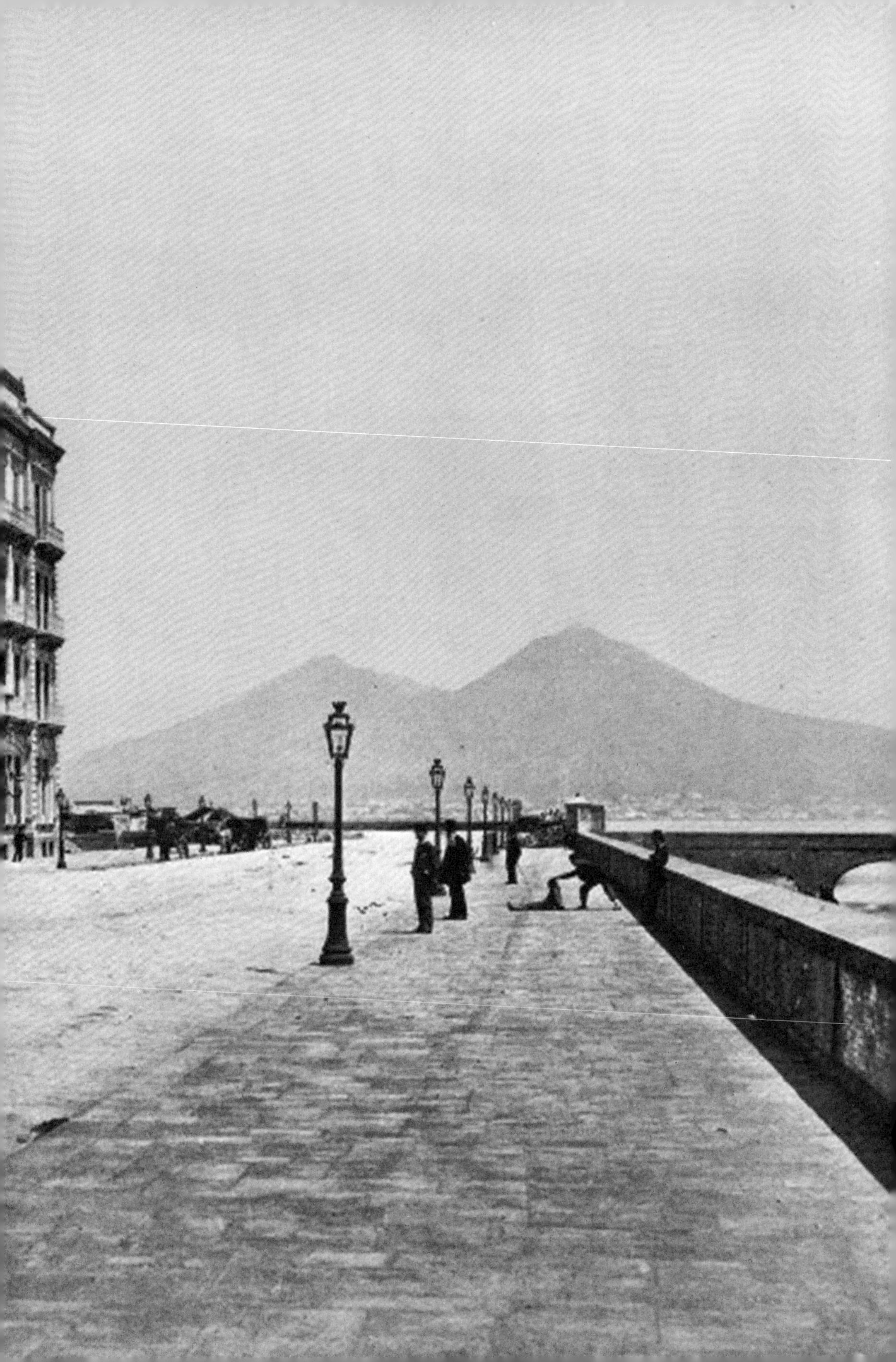

Letter to Reginald Turner, September 23 1897 (Naples, Hôtel Royal des Étrangers)

My dear Reggie, Bosie and I came here on Monday: we met at Aix: and spent the day at Genoa.

Much that you say in your letter is right, but still you leave out of consideration the great love I have for Bosie. I love him, and I have always loved him. He ruined my life, and for that very reason I seem forced to love him more: and I think that now I shall do lovely work. Bosie is himself a poet, far the first of all the young poets of England, an exquisite artist in lyric and ballad. It is to a poet that I'm going back. So when people say how dreadful of me to return to Bosie, do say *no*—say that I love him, that he is a poet, and that, after all, whatever my life may have been ethically, it has always been *romantic*, and Bosie is my romance. My romance is a tragedy of course, but it is none the less a romance, and he loves me very dearly, more than he loves or can love anyone else, and without him my life was dreary.

So stick up for us, Reggie, and be nice. [. . .]

Ever yours

Oscar

***

One of Oscar's purposes was to finish a poem written in exile in Berneval-le-Grand. During his imprisonment, a hanging took place on Tuesday, July 7 1896, that of Charles Wooldridge who was convicted of cutting the throat of his wife, Laura Ellen. He was aged 30 when executed. The poem narrates the execution of Wooldridge and highlights the brutalization of the punishment that all convicts share. Wilde juxtaposes the executed man and himself with the line "Yet each man kills the thing he loves [. . .] The coward does it with a kiss, The brave man with a sword." For the first time, he adopted the 'proletarian' ballad form, and suggested it be published in *Reynold's Magazine*, "because it circulates widely among the criminal classes—to which I now belong—for once I will be read by my peers—a new experience for me." The finished poem was published by Leonard Smithers on February 13, 1898 under the name C.3.3., which stood for cell block C, landing 3, cell 3.

Oscar also wished to translate and publish *Salomé*, as we can read:

Postcard to Robert Ross, September 25 1897 (Naples)

Dear Robbie,

An Italian here (age twenty-five)[76], a writer, is anxious to translate *Salomé*. I have no copy, nor has Bosie. Would you *lend* me yours? It would be very good of you, and I would return it honourably. I hope to have *Salomé* played here in the winter.

***

Letter to Robert Ross, October 1 1897 (Naples, Villa Giudice, Posilippo, now Via Posillipo, 37)

Dearest Robbie,

I have not answered your letter, because they distressed me and angered me, and I did not wish to write to you of all people in the world in an angry mood. You have been such a good friend to me. Your love, your generosity, your care of me in prison and out of prison are the most lovely things in my life. Without you what would I have done? As you remade my life for me you have a perfect right to say what you choose to me, but I have no right to say anything to you except to tell you how grateful I am to you, and what a pleasure it is to feel gratitude and love at the same time for the same person. I dare say that what I have done is fatal, but it had to be done. It was necessary that Bosie and I should come together again; I saw no other life for myself. For himself he saw no other: all we want now is to be let alone, but the Neapolitan papers are tedious and wish to interview me, etc. They write nicely of me, but I don't want to be written about. I want peace—that is all. Perhaps I shall find it.

Now to literature. Of course I want you to help me. I have sent Smithers my poem with directions for a type-written copy to be sent at once to you: please send me any suggestions and criticisms that occur to you. [. . .]

Bosie has written three lovely sonnets, which I have called "The Triad of the Moon"—they are quite wonderful.[77] He has sent them to Henley. I have also got him to send his sonnet on Mozart to the *Musician*.

Tomorrow I begin the *Florentine Tragedy*. After that I must tackle *Pharaoh*. We have a lovely villa over the sea; and a nice piano. I take lessons in Italian conversation from Rocco three times a week.

My handwriting is now dreadful, as bad as yours.

Ever yours

Oscar

---

[76] Author's Note: The 25-year-old man was Giuseppe Garibaldi Rocco.

[77] Author's Note: They were included in Douglas's second volume of poems, *The City of the Soul* (1899), which was published anonymously.

One can survive everything, nowadays, except death, and live down everything except a good reputation.
Oscar Wilde

In the letter October 1 Oscar refers to some articles published in the *Corriere di Napoli*, *The Naples Echo* and *Il Mattino*. After extensive research in newspapers of the time, we can state that many papers of the time confused the presence of Oscar Wilde with that of another person who arrived in Naples at the same time. The articles are shown below.

Oscar Wilde a Napoli from *Corriere di Napoli*, September 30 1897:

> An English friend of ours writes to warn us that those who affirmed the presence of Oscar Wilde, the notorious English aesthete, who returned from forced labor due to a conviction following unspeakable accusations, have fallen into error. Mr. Douglas, owner of Villa Gaiola (formerly Becchi) in Posillipo, is an English diplomat still in service and has nothing to do with Lord Alfred Douglas, Oscar Wilde's close friend. He is not even a very distant relative. The alleged Wilde is only a Spanish diplomat, a guest of Mr. Douglas.

This is what happened: the arrival of Oscar Wilde was first reported in *The Naples Echo*, an English-Italian bulletin which announced the visit of Mr. Sebastian Melmoth in the city of Naples. A few days later the same paper revealed the real name of Sebastian Melmoth: Oscar Wilde. The news spread to the other Neapolitan papers and the poet's presence was reported also by many gossip columns, or *mosconi*. But was it really Wilde? Oscar's peculiar reluctance to give statements added to the mystery, and when he moved to Villa Giudice the facts became even more complicated. Norman Douglas (whose last name was the same as Wilde's friend, Alfred Douglas) recounts in *Looking Back*[78] of an incident which occurred to him and a friend, Count de Monte Alegre, during their sojourn in Villa Maya in Posillipo:

> The Count, a Counsellor of the Embassy of Spain in St. Petersburg, renowned *bon viveur* and eloquent humorist, was suffering from a form

---

[78] Norman Douglas, *Looking Back: An Autobiographical Excursion* (New York: Harcourt, Brace, 1933).

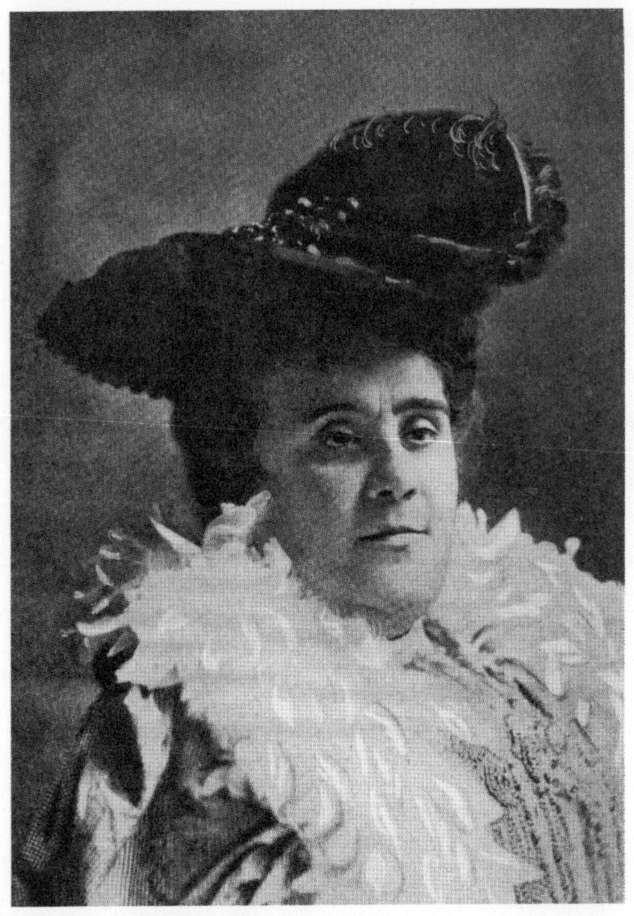

of paralysis which had reduced him to the point of being unable to walk, to which he was resigned and he was dragging himself from one place of care to another. Now obese and destroyed by pain, he had come to Naples for a change of climate, and also to listen to Leonard Bianchi.

Il Mattino had made vague mention (in the *moscone* Matilde Serao was awaiting confirmation of this) of Oscar Wilde, who had secretly taken refuge in a villa in Posillipo. Finally a reporter, scouring the roads of Posillipo, saw a couple in a carriage that made him jump for joy: an obese man with flaccid cheeks, of deformed aspect but of great distinction and, next to him, a young beautiful blond man, certainly an aristocrat. The carriage turned off on a slope, descended towards the sea and stopped at the Grotta di Seiano. There, the reporter was assured, lay the entrance to Douglas's villa. This great news, once published, was immediately denied by British Consul Neville Rolfe, a literate and habitual visitor of Villa Maya where, now and again, Lord Rosebery[79] sometimes stopped by in his beautiful yacht and Marion Crawford often visited from Sorrento.

Matilde Serao did not believe the denial and so the investigations continued and Oscar Wilde did not find his desired oblivion.

As an aside, it should be noted that Matilde Serao was a really incredible woman: she was born in the Greek city of Patras to an Italian father, Francesco Serao, and a Greek mother, Paolina Borely (or Bonelly). Her father had emigrated from Naples for political reasons to Greece. With her husband, Edoardo Scarfoglio, she founded *Il Corriere di Roma*, the first Italian attempt to establish a daily newspaper with the layout of a French newspaper. The newspaper was short-lived, and Matilde settled in Naples where she edited *Il Corriere di Napoli*. In 1892, with her husband she co-founded *Il Mattino*, which soon became the most important and most widely read newspaper in Southern Italy. She also founded and directed the newspaper *Il Giorno* in 1904 until her death.

On October 7, 1897 the following *moscone* appeared on the newspaper *Il Mattino* signed Gibus, a pseudonym used by Matilde Serao for her column:

IS HE HERE, OR NOT?

Someone has announced that Oscar Wilde, the English 'decadent' who provided such abundant matter to reporters some years ago about a repugnant trial, is in Naples. This announcement has given many people, including the humble undersigned, a certain amount of trepidation, bordering on panic. How so? Oscar Wilde in Naples? But this would be a calamity! The presence among us of that British aesthete, albeit— as announced—under a false name! We would be in close proximity to that most unbearable of nuisances that contemporary chronicles have as yet inflicted on patient publics! Do you recall the lengthy and deafening uproar which surrounded his name, which became notorious throughout the world as much for the foul faults attached to it, as for the prized works of a keen and sparkling wit?
At that time, there was no refuge from the Oscar Wilde trial: no newspaper, big or small, held back from daily dedicating at least a column to him; no scribbler to applying his analytical and critical spirit to the study of

---

[79] Prime Minister at the time of the Wilde trial and arch-enemy of the Marquess of Queensberry. He had in fact prevented him from becoming a peer of Britain, preferring his son.

the poet, the aesthete and the distinguished offender. Even his sentence to hard labor for a number of years sparked an outpour of erudition and debate on the notion of forced labor in England, on the bitter sentences of those condemned and on the harshness of Her Glorious Majesty's judges. Then, finally, the trumpets of the sad notoriety immodestly acquired by one who had been close to being crowned Poet Laureate of the English court became silent, either out of exhaustion or out of a belated sense of pity for the public's ears. Oscar Wilde was left to his misfortune, to his repentance and to his sufferings.

One could breathe a little: the Wildeian scourge seemed to have vanished. It would surely be a while until it would wear upon mankind's patience once more! One could almost be grateful to British judges for their severity in inflicting penalties on hateful perverts! But suddenly, there is talk once again of Wilde. Curiosity returns, and reporters set themselves to finding this wretch—repentant, perhaps reformed, wishing for peace, wishing to hide in silence and oblivion: they are ready to hound him, perhaps—or rather, certainly—to interview him and to describe his most minute occupations! And can we resist the rekindling of this disease that to all accounts had been vanquished? Oh no! Whether he is or he is not in Naples, this refined aesthete— refined in his own way, of course!—I protest in the name of good people, in the name of those who wish to live in peace, in the name of peace for Wilde himself (who has the right to ask for pity and discretion, since even great offenders sentenced to the gallows are entitled to this) against the infliction of an umpteenth Wilde chronicle!

But then, on balance, can that unfortunate one be hidden amongst us? It seems to me not: he must still be in a cruel English prison, atoning for his errors and mourning the bizarre exaggerations of his instinct. Except for this—which perhaps explains the misunderstanding which led to the rumors of his presence in Naples: investigations scrupulously conducted by my informants reveal that the other—in the words of the good Colautti "Wilde accomplice"—the young Lord Douglas who so indecorously bears the name of one of the greatest historical families of Great Britain, has now been residing for six or seven months in Naples, in the seductive quiet of Posillipo, in a secluded villa and dedicated, apparently, to literary pursuits. And may the Lord have mercy on him too, that callow youth, enamored of aesthetics, and leave him alone, in the company of his beautiful ghosts!

***

This intransigent article by Serao is part of an anti-Wilde movement that pervaded Italy at that time. This is followed soon after by Paolo Valera's book which states, among other things, the following:

> Oscarwildism is the religion of inverts. It is not a disease of certain men or of certain degenerates as many suppose. It is that of the cultivated, flaunted, widespread aestheticism, that has penetrated all classes. Men who worship men have not yet reached the brazenness of publicly posting their sexual perversions, nor to seeking comrades for their carnal revels in paid-for newspaper ads. However, in social gatherings they are not afraid to uphold the right of men to Socratic marriages, to sadistic frenzies and to same-sex turpitudes. Those who take on the feminine role belong to the upper classes, to the noble classes. . . Oscar Wilde is his own party, a religion in reverse, the first seed planted in the life of modern nations and raised as a flag to feminine extinction.
>
> I want people to talk about me–says Wilde—to public indifference I prefer insult and derision. The society of Oscar Wilde's is too ugly, too sick, too foul to allow to live. Let it be persecuted everywhere.[80]

Serao's article was followed by an interview with Oscar Wilde published in *Il Pungolo Parlamentare* (October 9–10 1897) signed by Eugenio Zaniboni (who was also the translator of Goethe's Italian edition of *Italian Journey*):

> The rumors that Oscar Wilde, who almost was appointed Poet Laureate of the Court of England and whose aesthetic theories instead got him condemned to forced labor, a sentence he served under brutal conditions, perhaps arrived several weeks ago, here in Naples, in a remote and delightful Villa at Posillipo, had spread in some artistic and journalistic circles, and had been commented with excess and implicit allusions of Platonic and Socratic Reminiscence. This aesthete, ferociously criticized by English intelligentsia by relentless judges, by newspapers and by the public opinion, although he is a vicious and corrupted persona, ended up becoming an interesting character and a celebrity which, outside his homeland, his wonderful novels and plays, rich in stylistic subtleties and artistic fictions, did not achieve.
>
> He who marked himself with sin, a monstrous one indeed, has some perverts idealizing him almost as an aesthetic canon of life. Has he

---

[80] Paolo Valera, *I Gentiluomini Invertiti* (Milan: Tipografia editrice E.M. Floritta, 1909).

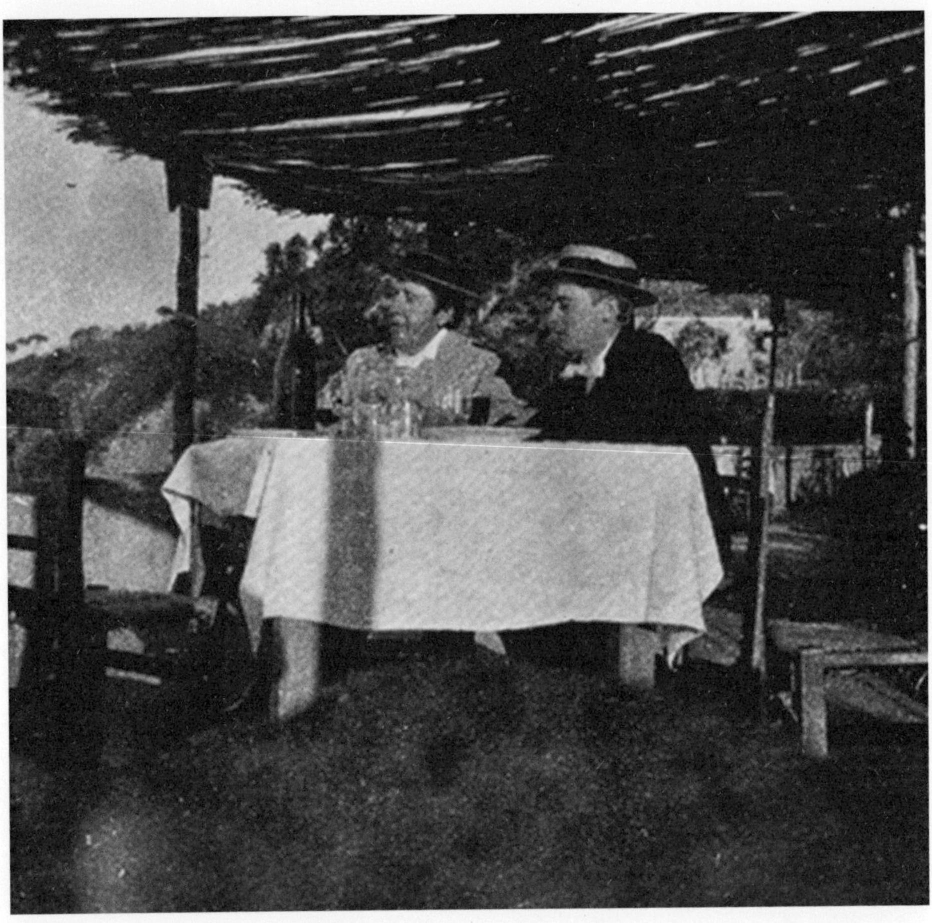

ameliorated his situation? He came down to Italy with that Lord Douglas whose name often arose during the course of the trial and their union, oh dear! it has many assume that the forced labor did not extinguish his aesthetic vice in the famous writer, which the English consider as a double incarnation of Evil. I, who had the strange curiosity to approach this Super Human and attempted to interview him, I cannot imagine the immeasurable greatness of his selfishness, which makes him foreign to everything that has no relation to his persona, trying as best as he can to achieve an ideal of life, that the sane and balanced can only regard as a monstrosity.

Wilde is at Villa Giudice in Posillipo and it was difficult to reach him: the difficulty was to reach him since he had given strict instructions of not wanting to be disturbed. So, he has therefore been in Naples for about a month: he took the at first a room at the Hotel Royal with his friend Lord Douglas, from the Hotel Royal he passed to Villa Giudice where they are living in splendid furnished apartments.

But how can one get around these strict orders? The custodian—to whom I sincerely confessed my desire—she could not answer me.

"*Signorino mio,*" said the good woman, "Milord doesn't want to see no one!" But this first stumbling failed attempt didn't discourage me, I pulled out all my dialectical skills and finally I managed to breach the guardian's soul: "*Mo' facimmo na cosa, ve chiammo 'o servitore 'e milord, isso ve se ve po' fa' trasì.*" (Now I'll call his servant, and we will see if he can let you in).

"Call me the Lord's servant", I nodded entering the villa and descending the beautiful shady avenue that leads to the apartments. The good woman signaled to wait at a door on the ground floor, a door with blue and white, opaque glass; Oscar Wilde's apartment was there.

"*Aspettate nu mumento!*" Wait a moment!

I waited.

The place was beautiful; surrounded by flower beds kept with great care; long shady paths, among the trees the vastness of the calm sea, of a livid color that widened to the horizon. A profound silence.

"*Chi desidera il Signore?*" Who seeks the gentleman?

The servant took me away from my contemplation.

"I would like to know who is at home, Mr. Wilde or Lord Douglas?"

"Lord Douglas is out, there is Mr. Wilde; I am his servant."

"Would you be so kind to announce me?"

But no . . . nobody can be received, orders are strict.

And here I needed a new dose of dialectical skill to convince this other someone who did not show any intention at all to be convinced otherwise. The servant slowly though agreed to be persuaded. He left a tray he had in his hands and entered his master's chambers. A few minutes later the glass door opened again, and the servant made a sign to me to enter. I went in and sat down.

Oh my goodness! What the Hell! Who had ever announced that servant dog? I saw a white mass affectionately moving towards me fearing that the oncoming greeting would be exaggeratedly amiable. I swear to you, my dear readers, it did not bring me great pleasure!

But suddenly that first affectionate glance dissipated completely; Wilde approached me again with a slow step and with an inquisitive and glacial look.

And then finally at last, I could see him well. He is a man of about forty, tall, a brightly lit English eye, with a noticeably blush complexion, the lip and the chin shaved with great care. The hair of a splendid blond hue with impeccable care descending his very elongated face, one of those horsy faces commonly found in the English.

The odd thing about this man is when he speaks to you: one of the upper incisor teeth, precisely the middle left incisor, is a single piece of gold secured in the gum, that gold closes some other corroded teeth as well; when the aesthete opens his mouth, that metal glitters strangely.

But the most particular note of Wilde is his elegant and refined way of dressing. He had a perfect white wool suit, those unsurpassable English wools, a rich silk shirt with embroidered lapels, under the collar of the shirt a knuckle tie, a ruby strip on top of the whiteness of the suite.

"Mr. Wilde," I started, just to waste some time, "I apologize; perhaps your servant did not correctly repeat my name. As a matter of fact, I thought that … But anyway, since your coming to Naples is already known, would you have the courtesy of telling me who you are here with?"

"My friend and I came to Naples about a month ago; we took accommodations first at the Hotel Royal des Étrangers; last Thursday we came here."

"And will you be staying long?"

"Well . . . we don't know. The place is delightful, maybe we'll stay some more time, at least; but for now I haven't decided yet what I'm going to do."

I knew enough about his current life. Some questions about the poet's previous misfortunes came to my mind and by logical deduction they tried to reach my lips. I chased away at the scabrous idea more than once, but I finally ventured:

"And have you left England a long time ago?"

"I . . . do not understand?"

I repeated the question: it was useless.

England must have had a strange effect on this Superhuman's nervous system. He widened his eyes as if I had asked him to square a circle, and then he stayed there, mute, motionless, almost as if he was chasing a long dormant memory.

I realized I had blown my chance, so I said goodbye and left.

He gave me a slight nod and withdrew.

***

But in all this, were Posillipo's lovers happy? It seems unlikely when we see the various photographic images taken by themselves or by the waiter under the pergola of a *trattoria* near via S. Lucia. White tie and bow tie, straw hat on head, they have, when all is said and done, a resigned expression. But although there was almost certainly nothing between them sexually, they loved each other fervently, at least for the first part of their cohabitation in Naples. Oscar was starting to learn some Italian. As we see on 1 October 19 1897, when Wilde wrote from the Villa del Giudice (Posillipo) to More Adey: "I am getting rather astonishing in my Italian conversation. I believe I talk a mixture of Dante and the worst modern slang."

One of the most controversial figures, but for Oscar of fundamental importance to get in touch with the Neapolitan literary world, was certainly Giuseppe Garibaldi Rocco, of whom we have already heard in the last letters when he was teaching Oscar Italian. Very little is known about Giuseppe Garibaldi Rocco (for sure his parents were in love with General Garibaldi!). It is well known that he had a position as the editor of the magazine *Strenna Margherita* in 1894, which saw contributions from well-known writers such as Matilde Serao, Salvatore Di Giacomo and Paolo Borrelli.

At all events, Giuseppe G. Rocco, or Arnaldo De Lisle, (a pseudonym he liked to use when he published his books) was a central figure in Wilde's Neapolitan living room. He was certainly a figure of reference for Oscar. Their conversations were ultimately all published in the introduction to the translation by Federigo Verdinois of *Il Delitto by Lord Arturo Savile* (*Lord Arthur Savile's Crime*), published in Naples in 1908 by the Società Editrice Partenopea with the subtitle *Il dovere del delitto* (*The Duty of Crime*). We presume that Giuseppe Rocco was homosexual, 'in the closet' as we can read between the lines. He was also confident enough to propose to Wilde that he should translate *Salomé* into Italian, and planned to have a Neapolitan performance with his own translation of the work. He was also the author of a gay novel, set in Naples, entitled *L'uomo femmina* (*The Female Man*, Società Editrice Partenopea, Naples, *ca.* 1899). In the office of the Neapolitan notary, Sodano, on October 25 1897, appears a notarized document which shows that Wilde wanted the whole transaction for the translation to be legally conducted:[81]

> Dear Mr. Rocco, I authorize you with the great pleasure to translate and arrange for the performance of my play *Salomé* on the Italian stage. Oscar Wilde.

***

---

[81] See Stefano Evangelista, *The Reception of Oscar Wilde in Europe* (London: Bloomsbury, 2010).

Excerpt from *Interview of Wilde* by Arnaldo (Rocco) De Lisle:

We were at the Gambrinus, beer was foaming in our glasses and Wilde, upon my request, was telling me some tales about his life.
"My names and surnames are Oscar Fingal O'Flahertie Wills Wilde. I was born in Dublin in 1854, and I belong to a noble Irish family: my father Sir William, was a doctor, an antiquarian and a scholar: my mother, lady Wilde, also delighted in writing verses, and did so with some success, my whole childhood was a rosy poem of joyousness. As a young man, I was powerfully drawn to study and I applied myself so diligently that when I was only eighteen, I won all the poetry prizes at Oxford University."
At this point he paused, suddenly drained his glass of beer, and remained rather pensive, as if he were regretting the contented times that had passed, when his life was still bereft of all the misery and humiliation by which it was to be stricken. He told me a lot about his first book, *Intentions*, published when he was only twenty-one years of age, and which made of him the idol of the London aristocracy, among whom he had carried his struggles, immediately after completing his university studies.
It was the period when—a spiritual iconoclast, even as he allowed himself to be idolized—he frightened his admirers, because of the affectation of that satanic dandyism which, as a new Baudelaire, made him exclaim in open society: "If you only knew how good it is to feed on the brains of a newborn baby!". (He used to proclaim such to cause scandal, and that, between two glasses of champagne, put him in the mood to expound frightful anarchist theories).
Despite these morbidities, his charm was so exceptional that he was offered up as Tennyson's successor as poet at court; and he would certainly have been proclaimed such at Windsor Castle, if the scandalous trial of 1894 had not suddenly covered him with ignominy and filth.
Lord Queensberry accused him of corrupting his son Lord Alfred Bruce Douglas. Wilde, as you know, responded by bringing him to trial for defamation. This was the fatal weapon that he turned against himself: since there were dreadful revelations, the accusation of Lord Queensberry was proven to be true, and other facts came to light, demonstrating that Wilde was a degenerate, afflicted by one of those vices that superficial men consider condemnable; and in fact the poet was condemned to two years of hard labor, with "punishments that bring to mind the cruelty

of the Holy Office," as Antonio Cervi rightly observes in his article of December 20 1900.

I said "one of those vices that superficial men find disgraceful" because scholars of sexual psychopaths know it to be an organic vice, transmitted by a tragic atavistic degeneration, and for which those who had it as their inheritance should be more worthy of pity than of contempt. And to say that the false moralists, who see no further than a hand's width, didn't limit themselves to insulting the man, but, showing unparalleled lunacy, they also wanted to ban the art.

And Wilde, during our encounter and interview, resembled very much, both by the solemnity of his bearing and by his shaved and proconsular countenance, an ancient Caesar. You may also add that Henri de Régnier, in his biography, speaking of his sin, says: "Wilde believed he was living in Italy during the Renaissance or in Greece during the time of Socrates. He was harshly punished for this error of chronology even though in London such anachronism is frequent."

And then you aren't going to deny that fatal atavism that I mentioned above, the human injustice and the stupid hypocrisy, which made Douglas write the hymn *Lust and Hypocrisy*, in which his groaning heart exclaimed: "Hypocrisy reigns in this country, all men owe her something, and to repay their debts they can do nothing but say wicked words towards their fellow men. Alas, when will God, with his terrible sieve, want to cleanse this over-ripe harvest and change the night into the day?" But, both of the trial, and of his love for Douglas, Wilde said very little to me, indeed he made sure to escape all my investigative questions in this regard; he was rather entertained by talking to me about how he was kindled with passion for a pretty young woman, who later became the mother of his children.

Another very strange detail of his unbalanced and exceptional temperament, which made him love a woman to the point of marrying her and having offspring: a phenomenon incompatible with the morbid tendencies by which he was affected. "My life is drawing to a close," he intoned, after having swallowed up several small glasses of cognac in a row, immediately after the beer. "I accomplished all that I set to undertake in the world; my destiny required that I write five plays and I wrote them, a novel and I published it, some short stories and verses, and of both of those I've reached the predetermined number: I enjoyed all the exceptional part of happiness that had been granted to me, and I suffered all the sufferings that I had to, and could suffer: now there is nothing left for me to do but wait for death, which will come to visit me in three years, since I must die at the age of 44."

And in saying this he burst out laughing with his mocking smile, which looked like a sneer and showed his two golden teeth, oddly shining in his large fleshy lipped mouth.

Then, with perfect serenity in his voice, he explained to me: "All my destiny is inscribed here, in the palm of my hand. I have an absolutely psychic hand, the fortune-teller told me, and we must believe in fortune-telling: it is the most exact and the most useful of all sciences. We should not deceive ourselves! Every man is predestined to carry out a certain existence: we are nothing more than simple puppets in a grotesque rat trap!"

Indeed, Wilde wrote nothing more and died at the age of forty-four precisely! Here one can see how fatalism combined with autosuggestion can commit crimes of such a distinctive type.

Wilde's weakness was precisely this great ability to be influenced both by his own ideas and by those of others, and even by certain environments. He became an atheist, and a sincere atheist, when with unbelievers, and vice versa. In the Rome of the great cathedrals, he let himself be conquered by the mystical charm that emanated from the shadows of the naves, from the smell of the incense, from the sacred images, and I saw him, a pagan soul, a born Protestant, kneeling and praying fervently at the foot of a crucifix, in the Church of St. Peter!

Product of that superstitious fatalism that made him wear two ancient rings, which he believed had belonged to Nero, no less. And to one of them, he attributed the power to attract contentment, to the other one, misfortune. Since, he said, "I have never confused, as almost all men do, my share of contentment with my share of misfortune. I was for a long time the happiest of men, now I well deserve to be the most unhappy. So, I'm under the influence of the bad ring right now."

Having emptied almost half a dozen small glasses of cognac, Wilde wanted to leave; he stood up and prepared to leave without having paid for his drinks.

"Allow me to pay," I told him, and I had a coin tinkling on the marble table to call the waiter. "Don't worry," he said, "you'll waste your time. When you call for them, the waiters never come, you must leave and they will certainly run right after you, and you will pay faster." Indeed, he was right. We had not even crossed the threshold of the café that three waiters ran to meet us demanding their payment. Wilde looked at me and laughed at his felicitous gimmick and said goodbye to me, inviting me to lunch for the next day at the Royal Hotel, where he lived with Lord Douglas, who was supposed to have lunch with us. That did not turn out to be the case. Only Wilde settled down at the table in front of me with a troubled look.

"And Lord Douglas?" I inquired.

Placing his hand upon his heart, a customary gesture for him when some melancholy notion tormented him, he said in a mournful voice:

"Poor lad! The Muses played a dreadful trick upon him. He wanted to write verses that were too beautiful, and he poisoned himself!"

"What are you telling me?"

"The truth. You must know that I have never been able to work well, unless I first read a dozen pages of that wonderful book that is *The Temptations of St. Anthony* by Flaubert and take two or three pills of hashish. Douglas knew this, and last evening, as he prepared to write verses, in my absence, he wanted to imitate my system; he miscalculated the dose and was poisoned; last night he was delirious and had tremendous hallucinations. I quickly called Dr. Masullo, who assured us that the episode would not have fatal consequences and that the patient will soon be able to leave his bed.

We are waiting for his recovery to leave the hotel and go to live in Posillipo, where we have procured a nice flat at Villa Giudice. Here it is too expensive, in Naples, at the hotel, just imagine that in a single week we've paid a bill of a thousand liras. I'm not richer than Douglas who has three thousand liras a month from his mother, so we must live as cost-effectively as possible."

***

During this time Wilde realized that Douglas was not only beautiful but totally unpredictable. His character was also easily irritated. He wanted to be loved and wanted to be considered at the same intellectual level. Certainly, one way to establish this equality was the undeniable economic power it exercised over poor Wilde, who depended upon him in every way. As a result, their relationship was not peaceful. Very often, after furious quarrels, they preferred to walk separately around Naples and its surroundings. But the *Ballad* must go on and be published in England and America. It was the only way out for Wilde.

***

Letter to Leonard Smithers, October 1? 1897 (Posilippo, Villa Giudice)

Dear Smithers,
Your letter has just arrived, and as the enclosure seems to have slipped out I wired at once to you to ask you to *telegraph* the £20 through Cook's office. I do hope you will do so. The crisis is of a grave and usual character—were it unique I would not feel so agitated. [. . .] How *can* you keep on asking is Lord Alfred Douglas in Naples? You know quite well he is: we are together. He understands me and my art, and loves both. I hope never to be separated from him. He is a most delicate and exquisite poet, besides far the finest of all the young poets in England. You have got to publish his next volume; it is full of lovely lyrics, flute-music and moon-music, and sonnets and ivory and gold. He is witty, graceful, lovely to look at, lovable to be with. He has also ruined my life, so I can't help loving him—it is the only thing to do.
My wife's letter came too late. I had waited four months in vain, and it was only when the children had gone back to school that she asked me to come to her, whereas what I want is the love of my children. It is now irretrievable, of course. But in questions of the emotions and their romantic qualities, unpunctuality is fatal. I dare say I may have more misfortunes yet. Still, I can write as well, I think, as I used to write. Half as well would satisfy me. [. . .]
Ever yours
Oscar Wilde

***

Letter to Robert Ross, October 3? 1897 (Naples, Posilippo, Villa Giudice)

My dear Robbie,
I hope you have received a type-written copy of the poem by this. [. . .] I'm awaiting a thunderbolt from my wife's solicitor. She wrote me a terrible letter, but a foolish one, saying "*I forbid you*" to do so and so: "I will not *allow* you" etc.: and "I *require* a distinct promise that you will not" etc.[82] How can she really imagine that she can influence or control my life? She might just as well try to influence and control my art. I could

---

[82] Author's Note: Constance's letter has perished, but on September 26 1897 she wrote to Carlos Blacker (MS. Blacker): "I have today written a note to Oscar saying that I required an immediate answer to my question whether he had been to Capri or whether he had met anywhere that appalling individual. I also said that he evidently did not care much for his boys since he neither acknowledged their photos which I sent to him nor the remembrances that they sent to him. I hope it was not too hard of me to write this, but it was quite necessary."

not live such an absurd life—it makes one laugh. So I suppose she will now try to deprive me of my wretched £3 a week. Women are so petty, and Constance has no imagination. Perhaps, for revenge, she will have another trial: then she certainly may claim to have for the first time in her life influenced me. I wish to goodness she would leave me alone. I don't meddle with her life. I accept the separation from the children: I acquiesce. Why does she want to go on bothering me, and trying to ruin me? Another trial would, of course, entirely destroy me. On the whole, dear Robbie, things are dark with storm.

The solitude of our life here is wonderful, and no one writes to either of us. It is lucky that we love each other, and would be quite happy if we had money, but of course Bosie is as penniless as usual. Up to the present I have paid for almost everything. [. . .] It is very curious that none of the English colony here have left cards on us. Fortunately, we have a few simple friends amongst the poorer classes. [. . .]
Oscar

***

Letter to Robert Ross, October 8 1897 (Naples, Posilippo, Villa Giudice)

My dear Robbie,
Thanks so much for your letter. [. . .] With much of your criticism I agree. The poem suffers under the difficulty of a divided aim in style. Some is realistic, some is romantic: some poetry, some propaganda. I feel it keenly, but as a whole I think the production interesting: that it is interesting from more points of view than one is artistically to be a regretted.
With regard to the adjectives, I admit there are far too many "dreadfuls" and "fearfuls." The difficulty is that the objects in prison have no shape or form. To take an example: the shed in which people are hanged is a little shed with a glass roof, like a photographer's studio on the sands at Margate. For eighteen months I thought it was the studio for photographing prisoners. There's no adjective to describe it. I call it "hideous" because it became so to me after I knew its use. In itself it is a wooden, oblong, narrow shed with a glass roof.
A cell again may be described *psychologically*, with reference to its effect on the soul: in itself it can only be described as "whitewashed" or "dimly-lit." It has no shape, no contents. It does not exist from the point of view of form or colour.

---

[83] Author's Note: *Cristo alla festa di Purim* by Giovanni Bovio (1841–1903).

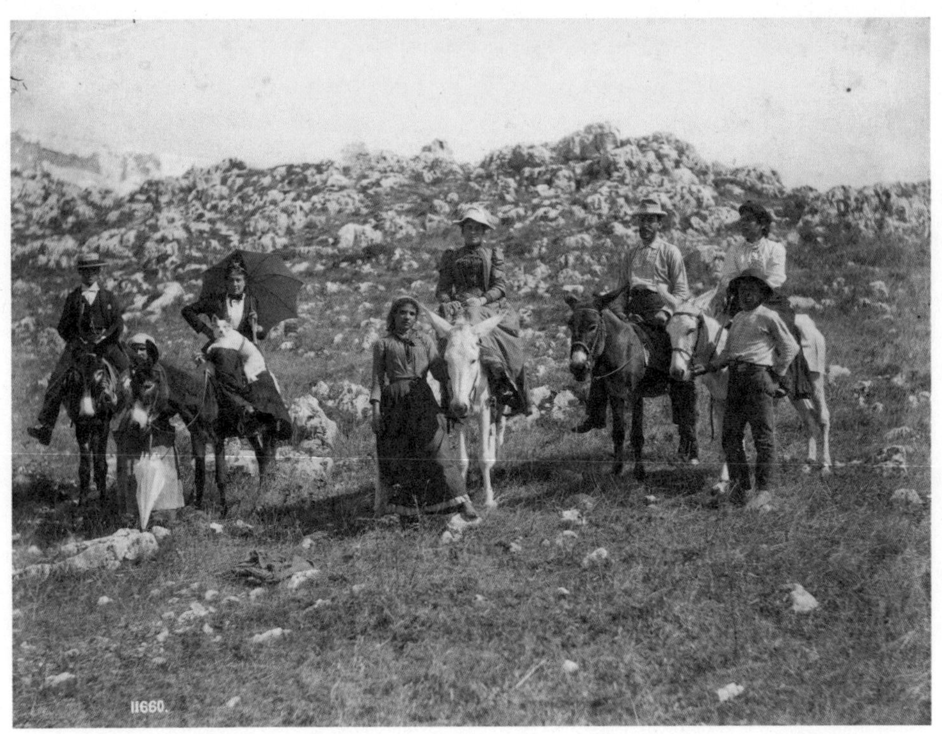

In point of fact, describing a prison is as difficult artistically as describing
a water-closet would be. If one had to describe the latter in literature,
prose or verse, one can merely say it was well, or badly, papered: or clean
or the reverse: the horror of prison is that everything is so simple and
commonplace in itself, and so degrading, and hideous, and revolting in
its effect. [. . .] I have had no money at all for three days, so cannot buy
note-paper. This is *your* foolscap.
Ever yours
Oscar

***

Letter to Reginald Turner, October 14 1897 (Naples, Posilippo, Villa Giudice)

Dear Reggie,
I have not heard yet from you about lending me a copy of *Salomé*. [. . .]
But at the close of the month there arrives here the best Italian company
of actors there is. They have already played the *Cristo* of Bovio;[83] a
religious drama, of course, and would like to do *Salomé*. It would help
here greatly to have it done as the papers have been rather offensive, and

I want to assert myself as *an artist*. Once I do that, they will leave me alone. So do try and get it for me. I have finished the great poem—six hundred lines now. I hope it will make a good effect. [. . .] Do write to me soon. Bosie sends his love.

Ever yours Oscar

***

Excerpt from *Interview of Wilde* by Arnaldo (Rocco) De Lisle

But, a few intimate news, so to speak, about the poet and his friend, I also obtained, and I present them to my readers. I take them as genuine, since they were supplied to me by persons who are close to the two travelers.

They took up residence at Villa Giudice, but Wilde, the first two nights, was forced to leave the dwelling at a late hour and go on foot to sleep in a Hotel on the Chiaia's Riviera, because of the mice and mosquitoes that infested his room. Several reporters, who were already on his heels, learning of these nocturnal jaunts, announced that Wilde devoted those hours to go in search of adventures.

The apartment of the two friends was comprised of six or seven elegantly furnished rooms, the two friends, apparently would remain there for some time.

They have in their employ a chef, Carmine, and two servants, Peppino and Michele. The malevolent neighbors at the Villa Giudice wanted to weave slanders on these two poor boys, who, however, with their beautiful chubby cheeks and their innocent eyes, seemed to laugh at these stupid rumors absolutely. Nothing is more normal than seeing Oscar Wilde or Lord Douglas going out at about one or two o'clock in the morning: as they set off alone around Posillipo, and coming back the next morning.

The two friends spend the day in constant strolls through Posillipo and often also travel to Naples (once the two areas of the city were very distinct, Posillipo being a residential area surrounded by countryside), sometimes they remain in the Villa to converse and then the conversation is often interrupted by abundant libations that continue until the lunch hour.

In fact, when I saw Oscar, his friend was not at home: he had left the night before and he had not yet returned at 10 in the morning. And so, I lingered a few more minutes along the beautiful avenues and, turning right, I saw the figure of Oscar Wilde: as the curtains at the windows

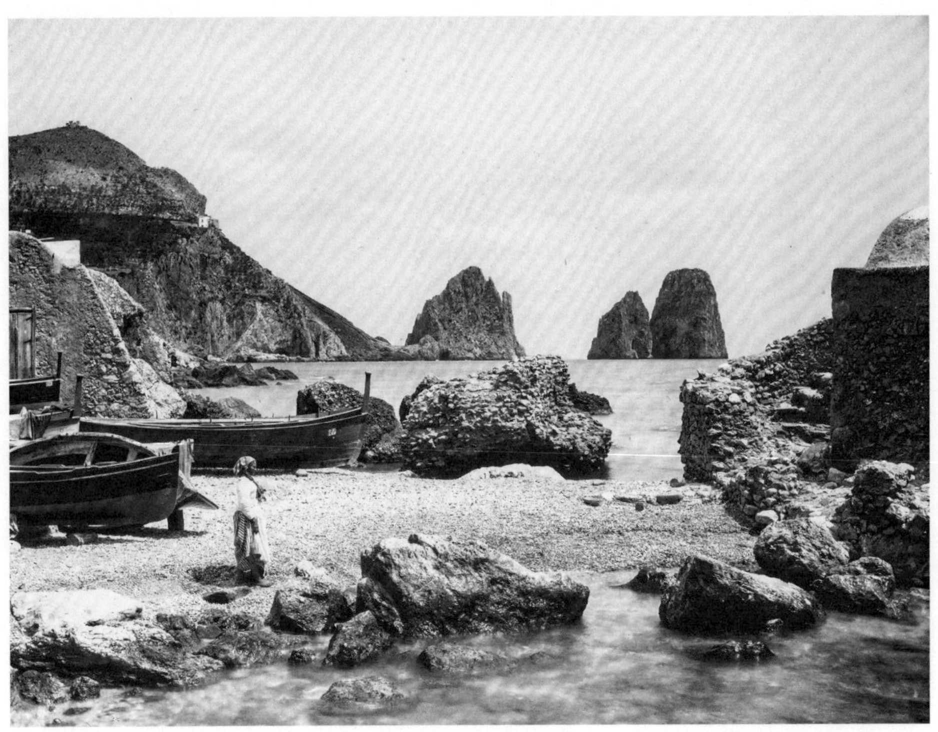

were a little set back on one side, I saw the poet near the small terrace, lying on a deckchair; his lazy lips pulled the smoke of a cigarette and his eyes wandered, wandering high on the ashy sky, where among the clumps of clouds the threat of imminent rain thickened.

I asked Douglas about their love one day in Posillipo, while Wilde was looking for the Inspiration for his poems in the golden reflections that the sun dazzled across the blonde hair of his adored Alfred and he answered me: *"Wilde started out loving my body and ended up staying in love with my soul."* Poor lunatics! And how grievously they atoned for their degeneration.

Many journalists interviewed him and, not understanding his language, although he spoke French quite perfectly, they said such and so much nonsense about him, that one day he came to me and asked me:

"Say, are there any newspapers on Capri?"

"I think not."

"Very well then, we'll go to Capri."

In fact, the next day I heard that they had left.

***

Letter to Reginald Turner, October 16? 1897 (Naples, Posilippo, Villa Giudice)

Dear Reggie, [. . .]
I have extracted, after three weeks of telegrams, £10 from Smithers! It is
absurd. However, with it we go to Capri for three days. I want to lay a
few simple flowers on the tomb of Tiberius. As the tomb is of someone
else really, I shall do so with the deeper emotion. [. . .]
Pray write whenever you have something better to do.
Ever yours
Oscar

***

Going to Capri was not that simple. There were two ways: either from Sorrento or
by the Postal Ship from Naples. They probably went via Sorrento. The trip from
Sorrento to Capri is well described by Maxime Du Camp in his book entitled *Capri*:

At the Pier there was a spear with six vigorous rowers. Semi-naked but
extremely civilized men who took to their oars with energy, shouting
to encourage themselves: *"Via forza ai remi, che questo bravo signore ci
farà comprare i maccheroni."* (Pull on those oars, lads, so that this good
gentleman will enable us to buy macaroni.) As soon as they docked
at the Marina Grande, they were attacked by a swarm of women who
screamed like possessed, insulted each other and grabbed their hair, and
all for the purpose of carrying their luggage. At that time, the porterage
jobs were carried out almost exclusively by women and the sight of a
caravan of women that ascended the "Scala Fenicia" with heavy loads on
the head constituted a usual scene.

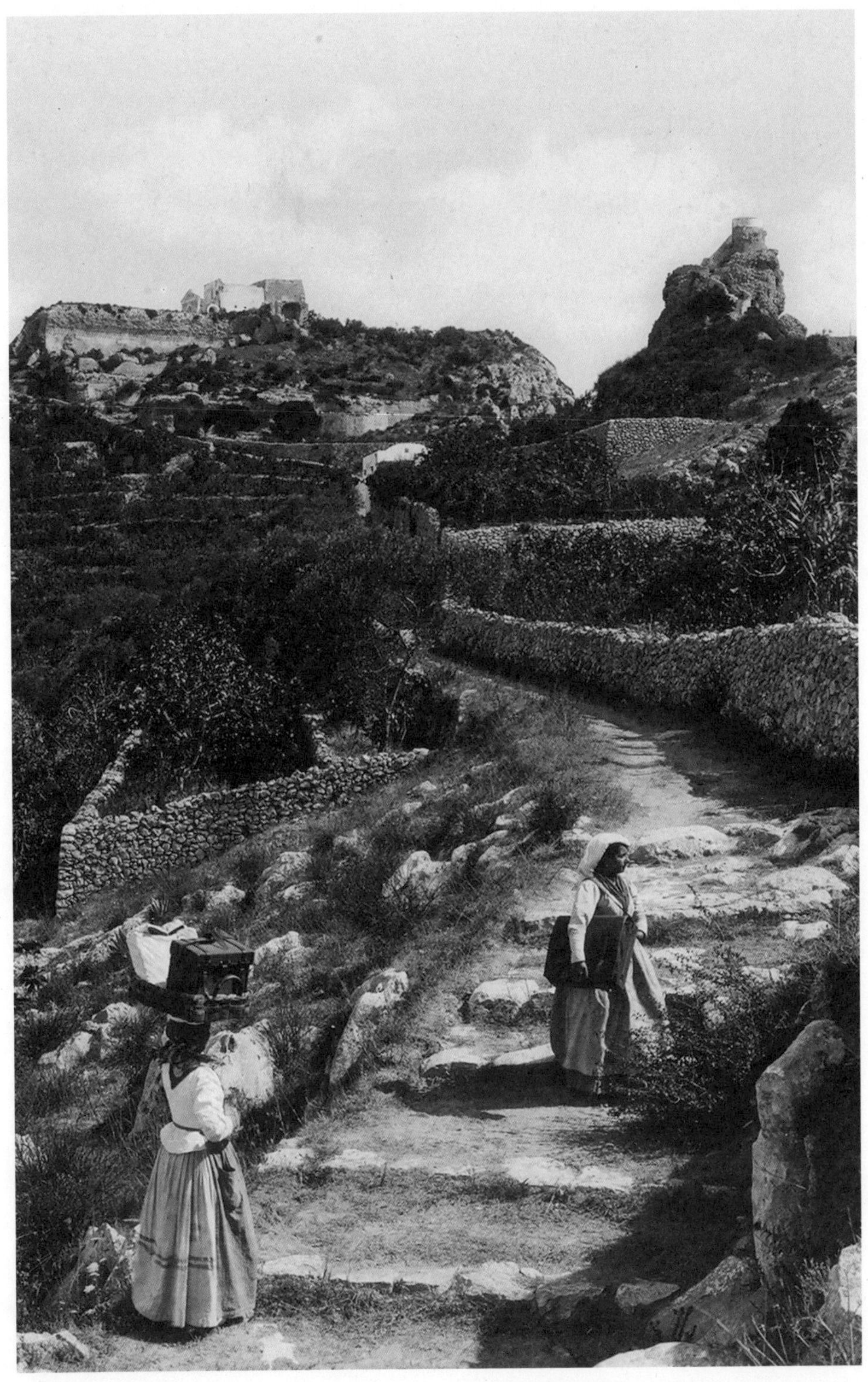

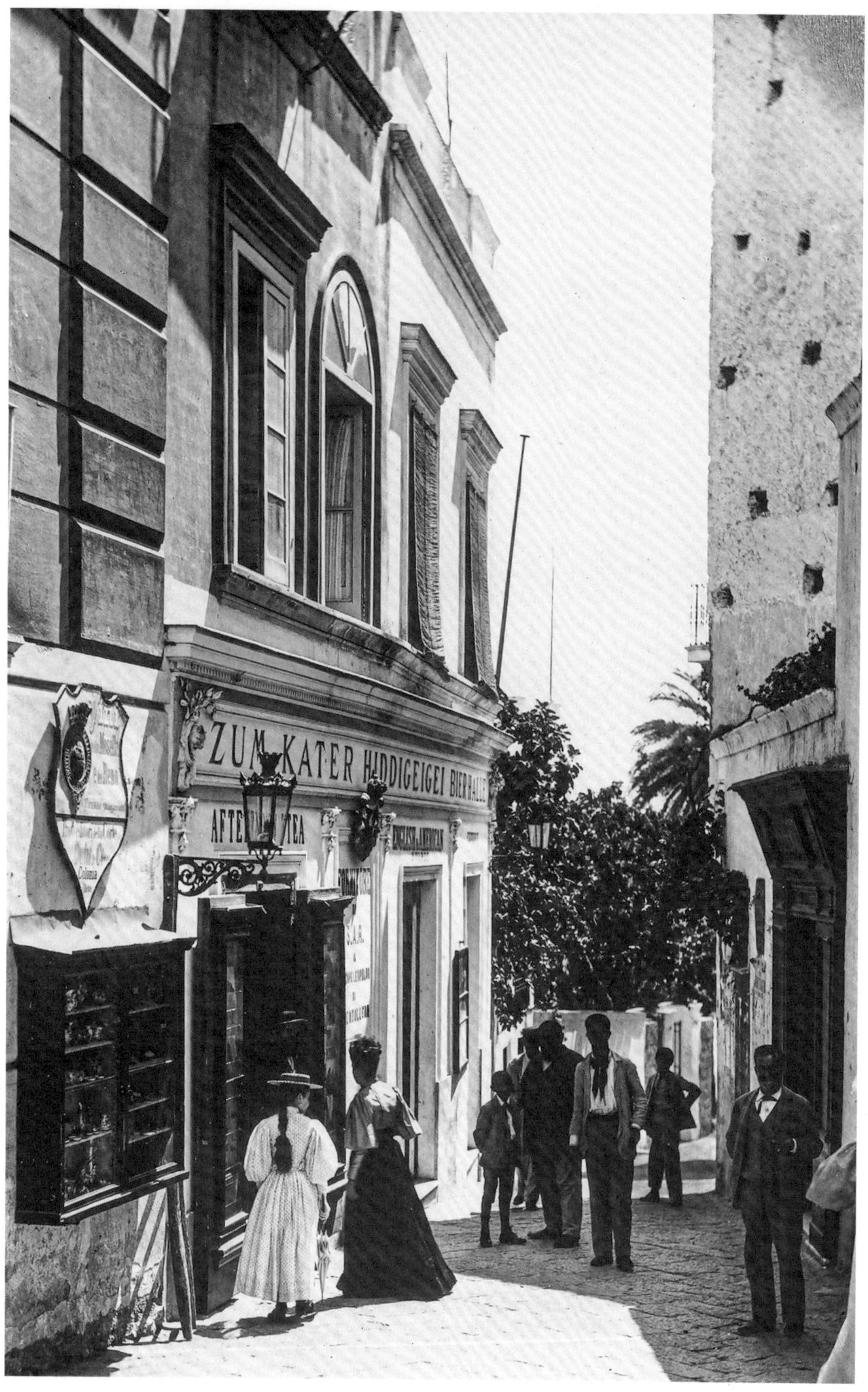

ZUM KATER HIDDIGEIGEI BIER HALLE
AFTERNOON TEA
ENGLISH AMERICAN
S.A.R.

Capri

Island of Pleasure

In the mid-nineteenth century, Capri filled with "picturesque and unusual people," mainly German and British, who sought refuge in the island away from the prying eyes of their own country.

Leaving the story of Capri to other books[84] we must remember that the island had a incredible reputation for being a place where all vices could be satisfied. This idea stemmed from the stories surrounding emperors Augustus (who lasciviously watched the gymnastic exercises of cadets—ephebes) and Tiberius, who according to Suetonius, decorated apartments in his beautiful Villa Jovis residence with pictures and statuettes in the most indecent poses so that each "erotic fantasy could draw inspiration from them." Suetonius also notes that Tiberius had trained little boys whom he called his "tiddlers" (*pisciculi*) to swim between his thighs to excite him with their tongues and nibble on his penis as if it were a nipple. At the end of the nineteenth century, the character of Capri was irrevocably transformed by the arrival of a German artist, Christian Wilhelm Allers, who at the beginning of the 1890s built a villa in Capri with Renaissance style furniture and medieval arms which acted as a backdrop to his paintings. According to Tito Fiorani:[85] "Allers had distinctly homosexual tendencies, and liked to surround himself with boys, whom he often used as models." [. . .] Allers's first boyfriend was a young sailor named Albertino, from Marina Grande, who became a general factotum in the villa. Later, Allers found love in other young boys who replaced Albertino and acquired the nicknames of *miezo culillo* (half-arse) and *meza recchia* ("*recchia*" is a corruption of "*recchione*," a shortened form of "*orecchione*", "big ear" which is slang for "gay." In non-verbal communication this is indicated by flipping one's earlobe back and forth.) Albertino and others boys posed as models in his studio until Allers received an expulsion order against him."[86]

***

In 1896, that while Oscar was in prison, Lord Alfred Douglas came to Capri and rented part of Villa Federico in Via Pastena where for over two months he hosted one of his future enemies and, at the time, one of Wilde's best friends, Robert Ross.

---

[84] In particular James Money, *Capri Island of Pleasure*. (London: Hamish Hamilton, 1986).

[85] Tito Fiorani, *Le dimore del mito* (Capri: Ed. La Conchiglia, 1996).

[86] Author's Note: In autumn 1902, there was a scandal. Friedrich Alfred Krupp, another famous person living in Capri, was accused by some Italian newspapers of homosexuality and pederasty. Some weeks later, Allers was found guilty in court. Krupp died: presumably by suicide. Allers managed to escape before the lawsuit began, which led to a sentence of four-and-a-half-years imprisonment, pronounced *in absentia*.

However, Wilde's stay in Capri did not start in the best of circumstances: upon his entrance with Bosie for dinner at the Quisisana hotel, all the English guests got up in unison from their tables, ready to leave the dining room should Oscar have remained.

Federico Serena, at the time owner of the hotel founded by Dr. Clark as a sanatorium and then transformed into a prestigious hotel, considered it best to escort him unequivocally to the door. The sad episode is very well described by Roger Peyrefitte in his book about Baron Fersen[87] in which he describes how the following day Fersen himself brought flowers to Wilde.
This episode was also well described many years later by Édouard Schneider in *Comoedia* (April 21 1923).

Oscar Wilde in the Island of Tiberius.

The encounter with Capri and the Pharisees was one of the last injuries suffered by Oscar Wilde. It is known that after the terrible months in Reading the poet came to the Gulf of Naples in search of refuge. He took lodgings in a room in Posillipo, but often he went around the coast and the islands bearing with him his sadness; one day he came to Capri. The episode I am about to tell must certainly be taken as true because it was reported by a witness worthy of trust. It was the time when the sun at sunset drowns its last rays. The foreign doctor (Axel Munthe) who has lived in Anacapri for more than thirty years and has become its most dignified citizen, was coming down the main road that descends to the town and had stopped in the square. After a moment he noticed two men who, without speaking, were slowly pacing along the pavement; they looked like souls in torment. He approached and recognized one of the two. His surprise at seeing him in that place at an hour when every house gathers together its guests, did last long. He introduced his companion who was none other than Oscar Wilde. Neither of them had dined and were breathing the cool of the evening while waiting for the steamship that was to take them to Naples at dawn. "I was denied bread," said the poet with amiable resignation. His companion recounted that as soon as they had taken their seats in the hotel dining room where they had gone to dine (the Quisisana), the embarrassed owner had, with perfect ceremony, strongly urged them to seek to be served elsewhere. Some distinguished foreigners, British citizens, had recognized the cursed poet and did not intend to tolerate his proximity. The two men had risen to look for a more welcoming roof; but the second refuge was no more hospitable than the first. In fact, the identical treatment was reserved for them.

---

[87] Roger Peyrefitte, Baron Jacques d'Adelsward Fersen, *L'exilé de Capri* (Paris: Flammarion, 1959).

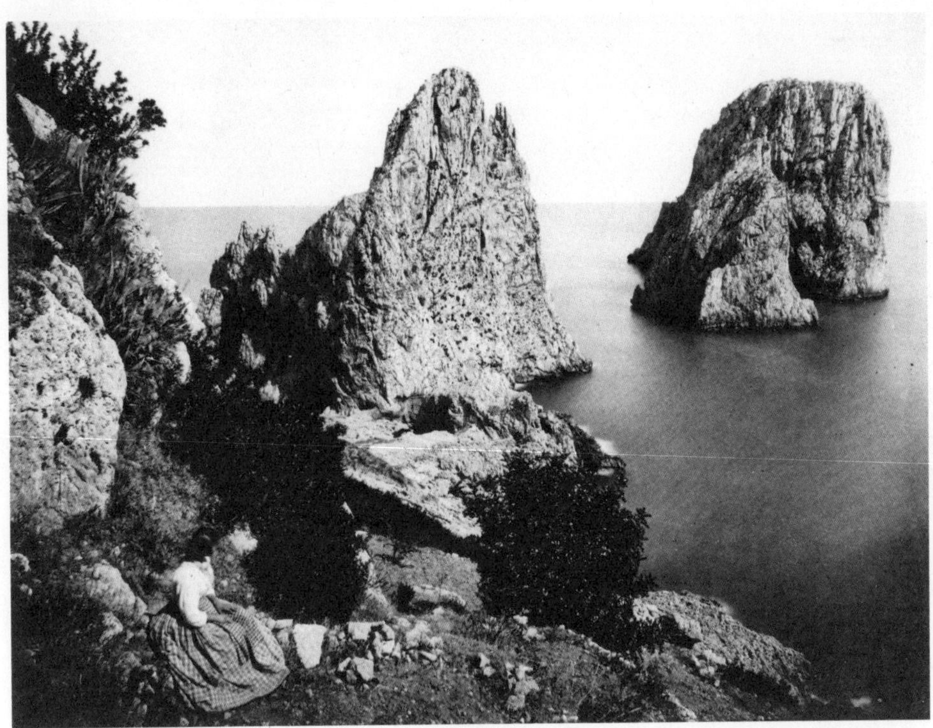

This second experience was enough and they thought no more than to flee. But now there was the problem of a roof beneath which to rest during the hours that separated them from the departure, their hotel (the Pagano) now being full. Not without insistence the doctor persuaded them to give up their hasty project and welcomed them into one of his properties (Villa San Michele) [. . .]. Inevitably I think of that touching page of *De Profundis* in which Wilde remembers that day in November 1895 in which, led from London to the station of Clapham Junction, he remained for half an hour at the central platform in a prisoner's uniform, handcuffs on his wrists, piteous and grotesque, a spectacle for the crowd that laughed in his face. "After that, for a whole year, every day, at the same time, I used to cry." Later this cry of pain would reach its extreme consequences: "For those who do not have enough imagination to go beyond the outward appearance of things and come to pity," he would write, "what 'pity' can there be except that of contempt?"

The return from Capri, after these unpleasant incidents, was not, however, the most settling. Villa Giudice was always haunted by mice and Oscar was forced to stay at the Hotel Royal again, trying to chase away the "unwanted guests." However, the number of interviews that came out after Oscar's death and that refer to his Neapolitan stay is impressive.

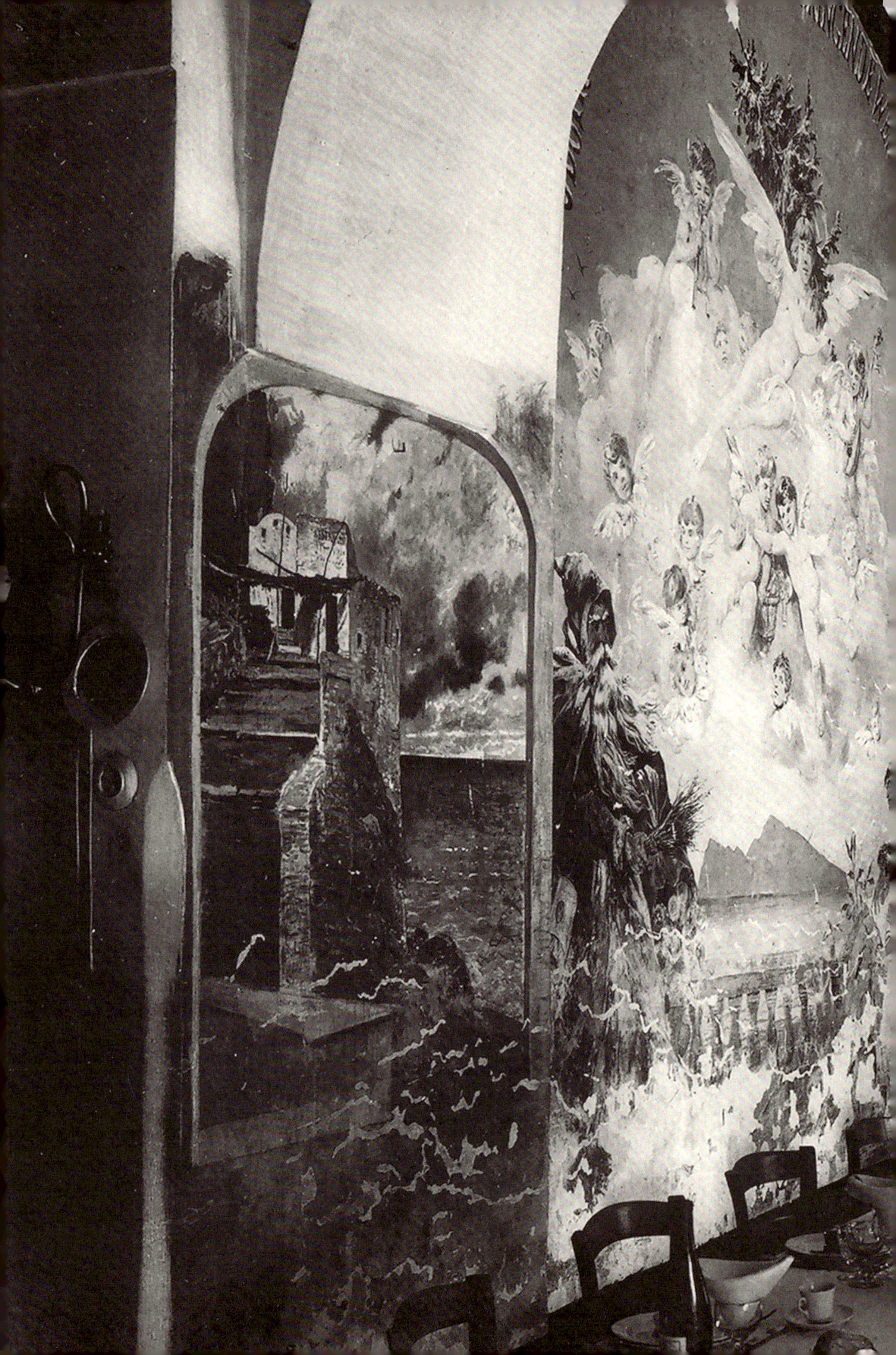

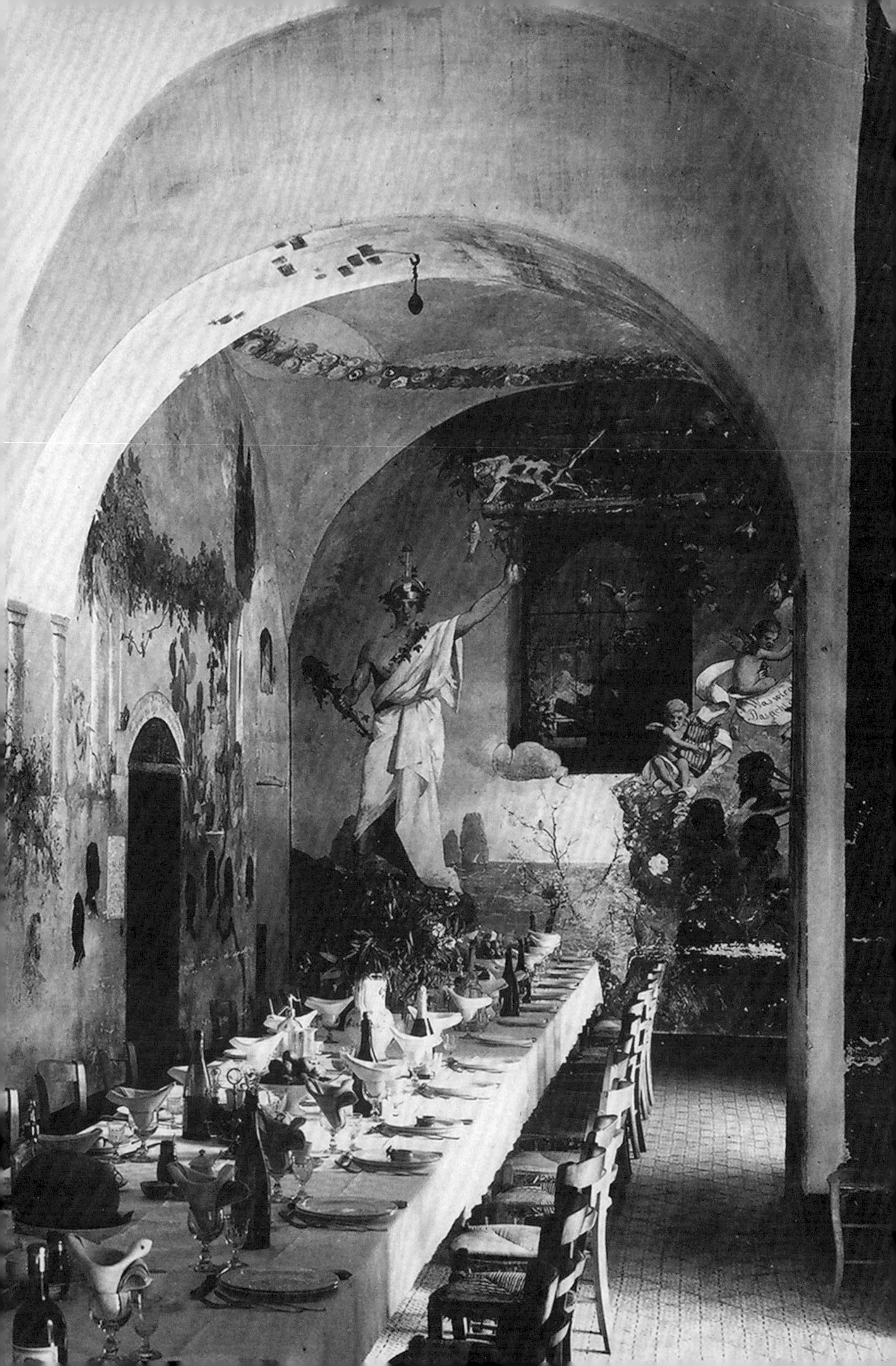

We refer to an article by Borrelli published in 1903 by *Esperia*, the Neapolitan Literary Magazine:

They chose not to—because were unable to—understand the difference between the perverted and reprehensible man and the Artist who gave English literature such genuine masterpieces. What they said was: his was the art of degeneration, and the least we can do is forget it, if not abhor it! . . . But they did not recall that such monstrous degenerations were widespread in biblical times, in the imperial courts of Rome—even among the best of emperors, such as Titus and Vespasian—and that above all they provided the artistic *substratum* and often inspiration for a very famous Greek poet: I say that Anacreon, without Batillus (his lover) would have written far fewer lyrics.

Among the first things he asked me in Posillipo was whether I knew any sorceress who could rid the house of the mice that infested it, and prevented him from sleeping [. . .].

My advice was to get some cats; but he regarded me in horror, because he hated those beasts of luck, much like those peacocks whose feathers and stuffed skins had adorned the villa and which, upon his arrival, he had destroyed.

So I suggested: spread arsenic everywhere; but he shook his head, with dejected conviction: he wanted a sorceress, one of those old sorceresses, whom he had seen at work when he was young and had come to Naples the first time; those enchantresses who, with two flutes, would call mice and lead them off, in just a short time. I was silent, and humiliated; I did not know then, and still do not—of the existence of such experts in my own country. This episode is not surprising: in fact, Wilde was, as we have noted, very superstitious. Any trivial event could entail a good or bad omen. An offer of peacock feathers by an admirer signified that something terrible was about to befall him, or if his gaze rested on the number thirteen he must surely lose something . . .!

***

Letter to Robert Ross, October 19 1897 (Naples, Hôtel Royal des Étrangers)

My dear Robbie,

Thank you so much for all the trouble you have taken.

I now think, [. . .] that I had better publish in an English newspaper. I suggest *Reynolds*: it circulates among the lower orders and the criminal classes, and so ensures me my right audience for sympathy. Also, it has always been nice to me, and about me. [. . .]

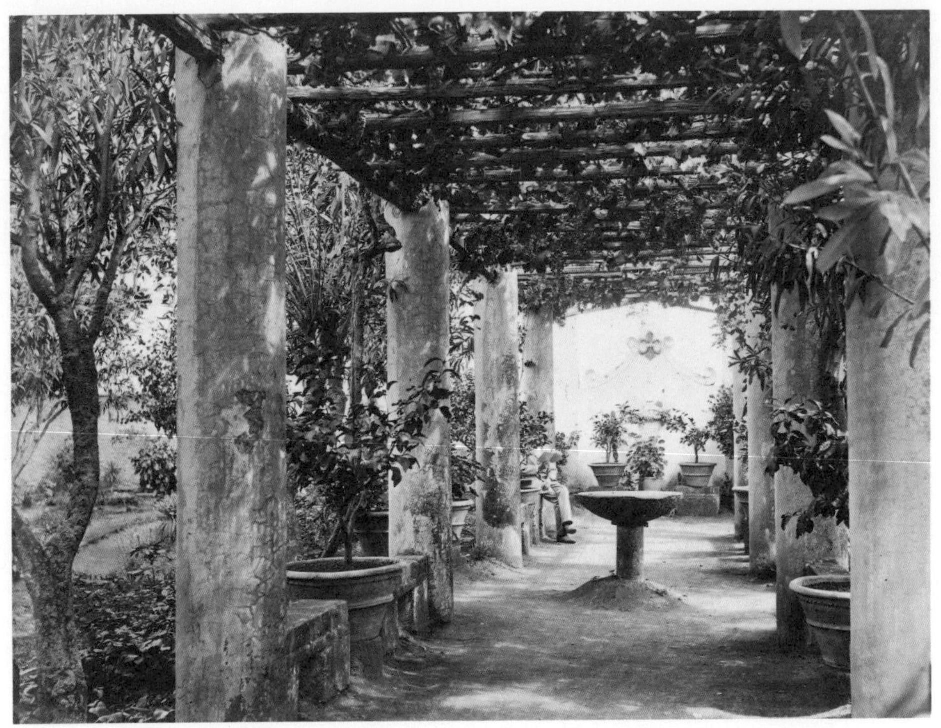

Bosie is at Capri. I came back yesterday, as there was scirocco and rain. He dines with Mrs. Snow.[88]
We both lunched with Dr Munthe,[89] who has a lovely villa and is a great connoisseur of Greek things. He is a wonderful personality.
I hope you will not go to Canada. What am I to do without you in London?
Ever yours
Oscar

***

His friendship with Rocco, however, provides us with a few more private glimpses of his stay:

Excerpt from *Interview of Wilde* by Arnaldo (Rocco) De Lisle

I went to visit them one day. And I found him in the company of several rascals he gathered from the Neapolitan rabble. Wilde struggled to expose

---

[88] Author's Note: An American lady living on Capri. Norman Douglas wrote in *Looking Back* (1934) that "a vision of her helped me to portray the Duchess" of San Martino in *South Wind* (1917). She used to host cultural events in her house.
[89] Author's Note: Axel Munthe (1857–1949), Swedish doctor and author of *The Story of San Michele* (1929).

a whole complicated theory of aesthetics to them, wanting to make them understand that they were wrong in being proud of the fact that he thought them handsome, since beauty really was not in them, but the delightful enchantment was located in his soul, and that, from it, not from them, emanated the radiant charm.

Those little tramps naturally laughed at it, understanding nothing, and thinking about exploiting the morbid mental turmoil from which he was afflicted and misled!

Poor Madman!

Lombroso's theory "genius is insanity" found in him its highest expression. On another occasion, while we were discussing *Salomé* at the Caffè Calzona,[90] he suddenly brought his hand upon his heart and remained silent, motionless, with an expression of pain on all the muscles of his face, as if he had been struck by a syncope.

"Are you feeling ill?" I asked him, as I prepared to assist him.

"My love, my love," he babbled, "my love just passed by, there they are!"

As he was saying this, he pointed to one of those dirty, tattered street-urchins who turn somersaults in front of foreigners in the areas in front of the Gallery! Rather than letters, he would send telegrams: his favorite mode of conversation was the apologue. [. . .]

Just like a good Oxford humanist, Oscar Wilde could very well have made use of Latin and Greek. He favored Hellenic and Roman antiquity. His subjects were all imaginary: he was an unrivalled storyteller, he knew them by the thousands, interlinked one with the next. It was his favorite manner of expressing all that he wanted: a subtle pictorial hypocrisy of his thought; one evening, he told one which I believe was an allusion to himself.

"Once upon a time," he said, "there was a young man who lived in a city that was reflected in the sea: every morning he would go strolling on the beach at length and, on his way back, he'd always recount stories of seeing mermaids. Now, one day it happened that he actually met a mermaid. She was bathing in the blue water: he saw her, but upon his return, as he was asked about what he had seen, that day, he did not answer: he remained silent." It was not a good idea to push Oscar Wilde too far on the significance of such allegories: it was enough to savor their sudden grace, without shaking the veils of this phantasmagoria of spirit that instilled into his conversation something that resembled the narrated *One Thousand and One Nights*.

---

[90] Author's Note: Caffè Calzona was founded in Naples in 1890 in the Galleria Umberto I. The café was well known for having a performance spectacle every night.

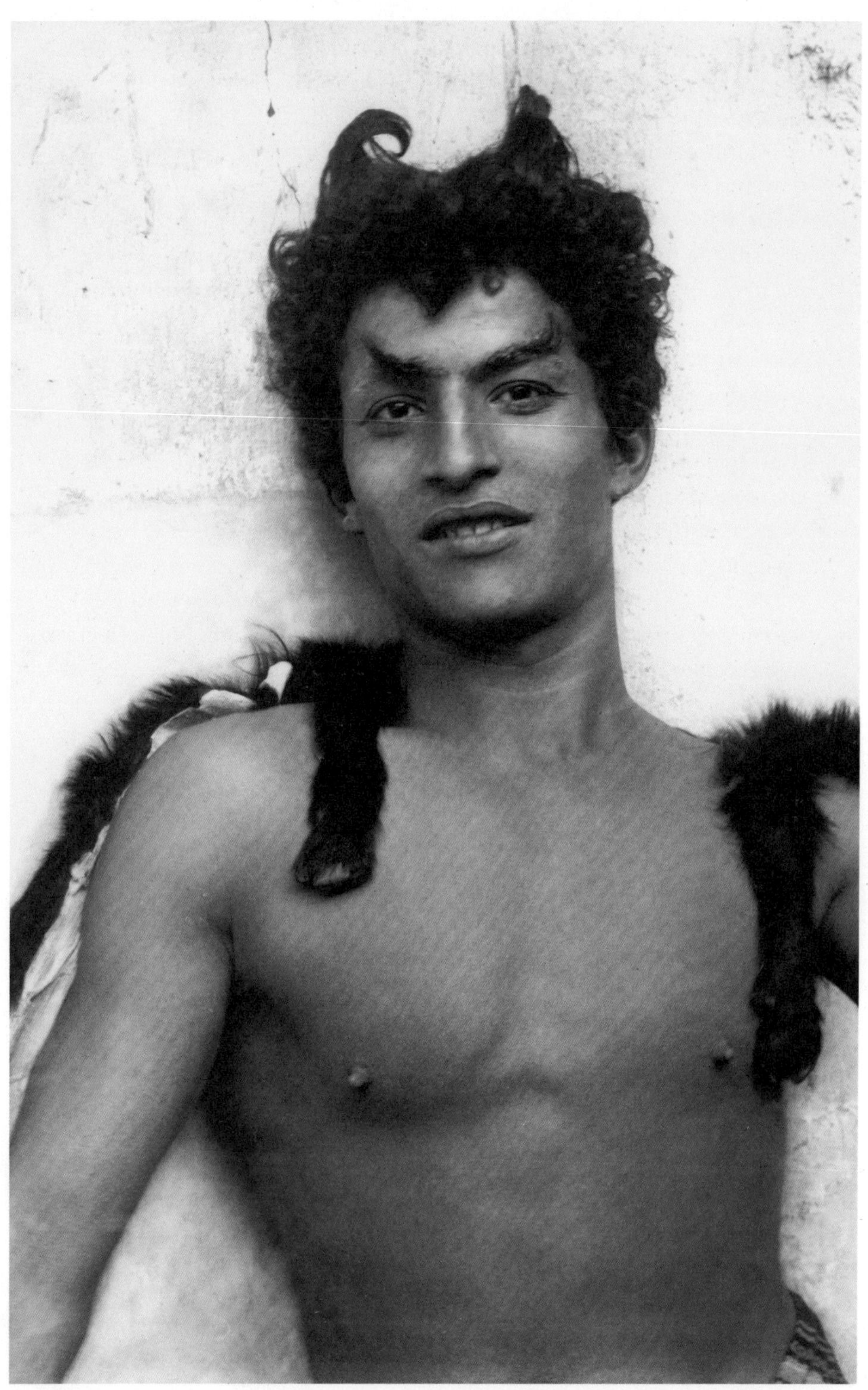

The golden-edged cigarette would go out and light up again without rest between the lips of the narrator. The hand, drawing a slow gesture, animated the scarab on the ring finger with green light. The face was transformed into the pleasing mimicry, the voice lasted tirelessly, a bit slow, but always the same.

Oscar Wilde would persuade and amaze. One thing set him apart, that of testifying to the improbable. The frailest doubts took, with his words, the momentary aspect of indisputable truth. From a fairytale he brought out a precise and real scene, from a fact he drew a fairytale. He listened to his inner Scheherazade, and it seemed that he himself was the first to be amazed at his fables and his peculiar inventions.

This special gift, this talent for storytelling, made Oscar Wilde's conversationalists more than the chosen ones [. . .]. Oscar Wilde pleased and delighted, instilling the belief that he was happy, a master of life. Had he not experienced his imagination shine with wonderful human thoughts; had he not shown that he could arrange them in novel ways?

He had already bestowed upon his life some genuinely eccentric but harmless gestures, such as serving rose dishes at lunchtime or hiring a leading tailor to make a "pauper" habit for a beggar he saw every day at the door of his home. The sight of that beggar grieved him. Oscar Wilde had already traveled extensively. He had traveled America in knee-length trousers, with a sunflower in his hands, he had journeyed through Italy flaunting a Byronian dandyism. He was seen in France, sailing along the Normandy coast with a yacht. His boat sailed the Loire just above the water. In London, he enjoyed the elegant life that great fortunes create. He was admired, and he admired himself with profound complaisance [. . .]. These were his happiest years before prison.

Jolted ghost, massive caricature, Wilde would bend over a Manhattan or a large whiskey soda, and for the curious, for his friends, for no matter who, he would re-improvise some of his improvisations and repeat a few of his paradoxes with a weary appearance.

It was mainly for himself that he rekindled these visions of his. He longed to wake up and cradle himself, to convince himself that he was still thinking, that he was still an artist and a sage. In fact, he knew all these things. He knew one by one Dante Alighieri's commentators, and their comments, the sources of Dante Gabriele Rossetti, the different facts and the battles, and of everything he talked about and discussed he was like a learned scholar and a recent graduate, after which he smiled his purgatory grin, and burst out laughing, for no reason, at a laugh that shook his rather

chubby belly, his fleshy cheeks and the gold of his poor decayed teeth. [. . .]
Every day brings him new suffering: he no longer has any admirers, nor
real friends, he lives under the weight of the worst neurasthenia.
The lack of money afflicts him: his pension of 10 lire per day from his
family, is no longer rounded up either by the advances or by the publishers'
fees: he should work, write comedies, for which he has already signed the
contracts, and he no longer has the strength for it, being unable to get
out of bed before three in the afternoon. He doesn't become embittered,
he wears himself out; he stares at his bed for an entire day, under the
pretext that, in a restaurant, the clams poisoned him, and he only gets up
begrudgingly and with the secret thought of the death of which he will die.
He then tells all his little tales: it is the bitter and dazzling flare of a
supernatural firework.

***

Letter to Reginald Turner, October 19 1897 (Naples, Hôtel Royal des Étrangers)

Dearest Reggie, [. . .]
The translation [of *Salomé*] is in the hands of Rocco—a poet here—who
knows French well. I hope it will be all right.
The French papers describe me as living, broken down in health, in the
lovely villa of the son of Lord Douglas! [. . .]
Ever yours
Oscar

***

Letter to Stanley V. Makower, October 21 1897 (Naples, Posilippo, Villa Giudice)

My dear Stanley, [. . .]
I am supervising an Italian version of *Salomé*, which is being made here
by a young Neapolitan poet. I hope to produce it on the stage here, if I
can find an actress of troubling beauty and flute-like voice. Unfortunately,
most of the tragic actresses of Italy—with the exception of Duse—are
stout ladies, and I don't think I could bear a stout Salomé. [. . .]
Believe me,
sincerely yours
Oscar Wilde

***

Two problems now haunted Oscar: finishing the *Ballad* (the only way he could get some money) and solving the payment of his alimony to his ex-wife Constance.

***

Letter to Robert Ross, November 16 1897 (Naples, Posilippo, Villa Giudice)

> My dear Robbie,
> I received this afternoon a letter from Hansell to say he was going to decide that I was to be deprived of my absurd income because I was with Bosie. I don't suppose that anything will prevent him from doing this, but I felt it due to myself and to Bosie to write to him a letter of protest, on the ground that I do not think it just or socially-speaking accurate to describe Bosie as a "disreputable person." After all, no charge was made against him at any of my trials, nor anything proved, or attempted to be proved.
> Nor do I think that it is fair to say that I have created a "public scandal" by being with him. If newspapers chronicle the fact, that is their business; I can't help that. If I were living here with you they would chronicle my being here with equal venom and vulgarity: or if I were living with someone of unblemished reputation and unassailable position. I think I should only be held accountable for any scandal caused by my getting into trouble with the law. My existence is a scandal. But I do not think I should be charged with creating a scandal by continuing to live: though I am conscious that I do so. I cannot live alone, and Bosie is the only one of my friends who is either able or willing to give me his companionship. If I were living with a Naples renter I would I suppose be all right. As I live with a young man who is well-bred and well-born, and who has been charged with no offence, I am deprived of all possibility of existence. [. . .]
> Ever yours, dearest Robbie,
> Oscar

***

Wilde's encounters with Rocco continued to be a pleasant interlude between ordinary troubles:

Excerpt from *Interview of Wilde* by Arnaldo (Rocco) De Lisle

> You could not be with him talking for five minutes, without him telling you about plots for stories, novels, dramas, romances and all very original, and with a different artistic outlook.

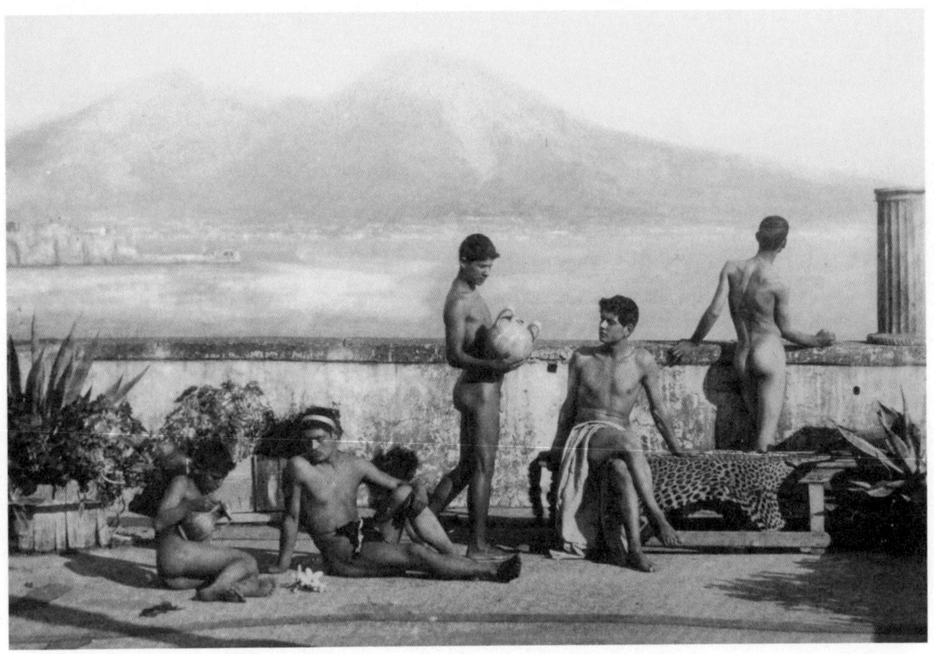

One day he suggested to me that I write a novel, a psychological study on the Neapolitan underworld, in which I should introduce a young scoundrel, who, finding himself in prison for the first time, envies the fate of his other cellmates, who in the evenings tell of all the misdeeds they committed; he feels humiliated having only a very small crime to his credit. So, such was the power of the seduction of crime upon him, that, so that he would be able to talk about himself, he gets up one night and strangles the most feared member of the Camorra.

He loved such studies of the underworld, feeling attracted to it by an irresistible force: he would have liked to live among the lower social classes, and be, like the Parisian Aristide Bruant, their singer, their standard-bearer!

He also loved parables, wrote beautiful ones and invented them at every turn. That of the very intelligent horse who thinks he can win the race by arriving last. Or that of the servant who, one day, after receiving a new garment from his master, believes himself to be a gentleman and no longer wants to serve him. And he told me so many of them.

He often said: "We must never look at people's faces during the day: they then wear the mask that best suits them to please those with whom they speak; pious if with a pious man, in a dejected demeanour if they're supposed to pretend to be afflicted. You must look at them either in the evening or secretly, when they do not know they are being observed, to catch the truth of their innermost soul."

As far as political ideas, he was a revolutionary, not because of the principle that by modifying a form of government, one could achieve a better one, but simply because he was against everything that represented any social order.

For him, there should be no laws, no guards: if they robbed him, he wouldn't have the thieves arrested. A bit like Tolstoy, he thought that those who steal needed to do it; this is not because of that heartfelt philanthropy that is at the bottom of Tolstoy's character, but rather because of that kind of extravagance that marked all his actions, and because of which it was actually impossible to get a precise idea of the man.

His spirit represented a unique phenomenon. Everything he said, he said convinced that he would not be believed, and precisely for this reason, as he spoke, in his voice there was always such a profound tone of mockery that it seemed to warn you: Take care! I will now tell you something extraordinary, which will surprise you, but do not lend it any faith, I always speak as an author when he is writing, I have no other purpose except that of arousing the greatest possible emotion. Like a great actor on the stage, who always seems to listen to his internal prompter.

And the waiter told me that one evening Wilde had returned home, followed by five soldiers: a sailor, an artilleryman, a grenadier, a *bersagliere* (Italian rifleman corps) and a little puppet, with whom he had spent the whole night.

"I asked myself," added the waiter, with that mischievous wit that is characteristic of Neapolitans, "waking up from time to time, who knows what corps 'mounts' guard right now!" And in Paris, one day, while loudly making licentious propositions to a young man in a café, he was beaten by several of the gentlemen around him with their canes!"

***

Finally, in November 1897, a draft proof of the *Ballad* arrived.

Letter to Leonard Smithers, November 19 1897 (Naples, Posilippo, Villa Giudice)

My dear Smithers,
your telegram has just arrived: and I am very much obliged to you for your kindness, as in the midst of my hideous worries the lack of any money at all was paralysing. Now, I can really think about my position,

and form some judgment as to whether it is worth while fighting on against the hideous forces of the world. Personally, I don't think it is, but Vanity, that great impulse, still drives me to think of a possible future of self-assertion. It seems absurd to be beaten by the want of money. And yet I feel that every problem in life must be solved on its own conditions. And Financial Problems can be solved only by Finance. Genius, Art, Romance, Passion, and the like are useless when the point at issue is one of figures. A solution for an algebraic problem is not to be found in the sense of Beauty, however developed. The proofs also have arrived: in old days of power and personality I always insisted that my proofs should be sent to me on the paper to be ultimately used. Otherwise I would not have been able to judge of the look of a page. Of course the paper of these proofs is awful, and the whole thing looks to me mean in consequence. The type is good [. . .]. The public is largely influenced by the *look* of a book. So are we all. It is the only artistic thing about the public. [. . .] Excuse this brief letter. I am in a hurry to buy cigarettes—the first for four days.
Sincerely yours
Oscar Wilde

***

But Oscar's real problems were yet to come. On November 23, Wilde wrote to Ross to try to figure out if Constance would have felt satisfied were he and Bosie to stay in different houses. Six days later Douglas wrote a letter replying to Edward Strangman having heard that they were still uncertain, but that they were approaching a decision.

***

Letter to Robert Ross, November 23 1897 (Naples, Posilippo, Villa Giudice)

My dear Robbie,
I have not heard yet from Hansell or Adrian Hope, nor do I know whether they will answer me or not.
Do you think that if I have engaged not to live with Bosie—in the same house–that that would be regarded as a concession of any kind? To say that I would never see him or speak to him again would of course be childish—we would not live in the same house again, if that will be regarded as an equitable concession. Or do you thing that everything is over, and that my wife will hear of nothing that would enable me to live? It is a dreary sordid tragedy, but I do think they should see that it is absurd to say that my wife cannot be expected to give me money to live with

Bosie. How I spend my money is surely a question for myself. If my wife became a teetotaller, would she have a right to say she would not give me money to spend on wine? If she objected to smoking, what I have to give up cigarettes? [. . .] I suppose Smithers has received the proofs by this time. Pray look over them carefully. I may have omitted something, or passed over an error.

The actor–manager here, Cesare Rossi, was astounded with *Salomé*, but said he had no actress who could possibly touch the part. I am going to try Duse, but have not much hope. My books have come from Dieppe by long sea, but I have not the money to get them out, so I have to do without them for the present; it is great nuisance.

The *Gil Blas* has an interview with me which I send you.[91]

Ever yours

Oscar

***

Wilde read the *Salomé* translated by Rocco and, after Wilde approved the translation, Rocco tried through his friends to contact the famous actress, Duse, to perform the *Salomé*.

***

Letter to Leonard Smithers, November 28? 1897 (Naples, Posilippo)

Dear Smithers, [. . .]

I wish you would start a Society for the Defence of Oppressed Personalities: at present there is a gross European concert headed by brutes and solicitors against us. It is really ridiculous that after my entire life has been wrecked by Society, people should still propose to exercise social tyranny over me, and to try to force me to live in solitude, the one thing I can't stand. I lived in silence and solitude for two years in prison. I did not think that on my release my wife, my trustees, the guardians of my children, my few friends, such as they are, and my myriad enemies would combine to force me by starvation to live in silence and solitude again. After all in prison we had food of some kind: it was revolting, and made as loathsome as possible on purpose, and quite inadequate to sustain life in health. Still, there *was* food of some kind. The scheme now is that I am to live in silence and solitude and have no food at

---

[91] Author's Note: his interview, signed Gédéon Spilett, appeared in *Gil Blas* on November 22: 54–55. Part of the interview appears earlier in this volume in the chapter "Oscar's life after his imprisonment at Reading."

all. Really, the want of imagination in people is appalling. This scheme is put forward on moral grounds! It is proposed to leave me to die of starvation, or to blow my brains out in a Naples urinal. I never came across anyone in whom the moral sense was dominant who was not heartless, cruel, vindictive, log-stupid, and entirely lacking in the smallest sense of humanity. Moral people, as they are termed, are simple beasts. I would sooner have fifty unnatural vices than one unnatural virtue. It is unnatural virtue that makes the world, for those who suffer, such a premature Hell.

All this has, of course, direct reference to my poem: and indeed is the usual way in which poets write to publishers. [. . .] The popularity of the poem will be largely increased by the author's painful death by starvation. The public love poets to die in that way. It seems to them dramatically right. Perhaps it is.

Even yours

O. W.

***

Letter to Leonard Smithers, November 30? 1897 (Naples, Posilippo, Villa Giudice)

My dear Smithers,

Your letter just received. [. . .] With regards to the notes of interrogation, I really think that it would be best to discuss vital points like this *en tête-à-tête*, so I hope you will come out to Naples and see me.

As I have lost my entire income, of course I cannot live with Alfred Douglas any more. He has only just enough for himself. So he is going back to Paris, and I shall be alone here. I do not know if, now that we are going to separate, there is any likelihood of my income being restored to me. I unluckily have now no one to plead my cause aright. I have alienated all my friends, partly through my own fault, partly through theirs. The Paris *Journal* has a sympathetic paragraph to say I am starving at Naples, but French people subscribe nothing but sonnets when one is alive, and statues when one is not. [. . .] My handwriting— once Greek and gracious—is now illegible: I am very sorry: but I really am a wreck of nerves. I don't eat, or sleep: I live on cigarettes.

Ever yours

O.W.

***

Letter to Robert Ross, December 6 1897 (Naples, Posilippo, Villa Giudice)

My dear Robbie,
I know that it would have been impossible for you to have prevented
Hansell's decision: what hurt me was that no effort was made, and I still
hold that More was wrong in saying that my wife was "acting strictly
within her rights according to the legal agreement." Hansell is of the same
opinion. He writes to me that he gave his decision, not on the grounds of
the written agreement, but on the understanding that existed that I was not
to live with Bosie. He told me at Reading that he would decide so. At that
time I did not want ever to see Bosie again, so I didn't mind. Afterwards
was a different thing. [. . .] Bosie is of course a gilded pillar of infamy in this
century, but whether he is *legally* disreputable is another question. I knew
that I was running a fearful risk of losing my income by being with Bosie.
I was warned on all sides: my eyes were not blinded [. . .]. You have done
wonderful things for me, but the Nemesis of circumstances, the Nemesis
of character, have been too strong for me—and as I said to More I think I
was a problem for which there was no solution. Money alone could have
helped me, not to solve, but to avoid solving the difficulty. [. . .] And on
the whole I do think you make wonderfully little allowance for a man like
myself, now ruined, broken-hearted, and thoroughly unhappy. You stab
me with a thousand phrases: if one phrase of mine shrills through the air
near you, you cry out that you are wounded to death.
Ever yours
Oscar.

***

Following the 'default' suspension of Wilde's income, came the threat by Bosie's
family to cut off food. Lord Douglas had no choice but to return to his mother
giving everyone his version of the facts. Bosie wrote as follows:

When Wilde came to the Villa Giudice he was in fair health and
reasonable spirits. That he had eaten and drunk too much at Berneval
he freely admitted, but on the whole he was in good physical condition.
From the end of August to the middle of November he had the run of
my villa as my guest, and I paid the whole of the housekeeping expenses,
including the tradesmen's bills for food and wine, the servant's wages, and
so forth, to which expenses Wilde never so much as contributed a farthing
piece. So far as I am aware, the life he lived here was perfectly proper and

without reproach. He had brought with him from Berneval a rough draft of part of *The Ballad of Reading Goal*, which he read to me [. . .]. He told me that he had composed certain of the stanzas in prison and he added to them at Berneval. But there can be no question that the poem was completed at Naples. He laboured over it in a manner which I had never known him to labour before. Every word had to be considered; every rhyme and every cadence carefully pondered. I had *The Ballad of Reading Gaol* for breakfast, dinner and tea, and for many weeks it was almost our sole topic of conversation. For my own part, I, too, was busy with literary work, and I wrote at Naples during this period some of my best sonnets, and occupied myself with various translations. We had not an idle week during the whole time we were together [. . .]. The truth is that Wilde consistently made free use of such gifts as I possessed, that I assisted him to many a piece of dialogue and many a gibe which has helped to make him famous, and that I gave him very material aid and counsel in the matter of *The Ballad of Reading Gaol*. There are passages in this latter poem which he lifted holus-bolus from a poem of my own, and it must be remembered that, while up to the time that he left Reading Gaol, he had affected some scorn of the ballad form and knew next to nothing of its possibilities, I had given a great amount of attention to the study of that form and had produced *The Ballad of Perkin Warbeck* and the *The Ballad of St. Vitus*, which latter Wilde read for the first time at Naples, and with which he was mightily impressed.

It would be preposterous for me to claim more than my due as regards the literary side of our friendship, and I had perhaps better put the position this way: I have never denied that I learned things from Wilde and that, up to a certain point, I owe a good deal to him in the literary sense. On the other hand, in view of what he said, it is necessary for me to point out that Wilde owes just as much to me as I owe to him and, for that matter, a great deal more.

Although our life at the Villa Giudice was perfectly harmless and consisted mainly of fairly strenuous literary toil, the fact that we were together did not please certain Wilde's friends, and the scandal-mongers were set busy again [. . .]. Anybody who knows Europe at all, knows perfectly well that Naples was then, and is now, a resort of the most exclusive set of Italian aristocracy, and that there is a large and highly respectable English colony there. My grandmother, the late Hon. Mrs. Alfred Montgomery, lived there for twenty years, and there was not a person of position in the place by whom I was not known or with whom I was not on calling terms if

I cared to follow up my social duties. There is nothing at all about the reputation of Naples to differentiate it from Rome or Genoa or Florence or Venice or any other Italian city. [. . .] The reports naturally came to the ears of my people, who were much distressed and upset by them; and it was pointed out to me that I was doing myself great damage by befriending this man and that I ought to send him about his business. One of the attachés from the British Embassy at Rome, in which city I had spent the winter of 1896 with my mother, came to Naples, at the instigation of the Ambassador, expressly to see me, and to urge on me the advisability of dissociating myself from Wilde. He told me that the fact that I had Wilde as a guest in my house was causing all sorts of unpleasant gossip, and he even went so far as to say that it was not fair to them at the Embassy that I should persist in giving cause for such gossip, as they had all made a point of being civil and friendly to me when I was in Rome. He was very insistent, and when he found that I was not to be moved he got annoyed with me, told me I was a "quixotic fool" and that I should live to be very sorry for having befriended a "beast like Wilde," who would get everything he could out of me and then probably turn round and abuse me. I knew that Oscar Wilde was hard at work on his poem. I believed that his life was clean and that he had determined to keep from his old evil courses; and I knew that my life was just as proper as it always had been, and I consequently saw no reason for turning upon my friend [. . .]. I was thus forced to capitulate; but I did not do so without a struggle and without making provision for the man who was dependent upon me. I arranged to leave him at the Villa Giudice, the rent of which had been paid in advance, and I arranged that my mother should send him two hundred pounds, which would enable him to live in comfort for a month or two; and I further arranged to let him have additional money as he wanted it [. . .]. It is true that at the very moment when he was writing to me in acknowledgment of these sums and to express his gratitude for my kindness, he was complaining to Ross [. . .]. "It was," said Wilde, "a most bitter experience in a bitter life. He went to Paris." The last sentence should have had an addendum: it should have read: "He went to Paris with two hundred pounds of Lord Alfred Douglas's money in his pocket, which had been sent to him per Mr. More Adey and the Marchioness of Queensberry." But it doesn't.[92]

***

---

[92] Alfred Douglas, *Oscar Wilde and Myself* (London: Long, 1914).

Letter to Leonard Smithers, December 10? 1897 (Naples, Posilippo, Villa Giudice)

My dear Smithers, [. . .]
You ask me to make it up with Robbie. My dear fellow, I would gladly go on my knees from here to Naples if Robbie would be nice to me. I was upset and distressed at everything that had happened, and wrote bitterly, not about anything that was said about me but about what was acquiesced in about someone else. In my deed of separation with my wife a clause was inserted to say that if I lived with any disreputable person, in such a way as to cause public scandal, I was to lose my income. My wife's advisers said that Alfred Douglas was a "disreputable person," and More Adey wrote to me that he and Robbie felt bound to admit that my life was "acting strictly within the terms of her legal agreement." I was hurt at More Adey and Robbie acquiescing at once with this view.
I do not deny that Alfred Douglas is a gilded pillar of infamy, but I do deny that he can be properly described in a *legal* document as a disreputable person, and I felt that some little stand might have been made by his friends and mine, for both Robbie and More Adey have been on friendly terms with Alfred Douglas and been with him in Paris. Indeed, Robbie spent two months in Capri within last year. Of course, they could not have prevented my wife doing what she wished, but they could have protested, and that protest would have helped me. *Hinc illae lachrymae.* Which, however, have been more of my shedding than Robbie's. To me the loss of his affection is irreparable. I really now have not one friend, of all my old friends, left in the world.
Robbie's refusal to interest himself in my poem I feel is inartistic of him— my work as a poet is separate from my life as a man—and as for my life, it is one ruined, unhappy, lonely and disgraced. All pity, or the sense of its beauty, seems to me dead in the world. Two months ago, before this last worry began, Robbie wrote to me: "Remember always that you committed the unpardonable and vulgar error of being found out."
This is the attitude of the world and its relation to me. I think it is one harsh, ignoble and Pharisaic. [. . .] However I still hope that Robbie may be kind to me again. I am deeply sorry I gave him pain, but, like most people, he only realises the pain he gets and not the pain he gives. [. . .] The fact is that when a man has had two years of hard labour, people, quite naturally, treat him as a pariah dog. This is a social truth that I realise every day. I don't complain about it. There's no use complaining about facts. *Je constate le fait, c'est tout.* It comes from the decay of imagination

in the race, caused by the pressure of an artificial and mechanical Society. And, after all, when my own wife leaves me to die of starvation in Naples, without taking the smallest interest in the matter, I don't see why I should expect old friends to take the trouble to even answer or acknowledge my letters. [. . .] I hope O'Sullivan will arrive soon. I suppose; however, he will stop and say his prayers at Rome.

I would be greatly obliged if you can get me a copy of *Dorian Gray* and send it to me. There is a Neapolitan poet [Biagio Chiara],[93] and good English scholar, who wants to translate it, and I want the Italians to realise that there has been more in my life than my love for Narcissus, or a passion for Sporus: fascinating though both may be.[94]

Eleanora [*sic*] Duse is now reading *Salomé*. There's a chance of her playing it. She is a fascinating artist though nothing to Sarah.

Pray write constantly, especially when there is no necessity to do so.

Ever yours

O. W.

***

The "fascinating artist" (Eleonora Duse) replied to Giuseppe G. Rocco, refusing to see Oscar, who would have been honored to represent a drama that his august colleague Sarah had been unable to play due to problems with censorship and age!

Unfortunately, however, the author's bad reputation did not allow it. The same answer was given by Enrico Pessina to Luigi Conforti, who wanted to make at least a reading of it at the Circolo Filologico, of which Pessina was president.

Even Rossi and De Santis—team leader of some of the tour companies of the time—who at first had become enthusiastic about the work—no longer wanted to know. "The author came out of prison and was a pervert; the work had to perish."

From De Lisle :

In any case, despite everything, the first reading of the version of the play took place in the house of Giovanni Bovio, and all who attended—writers, poets, students and journalists—were left enraptured, but the most enthusiastic was Mrs. Bovio, who did not tire of complimenting the Author.

---

[93] Author's Note: The first edition of *Doriano Gray Dipinto* (an awkward title, literally "Dorian Gray painted") was actually printed by Bideri in Naples and dedicated by Chiara to his friend, the painter Nino Brusa.
[94] Author's Note: Sporus was Nero's favorite, who "married him" with a ceremony.

Wilde in taking his leave kissed the lady's hand. And, as soon as he got out into the street, staring fixedly into the eyes of the translator who accompanied him, and who had read the *Salomé*, said to him: "Do you know why I kissed Mrs. Bovio's hand? Why?? Because I wanted to ask her for forgiveness, within myself, for a perverse idea that crossed my mind while you were reading. She was staring at me hard, and I don't know why I thought of killing her."
To Rocco's astonishment, Wilde added: "And you, you never thought of killing anyone??
The morbid disposition of the individual was thus triggered from time to time, and precisely in these twists and turns of his consciousness, one must seek the reason for some of his predilections for people of the underworld."

One of Bovio's guests, the lawyer Luigi Conforti, was so struck by the poetical energy of Wilde's writing that he tried to organize a public reading in the Circolo Filologico di Napoli, but it proved impossible.

***

According to Rocco's vision the play had a misogynist undercurrent with some linguistic sophistication. For instance, "Rocco found an admirable solution for the ending: Herod's expression of disgust in his order to 'Kill that woman!' when he sees Salomé kissing the lips of the dead head of the Baptist, is translated by the Neapolitan as '*Uccidete quella femmina!*' Rocco, who understands how Herod despises the woman in Salomé in that moment, aptly chooses, instead of the more common *donna*, the word *femmina* (female), which is an idiomatic expression of traditional Southern Italian, chauvinistic male attitudes to women."[95]

Letter to Leonard Smithers, December 11 1897 (Naples, Posilippo, Villa Giudice)

My dear Smithers,
A holograph letter from you is indeed a curiosity of literature, and I treasure it for its manner no less than for its matter. [. . .]
My life cannot be patched up. There is a doom on it. [. . .]
I am now simply an ordinary pauper of a rather low order: the fact that I am also a pathological problem in the eyes of German scientists is only interesting to German scientists: and even in their works I am tabulated, and come under the law of *averages*! *Quantum mutatus*! [. . .]

---

[95] Evangelista, *The Reception of Oscar Wilde in Europe*.

I think that you had better send me no more proofs of the poem. I have the *maladie de perfection* and keep on correcting. [. . .] I would also like to see the cover. [. . .] Robbie has just sent me the *Weekly Sun*. I do not know if this is a sign of forgiveness on the reverse.
Ever yours
Oscar Wilde

***

Letter to More Adey, December 13 1897 (Naples, Posilippo, Villa Giudice)

My dear More,
I must thank you very sincerely for your kindness in sending me the cheque, and I am really sorry that you should have again been bothered by my affairs.[96] I am very much grieved that I wrote to you as I did, but I was upset, irritable, and horrid. All I said to Adrian Hope was that I considered that Bosie's actual position socially was in no way inferior to that of any of my friends, and I still think so. He holds his own with Society with amazing success. That was all I said. But I hope you will forgive me for the petulance with which I wrote to you. After all, you can understand what a wreck of all fine things I am. In old days I was judged by a different standard from others: I should be equally so judged now: only now the standard has to be lower, not higher. Gratefully yours
Oscar

---

[96] Author's Note: Copies of letters in More Adey's hand read as follows (Dated December 9 1897): "Dear Oscar, I enclose a cheque for £100, the amount I have just received from Lady Queensberry. She says she will pay the second hundred to me in a week or ten days. I write in great haste to catch the post. Ever yours More"

The truth is rarely pure and never simple.
Oscar Wilde

One of the last testimonies of this period in Naples comes from O'Sullivan[97] who was about to come as shown in the letter to Leonard Smithers of December 10. Their friendship was old-established and Wilde knew that he could always count on him, mainly from the financial point of view. In a moment of total depression, Oscar considered suicide again, as he told his friend.

The following conversation occurred between Wilde and O'Sullivan, as recorded in O'Sullivan's book:

"There is here at Naples" (Parco della Rimembranza), he said one evening, "a garden where those who have determined to kill themselves go. A short time ago, after Bosie had gone away, I was so cast down by the boredom of leaving the villa at Posillipo, and by the annoyance the some absurd friends in England were giving me, that I felt I could bear no more. Really, I came to wish that I was back in my prisoner's cell picking oakum. I thought of suicide."
"You?"
"Does that surprise you?"
"Yes—that is, I think that suicide is impossible for you now. It should have come before—much before—if at all."
"I was never really tempted to kill myself. I never thought seriously of that as a way out. What I felt was that I must drain the chalice of my passion to the dregs. But one night when there were no stars I went down to that garden. As I sat there absolutely alone in the darkness, I heard a rustling noise, and sighing, and misty, cloud-like things came round me. And I realized that they were the little souls of those who had killed themselves in that place, condemned to linger there ever after. They had killed themselves in vain. And when I thought that such would be the fate of my soul too, the temptation

---

[97] Author's Note: O'Sullivan, 14 years Wilde's junior, was still handsomely in funds when Oscar Wilde was released from Reading Gaol in 1897 and it was he who paid Wilde's travel expenses when he settled in Naples where he hoped to escape the trauma and humiliation that followed his trial and imprisonment. His friendship with Wilde, Aubrey Beardsley, Ernest Dowson and Arthur Symons placed him at the heart of that period of *fin-de-siècle* "Yellow Book" dandyism. Wilde speculated about his sexual inclinations and in an effort to find out sent him off on a jaunt to take a look at "a wonderful black panther" of a young man. His memoir about Wilde, *Aspects of Wilde*, is generally accepted by Wilde scholars as the most perceptive and accurate of contemporary biographies of Wilde. Vincent O'Sullivan, *Aspects of Wilde* (London: Constable, 1936).

to kill myself left me and has not come back." [. . .] O'Sullivan continued: "At Naples one night we had sat late in a restaurant. It was the first night of a new play in the theatre which was hard by. About half-past eleven the restaurant was invaded by a fashionable crowd who showed a great interest in Wilde's presence, and those who knew him by sight began pointing him out to others. To me it seemed just barefaced curiosity, inconsiderate but not insolent, and not hostile. Wilde, however, was profoundly disturbed. He seemed to choke. 'Let us go,' he said in a thick voice.

Outside, the city lay quiet and strange under the moon. We went a little way in silence. Then one of those tragic beggars of Naples arose in a doorway where he had been crouching and held out his hand. Wilde gave him money, and I heard him murmur in English: 'You wretched man, why do you beg when pity is dead?'

From that house I felt the inexorable curtain had begun to fall and that Oscar Wilde had lived.

At Naples he pointed out to me in the street an old woman. 'Unless that old woman asks you for money do not offer it to her. But if she asks you, be sure not to refuse.' Some days later we were sitting in a restaurant when the witch came by. She paused a moment, looked at us both steadfastly, and then went her way. Wilde was very much disturbed. 'Did you see that? She has looked in at the window. Some great misfortune is going to happen to us.'"

***

Soon after Douglas's departure Wilde left the safe haven of the Posillipo villa, with its paid rent, and spent the first £100 of Lady Queensberry's money on a trip to Sicily, with Elder, a Russian friend of O'Sullivan, where he stayed with the elderly Baron von Gloeden,[98] an infamous homosexual.

---

[98] Author's Note: Wilhelm von Gloeden was born near Wismar, Germany, on September 16 1856. His father, a wealthy baron, died when Wilhelm was just a boy. His stepfather, also a baron, was a counsellor and friend to Kaiser Wilhelm. Von Gloeden was classically educated in the highest circles of the Prussian elite. But Wilhelm had no interest in politics. Instead he loved art and became a student of antiquity. But his ability to sketch and paint was impaired by tuberculosis. In his early twenties Wilhelm was advised by doctors to look for a warmer and drier climate where he could spend some time. So he went to Sicily and became a photographer: beautifully composed, von Gloeden's photographs transformed working-class boys into images of antique legend. Many photographs held the image of two or more boys, or a young man with a younger boy, and had the ability to suggest mysterious (-un)known relationships. Soon he became very popular: hundreds of famous people signed Wilhelm's guest book, including Prince August Wilhelm of Prussia, King Edward VII of England (who carried von Gloeden's nude photos back to the U.K. in his diplomatic pouch), King Alphonse of Spain, composer Richard Strauss, Anatole France, Guglielmo Marconi and Oscar Wilde. Alexander Graham Bell, who came to Taormina with his wife, brought home examples of von Gloeden's work for the newly formed National Geographic Society. Some of these photos were subsequently published in the National Geographic magazine (October 1916) in an article entitled "Italy – The Gifted Mother of Civilization."

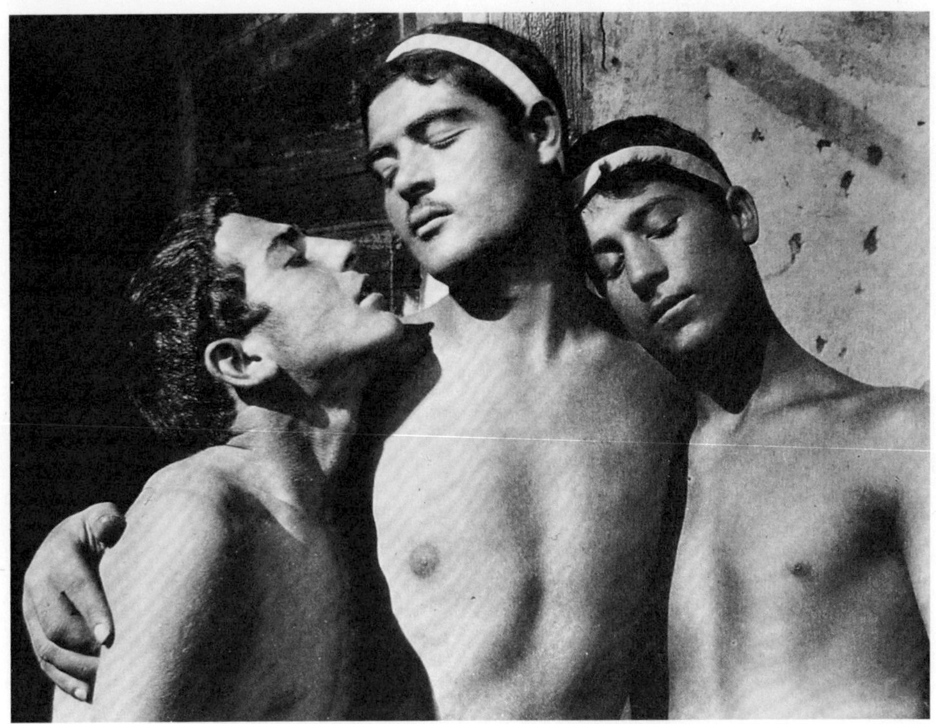

He also continued to practise and, at least to friends, defend homosexuality. On this he was unrepentant:

"A patriot put in prison for loving his country loves his country," he wrote to Ross, "and a poet in prison for loving boys loves boys. To have altered my life would have been to admit that Uranian love is ignoble. I hold it to be noble, more noble than other forms."[99]

Wilde remained in Naples until mid-January but moved, however, to Palazzo Bambino in via S. Lucia. In a conversation with O'Sullivan, Wilde noted as follows:

> Look at that boy, he reminds me of another Neapolitan faun, brown with those eyes that still seem to have the depth of the woods and that sensual grace of the whole person. From the way he looked at my stick, he must believe me very rich; unfortunately I have no money to invite him to lunch.

---

[99] Letter from Oscar Wilde to Robert Ross, February 18 1898(?); found in Rupert Hart-Davis, *The Letters of Oscar Wilde* (London: R. Hart-Davis, 1962).

Fortunately, eventually some promised money arrived, as evidenced by some correspondence:

Letter from More Adey, January 6 1898 (Wotton-under-Edge, Under the Hill)

> My dear Oscar,
> I have only just heard of your return to Naples. I had been waiting to write at length until I knew your address, as you did not mention what it would be at Taormina. However, I did write a very short letter to you at the Poste Restante there, on the chance of it reaching you, just to tell you that your second £100 has been paid in to me, and awaits your disposal in my bank. I came to Wotton-under-Edge the week before Christmas and shall be here until the end of the month. [. . .] It is rather late for me to say anything about the recent misunderstandings and disturbances, but while they were going on, and the atmosphere both here and with you was so electric, it was useless for me to say anything. Meanwhile however, I was doing everything I could possibly think of, to mitigate to both you and Bosie the unpleasantness of the situation and leave you freedom of action. You interpreted a sentence of mine about Mrs. Wilde's having acted strictly within her legal rights, to mean that I had somehow admitted that Bosie was a disreputable character. I made no admissions about Bosie of any kind. [. . .] Do write soon about beautiful plays and poems and nice new friends and your plans. It was nice going to Taormina with the Russian Elder, it would have been horrid for you left at Posilippo alone.
> Ever your friend
> More Adey

***

Only in Naples in winter, when the mud impoverished the scenery and "the rags cover the bronzes" did Oscar become prey to dark thoughts. The guides had discovered his favorite café (the Gambrinus, in Piazza Plebiscito), and would take tourists there who used to circle around his table.

The father of Graham Greene was a witness, as reported in his book *A Sort of Life*:

> A stranger hearing them speak in English asked whether he might join them over their coffee. There was something familiar and to them vaguely disagreeable about his face, but he kept them charmed by his with for more than an hour before he said goodbye. They didn't exchange names even

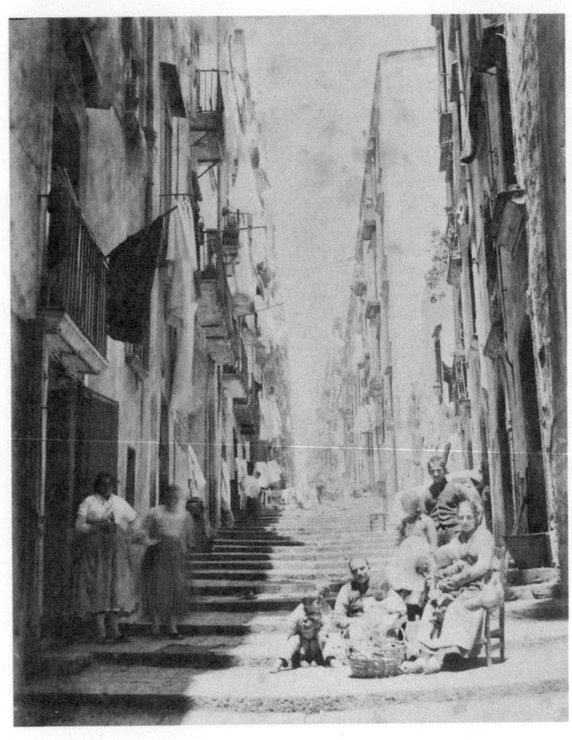

at parting and he left them to pay for his drink which was certainly not coffee. It was some while before they realized in whose company they had been. The stranger was Oscar Wilde, who not very long before had been released from prison. "Think," my father would always conclude his story, "how lonely he must have been to have expended so much time and wit on a couple of schoolmasters on holiday." It never occurred to him that Wilde was paying for his drink in the only currency he had.

I think this encounter must have been during the Christmas holidays of 1897–98 when his friend Bosie had departed and Wilde wrote of "ill-health, loneliness and general *ennui* with a tragi-comedy of an existence."[100]

***

Letter to Leonard Smithers, January 9 1898 (Naples, Santa Lucia)

My dear Smithers,
The revise has never arrived, and I waited from day to day for it. To wait longer would be foolish. I am sure it is all right. [. . .] The post here is

---

[100] Graham Greene, *A Sort of Life* (London: Simon and Schuster, 1971).

impossible, so pray bring it all out as soon as possible, without further consultation. I, as all poets, am safe in your hands.

As regards America, I think it would be better now to publish there without my name. I see it is my name that terrifies. I cannot advise about what should be done, but it seems to me that the withdrawal of my name is essential in America as elsewhere. And the public like an open secret. [. . .]

I have had many misfortunes since I wrote to you—influenza, the robbery, during my absence in Sicily, of *all* my clothes etc. by a servant whom I left at the villa, ill-health, loneliness, and general *ennui* with a tragi-comedy of an existence, but I want to see my poem out before I take steps.

Ever yours

O.W.

Return to Paris

*When I was young I thought that money was the most important thing in life;
now that I am old I know that it is.*
Oscar Wilde

The exact date of Wilde's return to Paris is not known, but he may well have carried out
the intention expressed in the last letter and reached Paris on Sunday, February 13, the
day on which Smithers published *The Ballad of Reading Gaol.*

On February 15 the *Daily Chronicle* had devoted two thirds of a column on the leader page
to the ballad, criticizing it favorably but concentrating on the horrors of prison life which
it portrayed. A review of *The Ballad* had appeared also in the *Academy* of February 26. The
anonymous critic complained that Wilde was "not as whole-souled a battler for truth as he
should be." Complimentary copies with a printed slip "compliments of the author" and
with a mark on the package "private" were sent to: Frank Harris, Fritz Thaulow, Dieppe;
Rev. Arthur Morrison, assistant Chaplain, Wandsworth Prison, Wandsworth; Oscar
Browning, Esq., King's College, Cambridge; Rev. Page Hopps, Leicester; the Baron von
Gloeden, Taormina, Sicily; Illustro Signor Alberto Stopford, Taormina, Sicily; Laurence
Housman, Esq., c/o Grant Richards, Publisher; and to his wife, Constance.

On February 19 1898, Constance wrote to her brother as follows:

> I am frightfully upset by this wonderful poem of Oscar's, of which so far I
> have only seen the extract in the D.C. I hear that it was sold out the day it
> was published and that orders are pouring in, and that is a good thing as it
> means money! It is frightfully tragic and makes one cry.

***

Letter to Robert Ross, March 2? 1898 (Paris)

My dear Robbie,
A thousand thanks for all the trouble you are taking for me. You, although
a dreadful low-Church Catholic, as a little Christian sit in the snow-white
rose. Christ did not die to save people, but to teach people how to save each
other. This is, I have no doubt, a grave heresy, but it is also a fact. [. . .]
The facts of Naples are very bald and brief.
Bosie, for four months, by endless letters, offered me a "*home*." He offered

me love, affection, and care, and promised that I should never want for anything. After four months I accepted his offer, but when we met at Aix on our way to Naples I found that he had no money, no plans, and had forgotten all his promises. His one idea was that I should raise money for us both. I did so, to the extent of £120. On this Bosie lived, quite happy. When it came to his having, of course, to repay his own *share*, he became terrible, unkind, mean and penurious, except where his own pleasures were concerned, and when my allowances ceased, he left.

With regard to the £500, which he said was "a debt of honour" etc. he has written to me to say that he admits that it is a debt of honour but that "lots of gentlemen don't pay their debts of honour," that it is "quite a common thing," and that no one thinks anything the worse of them. [. . .] It is, of course, the most bitter experience of a bitter life; it is a blow quite awful and paralysing, but it had to come, and I know it is better that I should never see him again. I don't want to. He fills me with horror.

Ever yours O. W.

***

Letter to Carlos Blacker, postmarked March 9 1898 (Paris, Hôtel de Nice)

My dear Carlos,

I cannot express to you how thrilled and touched by emotion I was when I saw your handwriting last night. [. . .] I am living here quite alone: in one room, I need hardly say, but there is an armchair for you. I have not seen Alfred Douglas for three months: he is I believe on the Riviera. I don't think it probable that we shall ever see each other again. The fact is that if he is ever with me again he loses £10 a month of his allowance, and as he has only £400 a year he has adopted the wise and prudent course of conduct.

I am so glad my poem has had a success in England. It appears with a French translation in the *Mercure de France* for April, and I hope to have it published in book form also, in a limited edition of course, but it is my *chant de cygnet*, and I am sorry to leave with a cry of pain—a song of Marsyas, not a song of Apollo; but Life, that I have loved so much—too much—has torn me like a tiger, so when you come and see me, you will see the ruin and wreck of what once was wonderful and brilliant, and terribly improbable. But the French men of letters and artists are kind to me, so I spend my evenings reading the *Tentation* by Flaubert. I don't think I shall ever write again: *la joie de vivre* is gone, and that, with will-power, is the basis of art.

When you come ask for Monsieur Melmoth. Ever yours Oscar

There is nothing in the world like the devotion of a married woman. It is a thing no married man knows anything about.
Oscar Wilde

For the sake of justice, we now try to see the issue from Constance's side: on March 4 1898, Constance Wilde wrote to Blacker:

Oscar is or at least was at the Hôtel de Nice, rue des Beaux-Arts. Would it be at all possible for you to go and see him there, or is it asking too much of you? He has, as you know, behaved exceedingly badly both to myself and my children and all possibility of our living together has come to an end, but I am interested in him, as is my way with anyone that I have once known. Have you seen his new poem, and would you like a copy, as if so I will send you one? His publisher lately sent me a copy which I conclude came from him. Can you find this out for me, and if you do see him tell him that I think *The Ballad* exquisite, and I hope that the great success it has had in London at all events will urge him on to write more. I hear that he does nothing now but drink and I heard that he had left Lord A. and had received £200 from Lady Q. on condition that he did not see him again, but of course this may be untrue. Is Lord A. in Paris? Do what seems right to you. C.

Again on March 10 1898, Constance Wilde wrote to Blacker:

I naturally would not have asked you to see Oscar, if I had thought there was any chance of your meeting that person whom I know that very naturally you loathe. I heard long ago that Oscar was not with him, and that he is on the Riviera with his mother, and that his allowance stops if he ever lives with O. again. The result of your writing to O., is that he has written to me more or less demanding money as of right. Fortunately for him, hearing that he was in great straits, I had yesterday, or rather the day before, sent him £40 through Robbie. He says that I owe him £78 and hopes that I will send it. I know that he is in great poverty, but I don't care to be written to as though it were my fault. He says that he loved too much and that is better than hate. This is true abstractedly, but his was an unnatural love, a madness that I think is worse than hate. I have no hatred for him, but I confess that I am afraid of him.

On March 20 1898, from Villa Elvira, at Bogliasco (Genoa) she continued:

My dear Mr. Blacker, I did send £40 to Mr. Ross [. . .]. The actual sum
that I owe him, if you call it owing, is at the rate of £12.18. a month.
£62.10. and not £80. I have said that I would give him £10 a month,
so at the most I owe him little more than £20! Also he had £10 of mine
which he more than ignores in his letter to you, for he says that he has
had nothing from me.
Oscar is so pathetic and such a born actor, and I am hardened when I am
away from him [. . .]. He owes, I am certain, more than £60 in Paris, and
if I pay money now he will think that he may write to me at any time
for more. I have absolutely no-one to fall back upon, and I will not get
into debt for anyone. The boys' expenses will go on increasing until they
are grown up and settled, and I will educate them and give them what
they reasonably require [. . .]. If I were living on someone else's money, it
would be a different thing and pride would not make me do even what
I hate. But Oscar has no pride. When he had this disastrous law-suit, he
borrowed £50 from me, £50 from my cousin, and £100 from my aunt.
The £50 I repaid my cousin, the £100 never has been, and I suppose
never will be, repaid. I was left penniless, and borrowed £150 from Burne-
Jones, and I have never borrowed a penny since. I still owe money in
London which I am trying to pay, but all these things are nothing to
Oscar as long as someone supports him! [. . .] I don't know what name
he is living under in Paris. Is it his own or the name he took when he left
England? If he was fixed anywhere, I could make an arrangement to pay
10 francs a day for his board to the hotel, not to him, for I know that he
would never pay it. In the winter I paid at the hotel here 9 francs a day. Of
course the good hotels are about 18 francs but I knew I could not afford
that and did not go to them [. . .]. At Heidelberg I paid about 4 marks a
day, only I know he would think it horrible, and I did not particularly like
it! [. . .] Love to all.
Yours ever
Constance Holland

***

Wilde's social activism for prison reform continued undaunted.

This following letter from Wilde appeared on March 23, 1898 in the *Daily Chronicle*,
under the heading DON'T READ THIS IF YOU WANT TO BE HAPPY TODAY:

Sir,

I understand that the Home Secretary's Prison Reform Bill is to be read this week for the first or second time, and as your journal has been the one paper in England that has taken a real and vital interest in this important question. I hope that you will allow me, as one who has had long personal experience of life in an English gaol, to point out what reforms in our present stupid and barbarous system are urgently necessary. [. . .] No prisoner has ever had the smallest relief, or attention, or care from any of the official visitors. The visitors arrive not to help the prisoners, but to see that the rules are carried out. Their object in coming is to ensure the enforcement of a foolish and inhuman code. [. . .] A prisoner who has been allowed the smallest privilege dreads the arrival of the inspectors. And on the day of any prison inspection the prison officials are more than usually brutal to the prisoners. Their object is, of course, to show the splendid discipline they maintain. The necessary reforms are very simple. They concern the needs of the body and the needs of the mind of each unfortunate prisoner. With regard to the first, there are three permanent punishments authorised by law in English prisons:

1. Hunger.

2. Insomnia.

3. Disease.

The food supplied to prisoners is entirely inadequate. [. . .] All of it is insufficient. Every prisoner suffers day and night from hunger. [. . .] The result of the food—which in most cases consists of weak gruel, badly-baked bread, suet, and water—is disease in the form of incessant diarrhoea. This malady, which ultimately with most prisoners becomes a permanent disease, is a recognised institution in every prison. [. . .]

Nothing can be worse than the sanitary arrangements of English prisons. In old days each cell was provided with a form of latrine. These latrines have now been suppressed. They exist no longer. A small tin vessel is supplied to each prisoner instead. Three times a day a prisoner is allowed to empty his slops. But he is not allowed to have access to the prison lavatories, except during the one hour when he is at exercise. And after five o'clock in the evening he is not allowed to leave his cell under any pretence, or for any reason. A man suffering from diarrhoea is consequently placed in a position so loathsome that it is unnecessary to dwell on it [. . .].

Every prisoner should be allowed to have access to the lavatories when necessary, and to empty his slops when necessary. The present system of ventilation in each cell is utterly useless. The air comes through choked-up gratings, and through a small ventilator in the tiny barred window, which is far too small, and too badly constructed, to admit any adequate amount of fresh air. [. . .]

With regard to the punishment of insomnia, it only exists in Chinese and English prisons. In China it is inflicted by placing the prisoner in a small bamboo cage; in England by means of the plank bed. The object of the plank bed is to produce insomnia. There is no other object in it, and it invariably succeeds. And even when one is subsequently allowed a hard mattress, as happens in the course of imprisonment, one still suffers from insomnia. For sleep, like all wholesome things, is a habit. Every prisoner who has been on a plank bed suffers from insomnia. It is a revolting and ignorant punishment.

With regard to the needs of the mind, I beg that you will allow me to say something. The present prison system seems almost to have for its aim the wrecking and the destruction of the mental faculties. The production of insanity is, if not its object, certainly its result. [. . .] Every prisoner should have an adequate supply of good books. At present, during the first three months of imprisonment, one is allowed no books at all, except a Bible, prayer-book, and hymn-book. [. . .] At present the selection of books is made by the prison chaplain.

Under the present system a prisoner is only allowed to see his friends four times a year, for twenty minutes each time. This is quite wrong. A prisoner should be allowed to see his friends once a month, and for a reasonable time. The mode at present in vogue is of exhibiting a prisoner either locked up in a large iron cage or in a large wooden box, with a small aperture, covered with wire netting, through which he is allowed to peer. His friends are placed in a similar cage, some three or four feet distant, and two warders stand between, to listen to, and, if they wish, stop or interrupt the conversation such as it may be. I propose that a prisoner should be allowed to see his relatives or friends in a room. The present regulations are inexpressibly revolting and harassing. A visit from our relatives or friends is to every prisoner an intensification of humiliation and mental distress. Many prisoners, rather than support such an ordeal, refuse to see their friends at all. [. . .] Every prisoner should be allowed to write and receive a letter at least once a month. At present one is allowed to write only four times a year. This is quite inadequate. One of the tragedies of prison life is that it turns a man's heart to stone. The feelings of natural affection, like all other feelings, require to be fed. They die easily of inanition. [. . .]

The officials who should not be allowed to hold any employment outside the prison, or to have any private practice, are the prison doctors. At present the prison doctors have usually, if not always, a large private practice, and hold appointments in other institutions. The consequence is that the health of the prisoners is entirely neglected, and the sanitary condition of the prison entirely overlooked. [. . .]. If prison doctors were prohibited from private practice they would be compelled to take some interest in the health and sanitary condition of the people under their charge.

I have tried to indicate in my letter a few of the reforms necessary to our English prison system. They are simple, practical, and humane. They are, of course, only a beginning. But it is time that a beginning should be made, and it can only be started by a strong pressure of public opinion formularised in your powerful paper, and fostered by it. But to make even these reforms effectual, much has to be done. And the first, and perhaps the most difficult task is to humanise the governors of prisons, to civilise the warders and to Christianise the chaplains.

Yours, etc.

THE AUTHOR OF THE BALLAD OF READING GAOL

***

Telegram to Robert Ross, April 12 1898 (Paris)

Constance is dead.[101] Please come tomorrow and stay at my hotel. Am in great grief. Oscar

***

Letter to Robert Ross, May 10 1898 (Paris)

My dear Robbie, [. . .]
I have had a very bad time lately, and for two days had not a penny in my pocket, so had to wander about, filled with a wild longing for *bock* and cigarettes: it was really like journeying through Hell. I was in the "circle of the Boulevards" one of the worst in the Inferno, and I could only get breakfast here, not dinner, so was dinnerless. [. . .]
Oscar

---

[101] Author's Note: Constance Wilde (aka Holland) died at Genoa on April 7 1898, aged forty, and was buried in the Protestant cemetery there.

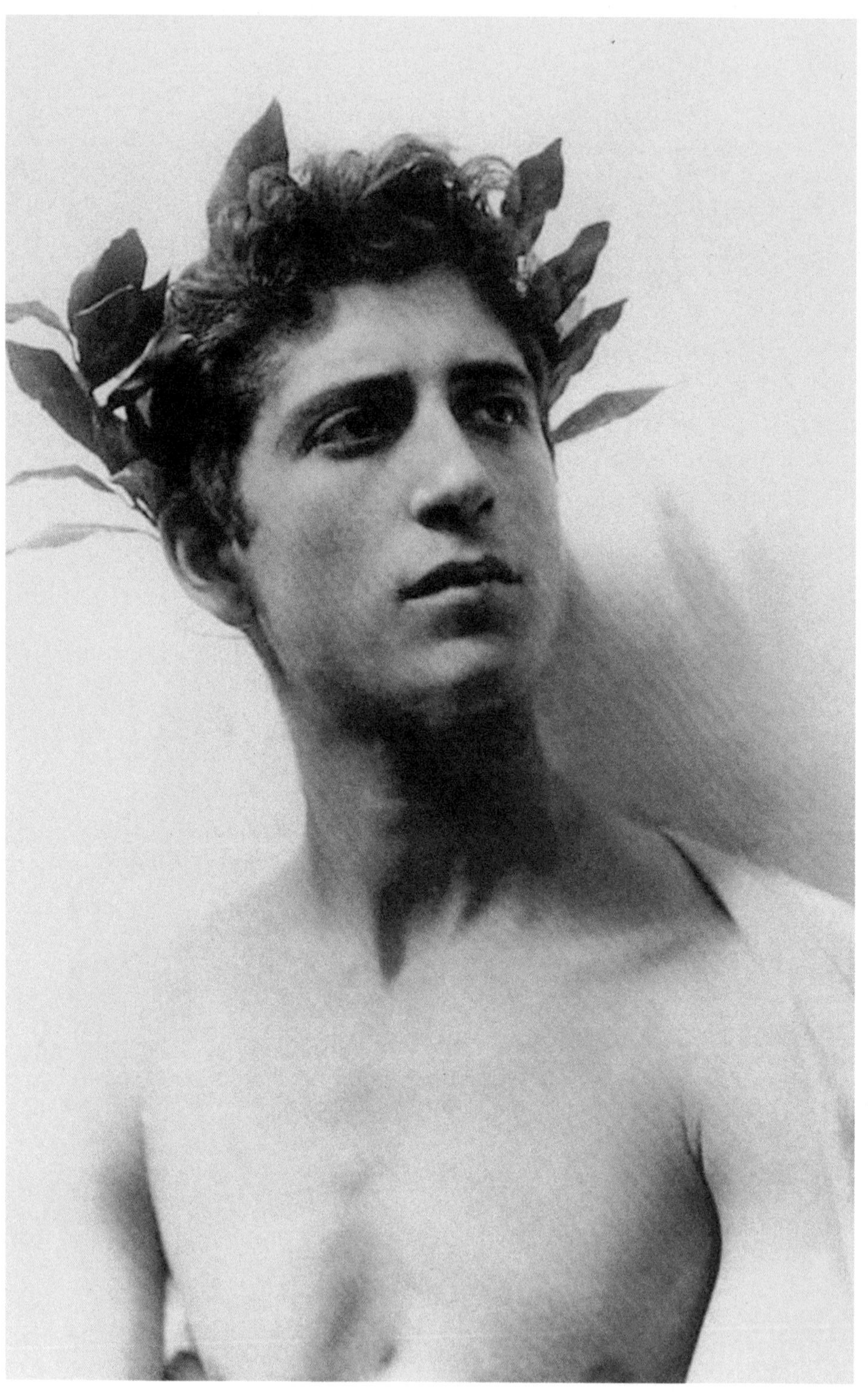

It is only by not paying one's bills that one can hope to live in the memory of the commercial classes.
Oscar Wilde

Except for brief stays in the South of France in the company of Frank Harris, Oscar spent his days between Paris and Italy in the company of Mr. Mellor, who, thinking that the poet's company could be the best cure for his chronic depression, invited him often in Sicily and Rome.

Who was Harold Mellor? We often hear of him in Wilde's last years. Here is how Oscar described him:

***

Letter to Robert Ross, January 2 1899 (Naples)

> There is a charming fellow called Harold Mellor (sent away from Harrow at the age of fourteen for being loved by the captain of the cricket eleven) [. . .]. He is about twenty-six, but looks younger. Sometimes a very pretty, slim, fair-haired Italian boy bicycles over with him. His name is *Eolo*; his father, who sold him to Harold for 200 lire, having christened all his children—seventeen in number—out of the *Mythological Dictionary*.

Ross in this period even went so far as to suggest that Oscar consider marrying. Oscar replied with bitter words to Ross's absurd proposal in the same letter:

> As regards my marrying again, I am quite sure you would like me to marry, this time, a reasonable, practical, simple, middle-aged boy, and I don't like the idea at all.
> Besides I am practically engaged to a fisherman of extraordinary beauty, age eighteen. So you see there are difficulties.

***

Letter to Reginald Turner, postmarked January 3 1899 (Naples, Hôtel des Bains)

My dear Reggie,

How are you getting on? [. . .] Do let me have a little news of you. Of course there is no good begging you to come out here, though there is wonderful sunshine each day. Sometimes the Mistral blows a little—it is a harsh Philistine wind—but on the whole the weather is utterly delightful.

My friend, my new friend, Harold Mellor comes here today to stay at the hotel, and tomorrow we go to Nice for the day. A great friend of mine, a Paris boy called *le petit Georges*, is now at Nice, and I have promised to run over and see him. He is like a very handsome Roman boy, dark, and bronze-like, with splendidly chiselled nose and mouth, and the tents of midnight are folded in his eyes; moons hide in their curtains. He is visiting Nice on speculative business. It is beautiful, and encouraging, to find people who can combine romance with business—blend them indeed, and make them one. I am in constant correspondence now with a Radley schoolboy, aged seventeen. His photograph, which he has sent me, and sends me constantly, is most beautiful. He seems to read nothing but my books, and says his one desire is to "follow in my footsteps!" But I have told him that they lead to terrible places. [. . .]

Oscar

***

Letter to Robert Ross, January 12 1899 (Naples, Hôtel des Bains)

My dear Robbie,

[. . .] I have been again to Nice with Harold Mellor, for three days. It was most pretty and gay, and music everywhere. I met one beautiful person, called André, with wonderful eyes, and a little Italian, Pietro, like a young St John. One would have followed him into the desert. [. . .] My Radley boy is called Louis Wilkinson—a horrid name—but his photograph is most interesting, and his poetry passionate and incoherent. He seems a most astonishing boy. He has dramatised *Dorian Gray!*[102]

Ever yours

Oscar.

---

[102] Author's Note: Between 1924 and 1926, almost at the same time as Cocteau's *Orphée* was being staged, Cocteau began a play adaptation of Wilde's novel, *The Portrait of Dorian Gray*. This book had fascinated and perversely attracted Cocteau during his youth. The manuscript for Cocteau's play adaptation was revived and recorded for radio in the 1990s thanks to the interest of R. Radiguet (one of Cocteau's lovers), Renato Miracco and other collaborators.

Letter to Robert Ross, March 1? 1899 (Switzerland, Canton Vaud, Gland)

My dear Robbie,
[. . .] I went to Genoa to see Constance's grave. It is very pretty—a marble
cross with a dark ivy leaves inlaid in a good pattern. [. . .] It was very tragic
seeing her name carved on a tomb, her surname, my name not mentioned
of course—just Constance Mary, daughter of Horace Lloyd, QC and a
verse from *Revelations*. I brought some flowers. I was deeply affected with
a sense, also, of the uselessness of all regrets. Nothing could have been
otherwise, and Life is a very terrible thing. [. . .]
Ever yours
Oscar

***

Letter to Leonard Smithers, postmarked March 30 1899 (Switzerland, Gland)

Gland, Switzerland
At the House of the Enemy
Among the Cities of the Plain
[. . .]
I leave on Sunday for Genoa—Albergo di Firenze. It is impossible for
me to go to Paris. I have not enough money. I am going to try and find
a place near Genoa, where I can live for ten francs a day (boy *compris*).
The chastity of Switzerland has got on my nerves. Neither Sporus nor
Ganymede treads these fields of snow, and Mellor is too repulsive for
anything. [. . .] On the other hand when I told him I was going away,
he went into floods of tears, and said that all his friends deserted him!
Tartuffe and Harpagon[103] sum him up, though on too grand a scale.
Kindly send me the *£20 in an order on Cook's at Genoa for £20.*
Ever yours
O. W.

***

Postcard to Robert Ross, postmarked April 7 1899 (Portofino)

This is really a lovely little place: only reached by mules or boats. S. M.

---

[103] Author's Note: Molière's hypocrite and miser.

Postcard to Robert Ross, postmarked April 7 1899 (San Fruttuoso)

Have not yet been here: but have decided to enter the *chiostro* [cloister]—
just the place for me. S. M.

***

Despite what has been said, from the end of 1899 Oscar and Mellor traveled again
together to Sicily, Naples and Rome.

The interview that follows is the last that Wilde gave in Naples.

Excerpt from *Interview of Wilde* by Arnaldo (Rocco) De Lisle:

If he could live again, he would be happy with his handiwork; he was keen
to create an extraordinary aura around himself, and his wish was more
than fulfilled, a legend was created that will remain unique in the history
of literature.
When he returned to Naples after an absence of a few months, he said
to me: "How unfortunate I am, I don't have a friend in this city, all my
acquaintances are in prison. I learned he'd met thieves, members of the
camorra and the like." [. . .] When I saw him again, for the last time,
in Rome, a year before his death, he invited me to lunch. Between one
course and the next—since the conversation had turned to the subject of
his insanity, (homosexual desire) to which, he believed all men were to
surrender themselves, even though, because of hypocrisy, they didn't have,
like him, the courage to admit it—gazing at me steadfastly, as if he were
asking me the most natural of questions, he asked me with a quiet voice:
"And you, never, not even when you were a young man in boarding school?"
"I've never been to boarding school, nor have such oddities ever crossed
my mind," I answered without a doubt. And he responded: "It's a matter
of temperament."—In this sentence the whole spirit of the poor madman
is revealed! One should not despise him but pity him!
I want to end this speech in its simplicity. Wilde, who suffered so much,
suffered even more from the reputation that he had gained rather than
the reputation he had contrived. The longest-lasting memory I will retain
of him was given to me one evening when I told him about his family,
although he didn't like to recall his lost treasures. That evening, however,
Wilde wanted me to hear his father's lamentations. He informed me of
the conversion of his son, Vivian, to Catholicism, saying with joy: and my

Vivian is only twelve years old, he remains whole hours lying on a couch, and if he is disturbed, he declares: "Leave me in peace, I think!" I hope he will forgive me for this oration, in which I wanted to mix history, emotion, justice, and the testimony of a friend of the evil days, who is neither an aesthete, nor a cynic, and whom I greet humbly, peacefully, in silence and in rest. And the silence and the rest he deserves, after having suffered so much and having so harshly expiated, without ever rebelling, indeed, even accepting his cruel fate with a stoically great resignation. Listen to him in the *De Profundis*, his posthumous book, which can be called his "*mea culpa*," his volume of repentance and atonement. In it, Wilde expresses himself like this: "I must thank destiny for everything that has made me suffer. The bed made only of boards, the nauseating food, the intricate ropes that I had to weave with my hands to make the tow, up to the point that the painful tips of my fingers became insensitive and started bleeding, the vile needs with which the days of punishment began and ended, the harsh commands, the horrible clothes that made the pain grotesque to see, the silence, the loneliness, the shame: I must transform all these into spiritual experiences. There is not a single defilement of my body that will not contribute to the spiritualization of my soul."

And shortly after he served his sentence, he said to his friend André Gide: "Jail completely changed me, and I was counting on that. My life resembles a work of art, an artist never starts the same thing twice, or that means he's a failed artist. My first conviction was perfect as far as that was possible. Now, it is complete. [. . .] Morals are of no assistance to me. I'm made for exceptions, not for rules. Religion is not of any help to me. My Gods inhabit temples built by the hands of men . . ."

Again, to his friend Gide, who invited him to Paris, he replied: "The general public is so terrible that they don't know a man except for the last thing he did. If I were to return to Paris, they would not want to see in me but the convicted man. Therefore, I will not show myself until I have written a new play. Up until that point I must be left in peace."

***

Letter to Robert Ross, April 16 1900 (Rome, Piazza di Spagna)

My dear Robert,
I simply cannot write. It is too horrid, not *of* me, but *to* me. It is a mode of paralysis—a *cacoethes tacendi* [craving for silence]—the one form the malady takes in me.

Well, all passed over very successfully. Palermo, where we stayed eight days, was lovely. The most beautifully situated town in the world, it dreams away its life in the Conca d'Oro, the exquisite valley that lies between two seas. The lemon-groves and the orange-gardens were so entirely perfect that I became again a Pre-Raphaelite, and loathed the ordinary Impressionists, whose muddy souls and blurred intelligences would have rendered but by mud and blur those "golden lamps hung in the green night" that filled me with such joy. The elaborate and exquisite detail of the true Pre-Raphaelites is the compensation they offer us for the absence of motion; Literature and Music being the only arts that are not immobile.

Then nowhere, not even in Ravenna, have I seen such mosaics. In the Cappella Palatina, which from pavement to domed ceilings is all gold, one really feels as if one was sitting in the heart of a great honeycomb looking at angels singing; and *looking* at angels, or indeed people singing, is much nicer than listening to them. For this reason the great artists always give to their angels lutes without strings, pipes without vent-holes, and reeds through which no wind can wander or make whistling.

Monreale you have heard of, with its cloisters and cathedral. We often drove there, the *cocchieri* most dainty finely-carved boys. In them, not in the Sicilian horses is race seen.

The most favoured were Manuele, Francesco, and Salvatore. I loved them all, but only remember Manuele.

I also made great friends with a young Seminarist who lived *in* the Cathedral of Palermo, he and eleven others in little rooms beneath the roof, like birds. Every day he showed me all over the Cathedral and I really knelt before the huge porphyry sarcophagus in which Frederick the Second lies. It is a sublime bare monstrous thing, blood-coloured, and held up by lions, who have caught some of the rage of the great Emperor's restless soul. At first, my young friend, Giuseppe Loverde by name, gave *me* information: but on the third day I gave information to him, and re-wrote History as usual, and told him all about the Supreme King and his court of Poets, and the terrible book that he never wrote.[104] Giuseppe was fifteen, and most sweet. His reason for entering the Church was singularly mediaeval. I asked him why he thought of becoming a *clerico*: and how. He answered "My father is a cook, and most poor, and we are many at

---

[104] Author's Note: Frederick II (1194–1250), Roman emperor, king of Sicily and Jerusalem, popularly known as *Stupor Mundi,* according to Dante, was born at his court and he was suspected by the Papal party of writing a book called *De Tribus Impostoribus* (that is, "the three impostors," or Moses, Jesus and Mohammed).

home, so it seemed to me a good thing that there should be in so small a house as ours one mouth less to feed for, though I am slim, I eat much: too much, alas! I fear." I told him to be comforted, because God used poverty often as a means of bringing people to Him, and used riches never, or but rarely. So Giuseppe was comforted, and I gave him a little book of devotion, very pretty, and with far more pictures than prayers in it; so of great service to Giuseppe, whose eyes are beautiful. I also gave him many *lire*, and prophesied for him a Cardinal's hat, if he remained very good, and never forgot me. He said he never would: and indeed, I don't think he will, for every day I kissed him behind the high altar.

At Naples we stopped three days. Most of my friends are, as you know, in prison, but I met some of nice memory, and fell in love with a Sea-God, who for some extraordinary reason is at the Regia Marina School, instead of being with Triton.

We came to Rome on Holy Thursday. H. M. left on Saturday for Gland, and yesterday,[105] to the terror of Grissell[106] and all the Papal Court, I appeared in the front rank of the pilgrims in the Vatican, and got the blessing of the Holy Father[107]—a blessing they would have denied me.

He was wonderful as he was carried past me on his throne, not of flesh and blood, but a white soul robed in white, and an artist as well as a saint—the only instance in History, if the newspapers are to be believed.

I have seen nothing like the extraordinary grace of his gesture, as he rose, from moment to moment, to bless—possibly the pilgrims, but certainly me. Tree should see him. It is his only chance.

I was deeply impressed, and my walking-stick showed signs of budding; would have budded indeed, only at the door of the chapel it was taken from me by the Knave of Spades. This strange prohibition is, of course, in honour of Tannhäuser.[108]

How did I get the ticket? By a miracle, of course. I thought it was hopeless, and made no effort of any kind. On Saturday afternoon at five o'clock Harold and I went to have tea at the Hôtel de l'Europe. Suddenly, as I was eating buttered toast, a man, or what seemed to be one, dressed like a hotel porter, entered and asked me would I like to see the Pope on Easter Day. I bowed my head humbly and said *Non sum dignus*," or words to that effect. He at once produced a ticket!

---

[105] Author's Note: Easter Day 1900 was on April 15.

[106] Author's Note: Hartwell de la Garde Grissel (1839–1907) had been a chamberlain of honour to the Pope since 1869. Wilde had met him in Rome.

[107] Author's Note: Leo XIII (1810–1903), pope from 1878.

[108] Author's Note: Wilde several times referred to Tannhäuser's pilgrimage as a penitent to Rome.

When I tell you that this countenance was of supernatural ugliness and that the price of the ticket was thirty pieces of silver, I need say no more. An equally curious thing is that whenever I pass the hotel, which I do constantly, I see the same man. Scientists call that phenomenon an obsession of the visual nerve. You and I know better.

On the afternoon of Easter Day I heard vespers at the Lateran: music quite lovely: at the close a Bishop in red, and with red gloves—such as Pater talks of in *Gaston de Latour* —came out on the balcony and showed us the relics. He was swarthy, and wore a yellow mitre. A sinister mediaeval man, but superbly Gothic, just like the Bishops carved on stalls or on portals. And when one thinks that once people mocked at stained-glass attitudes! They are the only attitudes for the clothed. The sight of this Bishop, whom I watched with fascination, filled me with the sense of the great realism of Gothic art. Neither in Greek nor in Gothic art is there any pose. Posing was invented by bad portrait-painters, and the first person who ever posed was a stockbroker, and he has gone on ever since.

Homer talks much—a little too much—of you. He slightly suspects you of treachery, and your immediate return seems to him problematic. Your allusion to his conduct on a postcard was mysterious. How was the "revision' painful? I have added one Pietro Branca-d'Oro to the group. He is dark, and gloomy, and I love him very much. I send you a photograph I took on Palm Sunday at Palermo. Do send me some of yours, and love me always, and try to read this letter. It is a labour of a week to read it. Kindest regards to your mother.

Always Oscar

***

Letter to Robert Ross, April 21 1900 (Rome)

My dear Robbie,

A thousand thanks for all your trouble. The cheque arrived safely this morning. Of course I got your telegram from Milan, and wrote to you at the Hôtel Cavour—a long, interesting, and of course seriously compromising letter. Should it fall into the hands of the authorities you will be immortal.

I have not seen the Holy Father since Thursday, but I am bearing up wonderfully well. I am sorry to say he has approved of a dreadful handkerchief with a portrait of himself in the middle, and basilicas at the corners. It is very curious the connection between Faith and bad art: I feel it myself. Where I see the Pope I admire Bernini: but Bernini had a

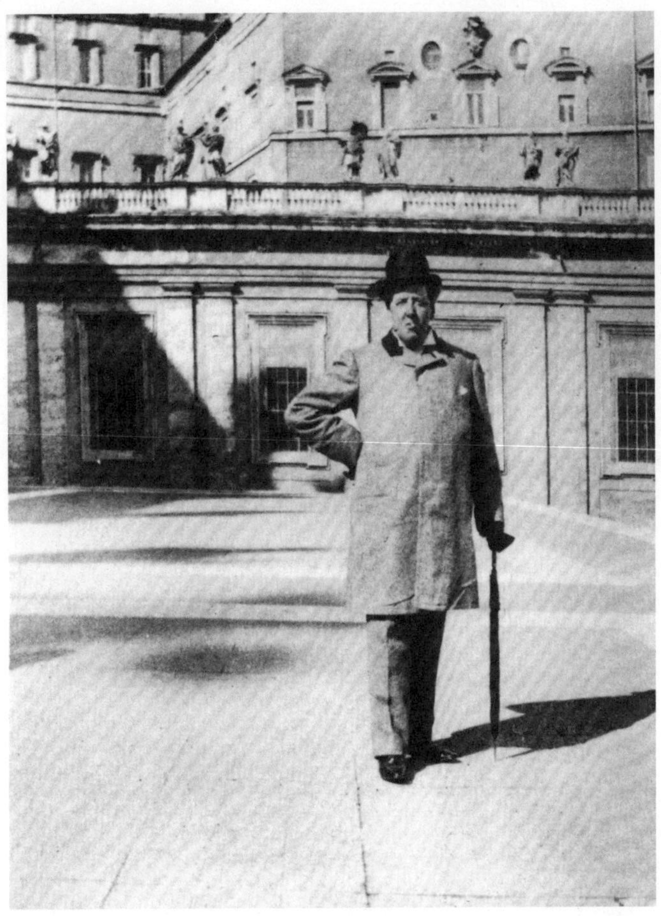

certain dash and life and assertion—theatrical life, but life for all that: the handkerchief is a dead thing.[109]

By the way, did I tell you that on Easter Sunday I was completely cured of my mussel-poisoning? It is true, and I always knew I would be. Five months under a Jewish physician at Paris not merely did not heal me, but made me worse: the blessing of the Vicar of Christ made me whole. Armand Point, the French painter, a bad Botticelli-Jones artist, is here, and has promised to do me a *tabella votiva*. The only difficulty is the treatment of the mussels. They are not decorative, except the shells, and I didn't eat the shells.

I have been three times to see the great Velasquez of the Pamfili Pope: it is quite the grandest portrait in the world. The entire man is there.[110] I also go

---

[109] Author's Note: Gian Lorenzo Bernini (1598–1680), Italian painter, sculptor and architect, designed the palace of Pope Urban VIII and the great colonnade of St Peter's.
[110] Author's Note: This portrait of Pope Innocent X (1574–1655) hangs in Palazzo Doria in Rome.

to look at the beautiful voluptuous marble boy I went to worship with you at the Museo Nazionale. What a lovely thing it is!

I have given up Armando, a very smart elegant young Roman Sporus. He was beautiful, but his requests for raiment and neckties were incessant: he really bayed for boots, as a dog moonwards. I now like Arnaldo: he was Armando's greatest friend, but the friendship is over. Armando is *un invidioso* [an envious person] apparently, and is suspected of having stolen a lovely covert-coat in which he patrols the Corso. The coat is so delightful, and he looks so handsome in it, that, although the coat wasn't mine, I have forgiven him the theft. [. . .] Yesterday a painful thing happened. You know the terrible, the awe-inspiring effect that Royalty has on me: well, I was outside the Caffè Nazionale taking iced coffee with *gelato*—a most delightful drink—when the King drove past. I at once stood up, and made him a low bow, with hat doffed—to the admiration of some Italian officers at the next table. It was only when the King had passed that I remembered I was *Papista* and *Nerissimo*![111] I was greatly upset: however, I hope the Vatican won't hear about it.

I enclose you a little cutting[112] that appeared in Palermo while I was there. My incognito vanished in three hours, and the students used to come to the café to talk—or rather to listen. To their great delight I always denied my identity. On being asked my name, I said every man has only one name. They asked me what name that was. "Io" [I] was my answer. This was regarded as a wonderful reply, containing in it all philosophy.

Rome is burning with heat: really terrible: but at 4.30 I am going to the Borghese, to look at daisies, and drink milk: the Borghese milk is as wonderful as the Borghese daisies. I also intend to photograph Arnaldo. By the way, can you photograph cows well? I did one of cows in the Borghese so marvellous that I destroyed it: I was afraid of being called the modern Paul Potter.[113] Cows are very fond of being photographed, and, unlike architecture, don't move. I propose to go to Orvieto tomorrow: I have never seen it, and I must revisit Tivoli. How long I shall stay here I don't know—a fortnight perhaps. Write always to Cook's. Love to More and Reggie.

Ever yours

Oscar

---

[111] Author's Note: Very black. A term in use among the Roman nobility, meaning "ultra-Catholic." There was at this time a great antipathy between regal and Papal circles, and the Pope was known as "the prisoner of the Vatican."

[112] Author's Note: On April 10 1900, the newspaper *Giornale di Sicilia* notes Wilde's time in Palermo under the heading "Note Mondane" (worldly notes): "Oscar Wilde, the aesthete, professes the principle that life is worthless if we live it like everybody else," (see Evangelista, *The Reception of Oscar Wilde in Europe*).

[113] Author's Note: Dutch animal painter (1625–1654) whose best-known picture is probably *The Young Bull* at the Hague.

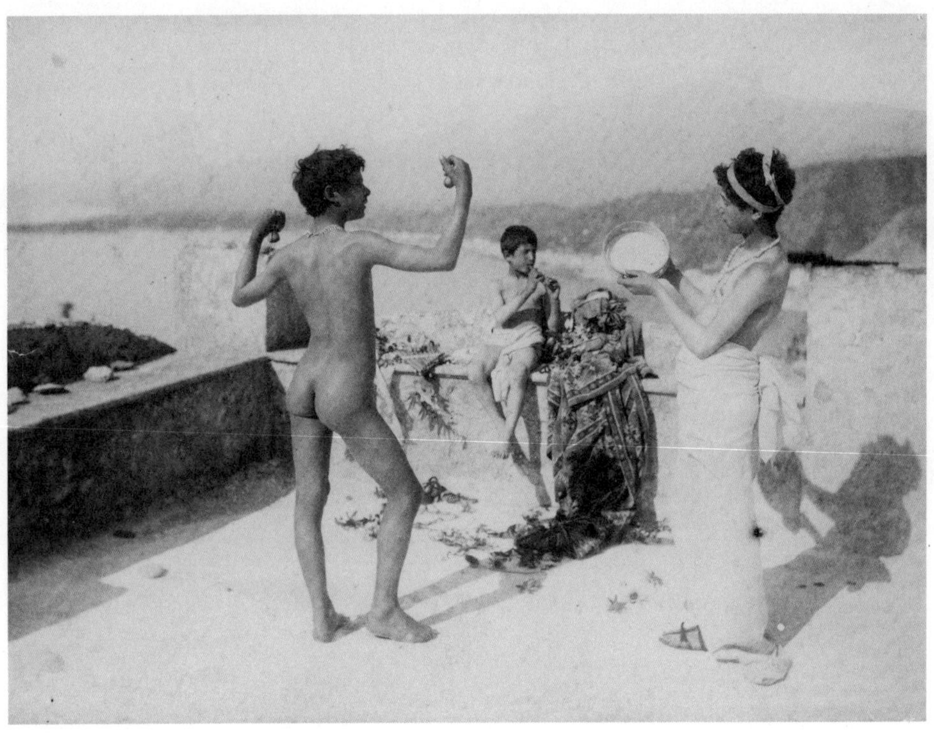

Letter to Robert Ross, 22 April 1900 (Rome)

Dear little Robbie,

I enclose the Sicilian cutting. I forgot of course: it is pleasant to pluck praise in the meadows of Persephone— recognition by asphodels.

Need I say that I see the Holy Father again tomorrow? I am thrilled with the prospect of an old pleasure, and I am promised a seat for the canonisation, or beatification, on the 24th. Rome is hot, so I don't know that I can stay, but I would like to go. It would annoy the withered Grissell, and fill me with holy joy.

Yesterday I went to *Albano*: how lovely it is! The day was beautiful, and the silent waveless lake a mirror of turquoise. It was wise enough to reflect nothing but its own beauty: would that the same could be said of all mirrors.

Omero was with me, and Armando, forgiven for the moment. He is so absurdly like the Apollo Belvedere that I feel always as if I was Winckelmann when I am with him.[114] His lips are the same, his hair, his somewhat vulgar,

---

[114] Author's Note: Johann Joachim Winckelmann (1717–1768), German archaeologist, historian and in some sense rediscoverer of Greek art. Lived for many years in Rome.

because quite obvious, pride; and he also represents that decadence of the triumph of the face over the body, never seen in great Greek art. Witness the thighs of Theseus, the breasts and flanks of Hermes.

His body is slim, dandy-like, elegant, and without a single great curve. He has not come out of the womb of giant circles.

I am at the Roma, the first time for ten days. Would you were here. Do you observe that I have fallen in love with you again? Our Indian winter.

Ever yours

Oscar

***

Letter to Robert Ross, April 27 1900 (Rome)

Dear Robbie,

would it bore you awfully to send me my allowance in an order on Cook here? It takes a week to cash a cheque. I know it will bore you, but then you are a little saint, not, I am glad to say, in conduct, which is nothing, but in soul, which is all. [. . .] Today, on coming out of the Vatican Gallery, Greek gods and the Roman middle-classes in my brain, all marble to make the contrast worse, I found that the Vatican Gardens were open to the Bohemian and the Portuguese pilgrims. I at once spoke both languages fluently, explained that my English dress was a form of penance, and entered that waste, desolate park, with its faded Louis XIV gardens, its sombre avenues, its sad woodland. The peacocks screamed, and I understood why tragedy dogged the gilt feet of each pontiff. But I wandered in exquisite melancholy for an hour. One Philippo, a student, whom I culled in the Borgia room, was with me: not for many years has Love walked in the Pope's pleasance.

No more paper.

Always yours

Oscar

***

Letter to Robert Ross, May 14 1900 (Rome)

Dearest Robbie,

You never write to me now, so I don't know if it is worthwhile informing you of my movements. However, I leave Rome tomorrow for Naples, thence by boat to Genoa, thence to Chambéry, where Harold Mellor awaits me, or should do so, with his automobile—and so to Paris. I suppose one of us will arrive safe; I hope it will be me.

Rome has quite absorbed me. I must winter here; it is the only city of the soul. I have been to Albano, and Nemi, and Tivoli, and seen much of Armand Point, who is really a dear fellow, gay and romantic, simple and intellectually subtle, with an inordinate passion for beauty in its most complete expression, and an inordinate love of life.

My photographs are now so good that in my moments of mental depression (alas! not rare) I think that I was intended to be a photographer. But I shake off the mood, and know that I was made for more terrible things of which colour is an element. Today I bade goodbye, with tears and one kiss, to the beautiful Greek boy who was found in my garden—I mean Nero's garden. He is the nicest boy you ever introduced to me. In the mortal sphere I have fallen in and out of love, and fluttered hawks and doves alike. How evil it is to buy Love, and how evil to sell it! And yet what purple hours one can snatch from that grey slowly-moving thing we call Time! My mouth is twisted with kissing, and I feed on fevers. The Cloister or the Café—there is my future. I tried the Hearth, but it was a failure.

Ever yours

Oscar

Write to Paris

Alcohol taken in sufficient quantities causes all the effects of an intoxication. Fortunately, there is wormwood. The first glass shows you things as you want to see them, the second shows us things as they are not: after the third, you see them as they really are, and there is nothing worse in the world.
Oscar Wilde

Trying to return to his previous life and to write again, between 1899 and 1900 Oscar sold a script of a play called *Love is Law* to Frank Harris for £175 and then sold the same script to several other friends and producers. The script was virtually identical to a play he had sketched out to George Alexander in 1894, which was provisionally entitled *Constance*. He also entered into a contract with a New York producer, Charles Frohman, who gave Oscar an advance of $500.

Elisabeth Marbury, a literary agent, wrote that when she showed Oscar the agreements with Frohman for signature, Oscar's hands trembled, and he signed it "Sebastian Melmoth." Elizabeth said to him, "This contract is being made with Oscar Wilde, who alone has the talent to fulfil it." She reports that "Wilde's tears blotted the page."[115] Maurice Gilbert, lover and friend who was with him until the last days, was visiting him daily "sharing with him all my medicine, showing him what little hospitality I can," wrote Wilde. Around this time—that is, around 1900—Oscar came to the realization that he could no longer write and would never return to being what he was. His friends began to worry that he spent too much time in the notorious Calisaya bar in Paris, a place he would never have frequented in the old days. As Vincent wrote, during those days, Oscar was "ruining what sympathy was left for him by showing himself drunk." Wilde in fact was now consuming large amounts of alcohol, including absinthe, brandy, and whiskey with soda. He had gained weight, and grown distinctly deaf in one ear, a problem that had troubled him in prison, and now he often spoke with his hand in front of his mouth to hide his bad teeth.

During the summer of 1900, Oscar had a new consolation: the International Exhibition. With Maurice Gilbert, lover and faithful friend, he visited Rodin's studio, and the great sculptor himself showed Wilde his "dreams in marble," *The Gates of Hell.*

---

[115] Elisabeth Marbury, "The last days of Oscar Wilde," in E.H. Mikhail, ed., *Oscar Wilde: Interviews and Recollections.*

At the Calisaya one night in August, in Paris, he ran through all his stories "like a last display of fireworks," as his friend Ernest La Jeunesse remarked. With them were Frank Harris, Maurice du Plessys and Gustave Le Ruge.

Excerpt from Guillot de Saix, *Le Chant du Cygne*, *Contes Parlés d'Oscar Wilde*, Paris, 1942, regarding one of Wilde's final nights in Paris, recollecting his days in Italy:

We were listening to him. He explains:
"You cannot know how much comfort Parisian ambience brings me; elsewhere, I would have become neurotic, here, in this hectic atmosphere, it is like a breath of freedom, of tolerance, which is not found anywhere else in the world, especially in that hateful London! In Paris, almost all my friends welcomed me with the same promptness as at the time of my successes. There was a time in my life when I really had nothing left to desire. I was rich, beloved, illustrious, and my health seemed perfect.
I was then resting in Sorrento in a delightful villa with a garden planted with orange trees, from my terrace, onto which the waves came crashing and lapping, I could follow with my gaze the soft and gentle curves of a voluptuous landscape, as beautiful as the body of an adolescent. I was in such a place, distractedly admiring the seascape dotted with white sails, when suddenly, I began to think, with a secret terror, that I was truly overly happy, that such an improbable happiness could only be a trap laid by my evil genius. And that idea haunted me for a long time. In the end, I remembered the adventure of that tyrant of antiquity, Polycrates, I believe, whose gesture was perpetuated by the Doges of Venice because of superstition and who, in order to prevent misfortune, threw a precious ring, which he cared for about above all else, into the sea.
I resolved to emulate Polycrates. It is true that his sacrifice was useless. But perhaps I would be a little more fortunate. So, I threw into the sea, as far as I could, a ring adorned with a large pearl that I kept in memory of a very dear friendship.
I thought I had, with that sacrifice, calmed down the evil gods, and found my peace again."
Ernest La Jeunesse mumbles, shakes his trinkets of rings and pendants, and, placing his monocle under his shaggy eyebrows, launches in with a eunuch's voice:
"Do I need to add that the ring was brought back to you as was that of Polycrates, found by a fisherman in the belly of a fish?"
Oscar Wilde gives a hint of a strange smile:

"You don't think you are saying this so well, but the misfortune lies in the fact that the fisherman who brought me the ring was handsome, really, overly handsome; so that when I left him, I couldn't help but leave the ring to him as a memento."

The poet, after a glance around the room meant to gauge what effect this hint of a confession had produced, falls back into silence and sucks a sip of one of those cocktails in which champagne mixes its fizz with whiskey's heaviness, through a straw. Ernest La Jeunesse and Maurice du Plessys start an aggressive discussion on the legend of the rings, and Gustave Le Rouge disappears.

When, towards the end of the last century, Oscar Wilde was a guest of Frank Harris, in the villa he owned at Napoule on the Côte d'Azur, he told him one day:

"At this moment, I am thinking of a poem, a *Ballad of the Young Fisherman*, a kind of a pair with *The Ballad of Reading Gaol*, but in which, instead of prison, I will sing of freedom, instead of pain, of the joy of living, instead of death, of love. There will be as much sun in it as there was darkness in the other ballad. Yes, I will make it a song of joy; much better than I did, of the other one, the song of suffering and of bleak desperation."

Sometime later, Frank Harris, returning from Monte Carlo, and joining Oscar Wilde, whom he had left a few days earlier, asked him:

"During my absence, did you write anything new?"

"No," Oscar replied in a listless tone, "I do not believe that I can write again. After all, why do it? What is the purpose of my efforts?"

"And your *Ballad of the Young Fisherman?*'

"I think about it. It cradles me and lulls me. I have composed three or four verses, which I know by heart."

He started to recite them, and the first one was very beautiful, it seems. When Harris begged him to write more, he sighed:

"Let me be, Frank. Every imposed task is too reminiscent of prison. And don't you doubt it, I'm horrified by the memory. It was degrading, inhuman. Let me live the few days I have left."

A friend of Oscar Wilde's, who did not want to be mentioned, passed on to me at least the subject of the poem, which agrees with certain memories wonderfully related by Édouard Schneider. It is said that Oscar Wilde conceived that Ballad keeping under his eyes the reproduction of the young Neapolitan fisherman sculpted by Rude, and it was at the Café Neapolitan in Paris, near the Opéra, that he spoke of those verses for the last time.

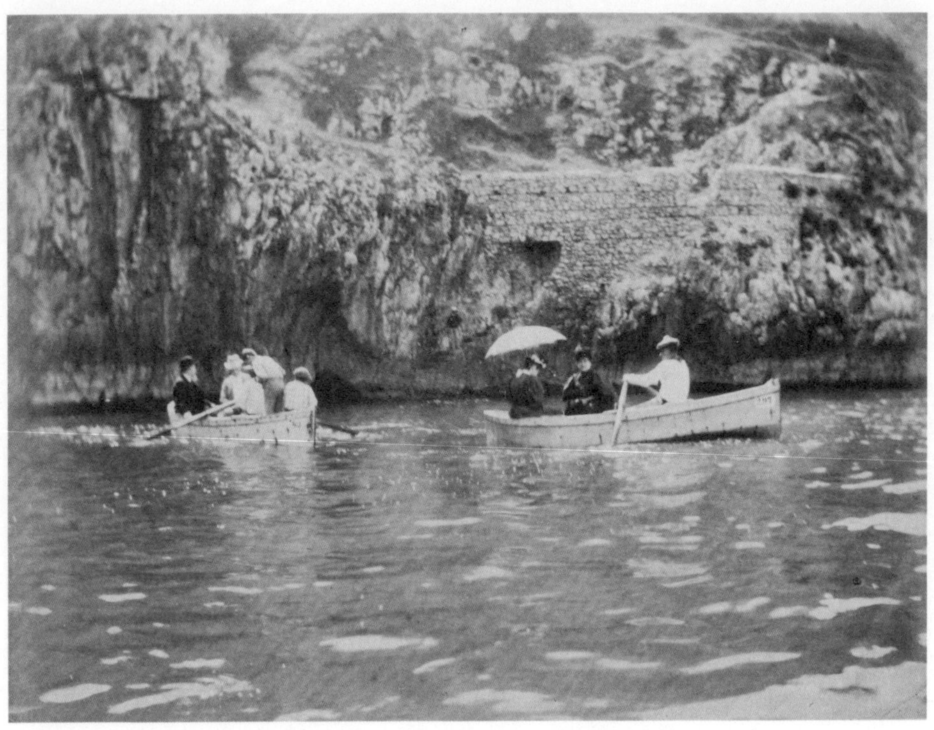

Following is Wilde's last known draft of *The Ballad of the Young Fisherman*. The ballad was never completed:

The Ballad of the Young Fisherman
(Oscar Wilde's last draft)

He was a young and handsome fisherman from the Sorrento countryside. Day and night, he dreamed of fishing a miraculous pearl from the sea.
One day a stranger passed by, carrying on his ring a pearl similar to the one the young fisherman dreamed of.
The young fisherman, like the fox spying on his prey, with his eyes fixed on that pearl, furtively followed the stranger on the beach.
The stranger walked along, always alone, looking sadly at the pearl of his gold ring.
He was convinced that that pearl had brought him misfortune and, to imitate Polycrates, in order to ward off fate, he threw the fateful ring into the sea.

But the young fisherman had caught him in the act.

He jumped into the waves and shortly afterwards, naked, dripping, smiling, and with his body covered with water pearls more beautiful than the pearl itself, brought the stranger the gorgeous ring. The man admired the young messenger that Destiny sent him, and quivering said to him: "Behold, you are so beautiful before me, you who are coming out of the sea as Venus did, that, for a kiss from your mouth, I would bestow this ring upon you."

The greedy young fisherman immediately accepted the barter, gave the required kiss and, cheerfully, went to the edge of the waves, allowing the sun to shine on the ring beautified by the pearl.

In his joy, he threw himself into the shimmering sea to swim in it like a golden fish.

The stranger, still holding on his lips the salty taste of that kiss, saw the head of the young and beautiful fisherman with its heavy black curls moving away on the water, like a sombre and frizzy flower.

A sudden thunderstorm forced him to return home.

But that same evening, when everything had quietened down, while taking his usual stroll on the beach, he saw, in the deep red of the setting sun, thrown back by the waves, motionless, the body of the young, handsome fisherman. The ring was no longer on his finger. It was, no doubt, too big. The sea had taken back the magnificent pearl that men had tried to snatch away from it. The stranger, who was a poet, composed the most beautiful of his songs on this. He took it up again and again and made it more and more perfect. He would repeat it to himself to the very rhythm of the waves in the evenings as he walked along the seashore. But he never dared write it down."

Suffering is one very long moment. We cannot divide it by seasons. We can only record its moods, and chronicle their return. With us time itself does not progress. It revolves. It seems to circle round one centre of pain.
Oscar Wilde

One night in 1900, at the Spanish café in Paris, the Comtesse Anna de Brémont (a friend of Oscar's mother) was sitting with friends when she saw Wilde coming towards her. She feared his effect upon her friends, and put up her fan. Yet one friend said to her after Wilde had gone, "I should have liked to meet him and find out what sort of monster he is." The comtesse was staggered by this comment, and passed a sleepless night. In the morning she rose early and walked along the Champs-Elysées to the Pont de la Concorde, where on impulse she embarked on one of the *bateaux-mouches* which took passengers to Saint-Cloud. On the way she heard a voice:

"Good morning, are you surprised to see me? Surely not. You are not the only restless spirit in this great Paris."
He had seen her the night before but had not wished to speak to her before strangers.
"Life held to my lips a full flavoured cup, and I drank it to the dregs," he said to her as to Maeterlinck, "the bitter and the sweet. I found the sweet bitter and the bitter sweet."
"Why do you not write now?" she asked.
"Because I have written all there was to write. I wrote when I did not know life, now that I know the meaning of life, I have no more to write." Then, less penitently, he said:
"I have found my soul. I was happy in prison because I found my soul."
Anna de Brémont felt close to tears, but they had reached the pier, and he said, "*Contessa*, don't sorrow for me," and left her.[116]

***

Oscar Wilde died in Paris on November 30, 1900.

---

[116] "Letters to Steele Mackaye," in Percy Mackaye, *Epoch: The Life of Steele Mackaye, Genius of the Theatre* (New York: Boni & Liveright, 1927).

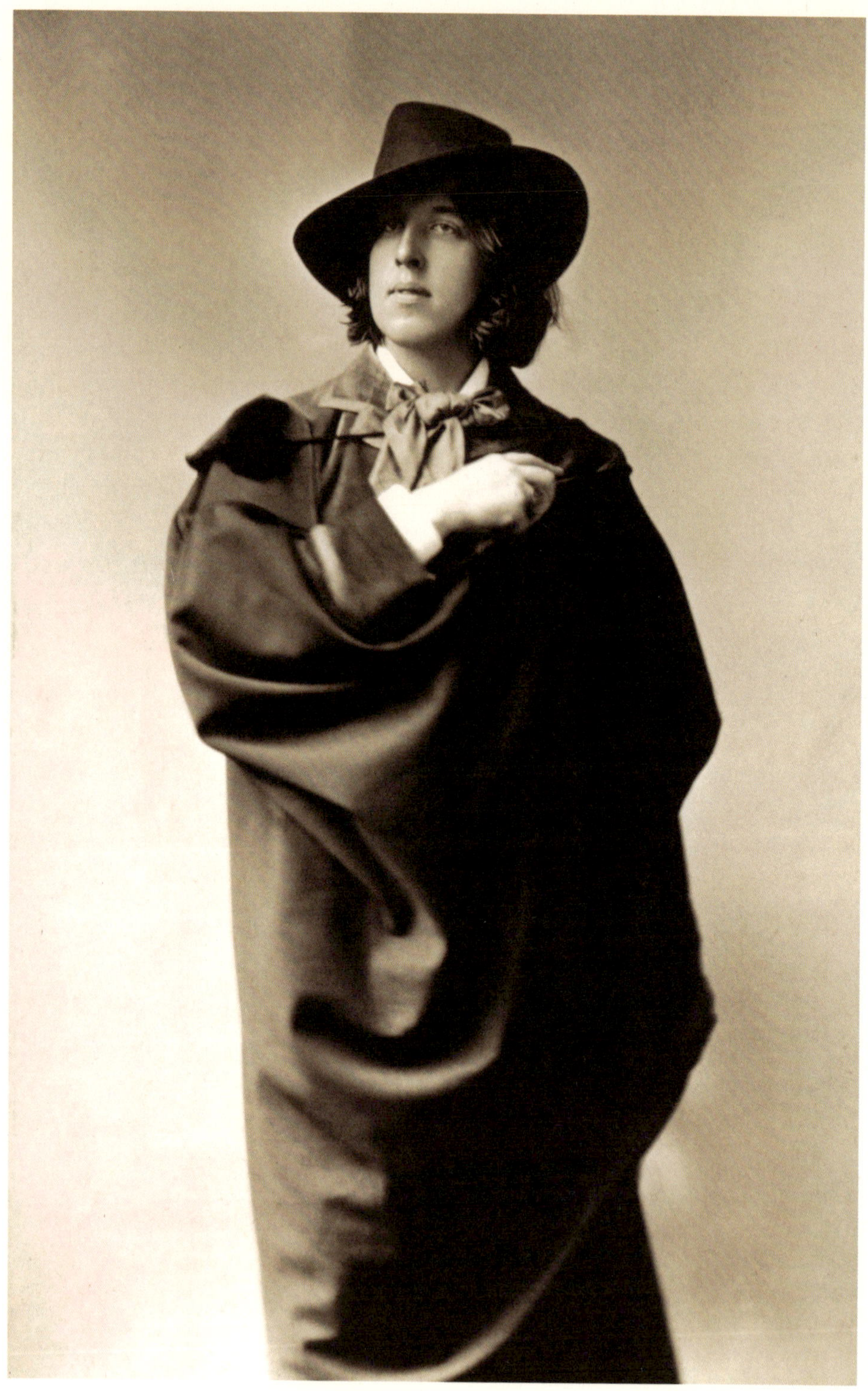

Renato Miracco

Renato Miracco is a curator and critic who was awarded the Order of Merit of the Italian Republic for Cultural Achievements in 2018. He served as cultural attaché for the Italian Embassy in Washington from 2010 to 2018 and as advisor to the Ministry of Foreign Affairs of Italy. Miracco has curated major exhibitions with Tate Modern in London, with the Metropolitan Museum of Art in New York and with London's Estorick Collection. His passion for Wilde dates from the early 1980s when he wrote his first essay on Wilde's stays in Italy entitled *Verso il sole. Cronaca del soggiorno napoletano* (Colonnese, 1981). Miracco's new book on Wilde is based on new materials that he has found in the last few years.

Philip Kennicott

Philip Kennicott is the Pulitzer prize-winning Art and Architecture critic of *The Washington Post*. He is also a two-time Pulitzer finalist (for editorial writing in 2000 and criticism in 2012), a former contributing editor to *The New Republic*, and a regular contributor to *Opera News* and *Gramophone*. His memoir, *Counterpoint*, about Bach's *Goldberg Variations*, will be published by Norton this year.

Adams, James Eli. *Dandies and Desert Saints: Styles of Victorian Masculinity*. Ithaca, New York: Cornell University Press, 1995.

Amor, Anne Clark. *Mrs Oscar Wilde: A Woman of Some Importance*. London: Sidgwick & Jackson, 1983.

Aldrich, Robert. *The seduction of the Mediterranean: Writing, Art and Homosexual Fantasy*. London: Routledge, 1993.

Arcara, Stefania. *Hellenic Transgressions, Homosexual Politics: Wilde, Symonds and Sicily*. Catania: Cavallotto, 1998.

Atkinson, George Thomas. "Oscar Wilde at Oxford." *Cornhill Magazine*, no. 3905 [1929].

Auden, Wystan Hugh. *Forewords and After Words in Improbable Life*. Selected by Edward Mendelson. London: Methuen, 1957.

Bartlett, Neil. *Who Was That Man?: A Present for Mr. Oscar Wilde*. London: Serpent's Tail, 1988.

Bentley, David. *English Criminal Justice in the Nineteenth Century*. London: Hambledon Press, 1998.

Bentley, Joyce. *The Importance of Being Constance*. London: Robert Hale, 1983.

Borrelli, Paolo. "Oscar Wilde a Napoli." *Esperia Rivista di Letteratura* (Aug–Oct 1903).

Brady, Sean. *Masculinity and Male Homosexuality in Britain, 1861-1913*. New York: Columbia University Press, 2006.

Brake, Laurel. *Print in Transition, 1850–1910: Studies in Media and Book History*. London: Palgrave, 2001.

Bray, Alan. *Homosexuality in Renaissance England*. New York: Columbia University Press, 1995.

Bowden, John Edward. *The Life and Letters of Frederick William Faber*. London, 1869.

Carpenter, Edward. *The Intermediate Sex*. London: G. Allen & Unwin, 1908.

Chandler, Glenn. *The Sins of Jack Saul*. London: Grosvenor House, 2016.

Chesney, Kellow. *The Victorian Underworld*. Middlesex: Penguin, 1972.

Cohen, Edward. *Talk on the Wilde Side*. New York: Routledge, 1993.

Cook, Matt. *London and the Culture of Homosexuality, 1885–1994*. Cambridge UK: Cambridge University Press, 2003.

———. "A Pickup in 1870." In Matt Cook, *London and the Culture of Homosexuality, 1885–1994*. Vol. 6, *My Secret Life*. Cambridge UK: Cambridge University Press, 2003.

Cox, Devon. *The Street of Wonderful Possibilities: Whistler, Wilde & Sargent in Tite Street*. London: Frances Lincoln, 2015.

Crawford, Mabel Sharman. *Life in Tuscany*. London, 1859.

Croft-Cooke, Rupert. *The Unrecorded Life of Oscar Wilde*. New York: David McKay, 1972.

Crompton, Louis. *Byron and Greek Love: Homophobia in 19th-century England*. Berkeley: University of California Press, 1985.

D'Amico, Masolino, ed. *Vita di Oscar Wilde attraverso le lettere*. Turin: Einaudi, 1977.

D'Arch Smith, Timothy. "Charles Sayle." In *Love in Earnest: Some Notes on the Lives and Writings of English Uranian Poets from 1889 to 1930*. London: Routledge And Kegan Paul, 1970.

————. *Love in Earnest: Some Notes on the Lives and Writings of English Uranian Poets from 1889 to 1930*. London: Routledge & Kegan Paul, 1985.

De Langlade, Jacques. *Oscar Wilde ou la vérité des masques*. Paris: Mazarine, 1987.

Delarue-Mardrus, Lucie. *Les amours d'Oscar Wilde*. Paris: Flammarion, 1929.

Dellamora, Richard. *Masculine Desire: the Sexual Politics of Victorian Aestheticism*. Chapel Hill, N.C.: University of North Carolina Press, 1990.

Dell'Orto, Giovanni. *Tutta un'altra storia. L'omosessualita; dall'antichità al secondo Dopoguerra*. Milan: Il Saggiatore, 2015.

De Saix, Guillot. *Le Chant du Cygne, Contes parlés d'Oscar Wilde*. Paris: Mercure de France, 1942.

Douglas, Alfred. "Prince Charming." *The Artist* (1415 April 1894).

————. *Oscar Wilde and Myself*. London: Long, 1914.

————, *Autobiography of Alfred Douglas*. London: Martin Secker, 1929.

————, *Without Apology*. London: Martin Secker, 1938.

————, *Oscar Wilde: A Summing Up*. London: Duckworth, 1940.

Douglas, Norman. *Looking Back: An Autobiographical Excursion*. New York: Harcourt, Brace, 1933.

Dowling, Linda. *Hellenism and Homosexuality in Victorian Oxford*. Ithaca NY: Cornell University Press, 1994.

Du Camp, Maxime. *Capri*. Translated by Atanasio Mozzillo. Massa Lubrense: Edizioni Lubrensi, 1985.

Durand-Davray, Henry. *Oscar Wilde: La Tragédie Finale*. Paris: Mercure de France, 1928.

Engels, Friedrich. *Der Ursprung der Familie, des Privateigenthums und des Staats*. Zurich, 1884.

Ellmann, Richard. *Oscar Wilde*. New York: Penguin Books, 1988.

Evangelista, Stefano. *The Reception of Oscar Wilde in Europe*. London: Bloomsbury, 2010.

Fiorani, Tito. *Le dimore del mito*. Capri: Ed. La Conchiglia, 1996.

Fitzsimons, Eleonor. *Wilde's Women: How Oscar Wilde Was Shaped by the Women He Knew*. New York: Overlook Duckworth, 2015.

Frankel, Nicholas. *Oscar Wilde, The Unrepentant Years*. Cambridge: Harvard University Press, 2017.

Franzeno, Carlo Maria. *La vita di Oscar Wilde*. Milan: Ugo Mursia, 1959.

Fryer, Jonathan. *Robbie Ross, Oscar Wilde's Devoted Friend*. New York: Carroll & Graf, 2000.

Gamberale, Luigi. *Un più reale Oscar Wilde*. Rome: Tip. dell'Unione Cooperativa Editrice, 1905.

Gargano Claudio, *Capri pagana, uranisti ed amazzoni tra ottocento e novecento*. Capri: La Conchiglia, 2007.

Gide, André. "Oscar Wilde. In memoriam." In *Oscar Wilde. Interviews and Recollections*, edited by E.H. Mikhail. London: Macmillan, 1979.

Goldberg, Jonathan. *Reclaiming Sodom*. New York: Routledge, 1994.

Greene, Graham. *A Sort of Life*. London: Simon and Schuster, 1971.

Haight, Gordon. *The Letters of George Eliot*. New Haven: Yale University Press, 1978.

Harris, Frank. *Oscar Wilde: His Life and Confessions*. New York: Brentano's, 1916.

———. *Oscar Wilde*. London: Constable, 1938.

Hart-Davis, Rupert, ed. *The Letters of Oscar Wilde*. London: R. Hart-Davis, 1962.

Hart-Davis, Rupert, and Merlin Holland, eds. *The Complete Letters of Oscar Wilde*. New York: Henry Holt, 2000.

Havelock Ellis, Henry. *A Note on the Bedborough Trial*. New York: privately printed, 1925. First published 1898 by Watford University Press.

Holland, Merlin, ed. *The Complete Works of Oscar Wilde*. London: Fourth Estate, 2003.

———. *Oscar Wilde. A Life in Letters*. London: Fourth Estate 2003.

———, *The Real Trial of Oscar Wilde: the First Uncensored Transcript of the Trial of Oscar Wilde vs. John Douglas, Marquess of Queensberry, 1895*. London: Fourth Estate, 2003.

Hyam, Roland. *Empire And Sexuality: the British Experience*. New York: St. Martin's Press, 1990.

Holland, Vyvyan. *Son of Oscar Wilde*. Oxford: Oxford University Press, 1988.

Hyde, Montgomery Harford. *L'Angelo Sofisticato, Vittoria Regina contro Oscar Wilde Omosessuale*. Milan: Mondadori, 1962.

———. *Oscar Wilde: The Aftermath*. New York: Farrar Straus, 1963.

———, *A History of Pornography*. London: Heinemann, 1964.

———, *The Love That Dared Not Speak Its Name. A Candid Story of Homosexuality in Britain*. Published in London under the title *The Other Love*, 1975. London: Heinemann, 1970.

———, *The Trials of Oscar Wilde*. New York: Dover, 1973.

———, *The Cleveland Street Scandal*. London: W.H. Allen, 1976.

Joplin, Louis. *Twenty Years in My Life, 1867–1887*. London: John Lane/Dodd Mead, 1925.

Jullian, Philippe. *Oscar Wilde*. Turin: Einaudi, 1972.

Kaplan, Morris. *Sodom on the Thames: Sex Love and Scandal in Wilde Times*. Ithaca:

Cornell University Press, 2005.

Katz, Jonathan Ned, *Love Stories. Sex between Men before Homosexuality*, Chicago: Univerity of Chicago Press, 2001.

Kempf, Roger. *Dandies*. Paris: Editions du seuil, 1977.

Kohl, Norbert. *Oscar Wilde: the Works of a Conformist Rebel*. Cambridge: Cambridge University Press, 1989.

La Jeunesse, Ernest, Frank Blei, and Percival Polland. *The Truth About Oscar Wilde*. Boston: John W. Luce, 1906.

Langtry, Lillie. "The Oscar I Knew." In *Oscar Wilde. Interviews & Recollections*, edited by E.H. Mikhail. London: Macmillan, 1979.

Lee, Laura. *Oscar's Ghost, The Battle for Oscar Wilde's Legacy*. Stroud: Amberley Publishing, 2017.

Leverson, Ada. *Letters to the Sphinx from Oscar Wilde: With Reminiscences of the Author*. London: Gerald Duckworth, 1930.

Lewis, John Royston. *The Victorian Bar*. London: Robert Hale, 1982.

Linnane, Fergus. *London's Underworld: Three Centuries of Vice and Crime*. London: Hodder and Stoughton, 1965.

Mackaye, Percy. "Letters to Steele Mackaye." In *Epoch: The Life of Steele Mackaye, Genius of the Theatre*. New York: Boni & Liveright, 1927.

Marbury, Elisabeth. "The Last Days of Oscar Wilde." In *Oscar Wilde: Interviews and Recollections*, edited by E.H. Mikhail. London: Macmillan, 1979.

Marquis of Queensberry, and Percy Colson. *Oscar Wilde et le Clan Douglas*. Paris: Arts et Metiers Graphiques, 1950.

Martin, Thomas. "The Poet in Prison." (1906) In *Oscar Wilde: Interviews And Recollections*, edited by E.H. Mikhail. London: Macmillan, 1979.

McKenna, Neil. *The Secret Life of Oscar Wilde*. New York: Basic Books, 2005.

Mayer, Hans. *Außenseiter*. Frankfurt am Main: Suhrkamp, 1975.

Mendes, Peter. *Clandestine Erotic Fiction in England 1800–1930*. New York: Ashgate, 1993.

Merle, Robert. *Oscar Wilde ou la Destinée de l'Homosexuel*. Paris: Gallimard, 1955.

———. *Oscar Wilde*. Paris: Hachette, 1955.

Money, James. *Capri Island of Pleasure*. London: Hamish Hamilton, 1986.

Mosse, George Lachmann. *The Image of Man: The Creation of Modern Masculinity*. New York: Oxford University Press,1996.

Moyle, Franny. *Constance. The Tragic and Scandalous Life of Mrs Oscar Wilde*. New York: Pegasus Books, 2012.

Murphy, William Martin. *Lily Yeats's Scrapbook*. 1889.

Norton, Rictor. *Mother Clap's Molly House: The Gay Subculture in England 1700–1830*. London: GMP, 1992.

O'Sullivan, Emer. *The Fall of the House of Wilde*. London: Bloomsbury Publishing, 2016.

O'Sullivan, Vincent. *Aspects of Oscar Wilde*. London: Constable, 1936.

———. *Some Letters to A. J. Symons*. Edinburgh: Tragara Press, 1975.

Page, Norman. *An Oscar Wilde Chronology*. London: Macmillan, 1991.

Pearson, Heskett. *The Life of Oscar Wilde*. London: Methuen, 1946.

Pemble, John. *The Mediterranean Passion: Victorian and Edwardians in the South*. Oxford: Oxford University Press, 1988.

Peyrefitte, Roger. *L'exilé de Capri*. Paris: Flammarion, 1959.

Raffalovich, Marc-André. "The World Well Lost IV." In *In Fancy Dress*. London, 1886.

———. "Il Processo Oscar Wilde." In *L'uranismo, inversione sessuale congenita*. Turin, 1896.

———, *L'Affaire Oscar Wilde*. Lyon, 1895.

———, *Uranisme et unisexualité: étude sur differentes manifestations de l'instinct sexue*. Lyon, 1895.

Robb, Graham. *Strangers: Homosexual Love in the Nineteenth Century*. London: Picador, 2003.

Roditi, Eduard. *Oscar Wilde*. Norfolk CT: New Directions, 1947.

Saul, Jack. *The Sins of the Cities of the Plain*. San Bernardino: Grosvenor, 2016.

Schiffer, Daniel Salvatore. *Oscar Wilde, Splendeur et misère d'un Dandy*. Paris: Editions de la Martinièr, 2014.

Shaw, George Bernard. "The Prosecution of Mr. Bedborough." *The Adult* 2, 8 (September 1898).

Sherard, Robert Harborough. *Oscar Wilde: The Story of Unhappy Friendship*. London: T.W. Laurie, 1902.

———. *The Life of Oscar Wilde*. London, 1911.

Sigel, Liza Z. *Governing, Pleasures, Pornography and Social Change in England 1815-1914*. London: Rutgers University Press, 2002.

Simon, William. *Postmodern Sexualities*. New York: Harper and Row, 1968.

Stokes, Jon. "Letters of George Ives." In *Oscar Wilde: Myths, Miracles and Imitations*. Oxford: Cambridge University Press, 1996.

Stoller, Robert Jessie. *Sex and Gender. The Development of Masculinity and Femininity*. New York: Science House, 1968.

Sturgi, Matthew. *Oscar: A Life*. Santa Cruz: Apollo, 2018.

Symonds, John Addington, and Ellis Havelock. *Sexual Inversion*. London, 1897.

Thompson, Vance. *The Two Deaths of Oscar Wilde*. London, 1930.

Trumbach, Randolph. "The Birth of the Queen: Sodomy and the Emergence of Gender Equality in Modern Culture, 1660–1750." In *Hidden from History: Reclaiming the Gay and Lesbian Past*, edited by George Chauncey, Martha Vicinus, and Martin Duberman. New York: New American Library, 1989.

Ulrichs, Karl Heinrich. *The Riddle of "Man-Manly" Love: the Pioneering Work on*

Male Homosexuality. Buffalo NY: Prometheus Books, 1994.

Upchurch, Charles. *Before Wilde: Sex Between Men in Britains' Age of Reform*. California: University of California Press, 2009.

Valera, Paolo. *I Gentiluomini Invertiti*. Milan: Tipografia editrice E. M. Floritta, 1909.

Von Platen, August. *Tagebücher*, edited by Rudiger Gorner. Zurich: Manesse-Verlag, 1990.

Weeks, Jeffrey. *Coming Out: Homosexual Politics from the Nineteenth Century to the Present*. London: Quartet Books, 1990.

Wilde, Oscar. *Salomé. Introduzione di Biagio Chiara*. Naples: Bideri, 1906.

————. *Il Delitto di Lord Arthur Savile: con un'intervista di Arnaldo De Lisle*. Naples: Società Editrice Partenopea, 1908.

————, *Letters of Oscar Wilde to Robert Ross, after Bernavel*. London: Beaumont Press, 1922.

————, *Some Letters from Oscar Wilde to Alfred Douglas 1892–1897*. San Francisco: J.H. Nahs, 1924.

————, *Sixteen Letters by John Rothenstein*. London: Faber, 1930.

Wolf, Naomi. *Outrages: Sex, Censorship and the Criminalization of Love*. London: Houghton Mifflin, 2019.

Zito, Eugenio, and Paolo Valerio. "I femminielli napoletani: un genere al (di) confine." In *Sesso e genere*, edited by Roberto Vitelli and Paolo Valerio. Naples: Liguori, 2012.

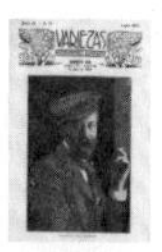

p. 7   Portrait of German photographer Wilhelm von Gloeden on the cover of the Italian magazine *Varietas* in July 1910.

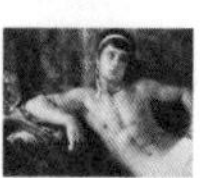

p. 12-13   Wilhelm von Gloeden, *Study of a reclining boy wearing jewelry, ca. 1899.*

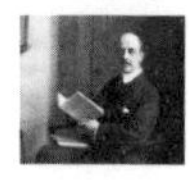

p. 14   Elliott and Fry, *Robert Ross*, 1911.

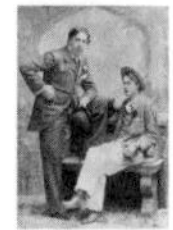

p. 15   Gilman & Co., *Oscar Wilde with Lord Alfred "Bosie" Douglas*, London, May 1893.

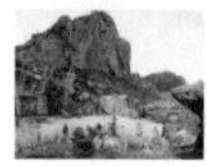

p. 18   Giacomo Brogi, *Group of fishermen on the beach at Marina Piccola at Capri*, Isle of Capri, *ca.* 1880.

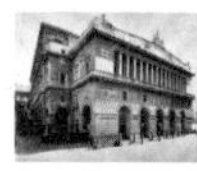

p. 19   Giorgio Sommer, *The arcaded facade of the Teatro San Carlo in Naples*, Naples, *ca.* 1880.

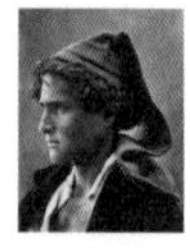

p. 21   Giorgio Sommer, *Man with stocking cap, No. 9*, Sicily, *ca.* 1870s.

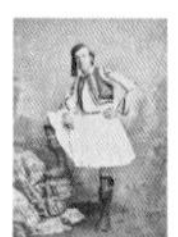

p. 26   Petros Moraites, Cabinet photograph of *Oscar Wilde in costume when in Greece*, Athens, April 1 1878.

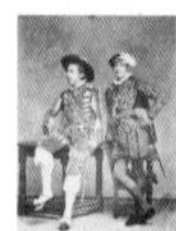

p. 29   J. Guggenheim, *Oscar Wilde in the costume of Prince Rupert 'with plum-colored breeches and silk stocking' in which he attended an Oxford fancy dress ball*, 1 May 1878.

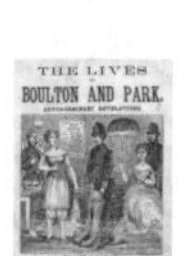

p. 34   Wilhelm von Gloeden, *Study of three male nudes*, Sicily, *ca.* 1900.

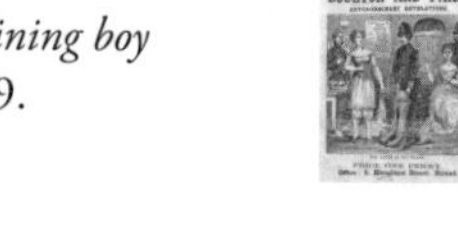

p. 47   *The lives of Boulton and Park, extraordinary revelations. The toilet at the station*, London, 1870.

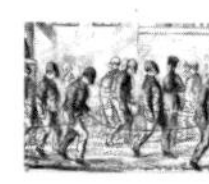

p. 51   Separate system of prisons showing the caps used to prevent communication still used in Wilde's day. Pentonville Prison, *ca.* 1840.

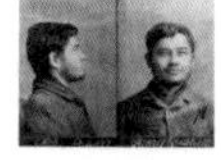

p. 57   Steve Parsons, *Reading Prison prisoner Henry Bushnell, ca.* 1895.

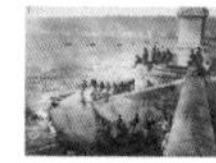

p. 60   Giorgio Sommer, *Fishermen in the port of Naples, ca.* 1880.

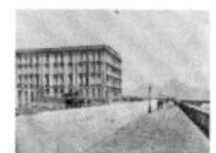

p. 66-67   Giorgio Sommer, *Hôtel Royal des Étrangers*, Naples, *ca.* 1897.

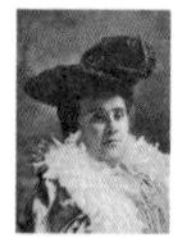

p. 71   Ken Welsh, *Matilde Serao*, Naples, *ca.* 1897.

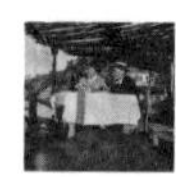

p. 75   *Oscar Wilde with Lord Alfred "Bosie" Douglas in Naples*, 1897. Probably taken by the waiter with Oscar's camera.

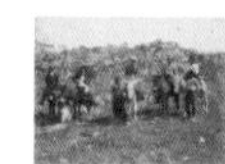

p. 85   Giorgio Sommer, *Excursion on donkeys to Villa Jovis in Capri*, Isle of Capri, *ca.* 1880.

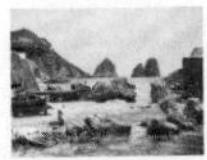

p. 87   Giacomo Brogi, *A woman on the beach of Marina Piccola at Capri, with the Faraglioni in the background*, Capri, *ca.* 1885–1910.

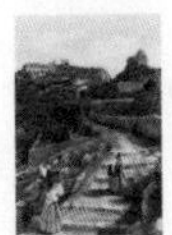

p. 89   Giacomo Brogi, *A characteristic view of the isle of Capri with the Torre di Tiberio in the background*, Capri, *ca.* 1900 (detail).

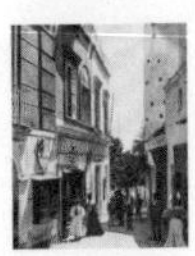

p. 90   Giacomo Brogi, *A view of the bustling Via Camerelle in Capri*, Isle of Capri, ca. 1900.

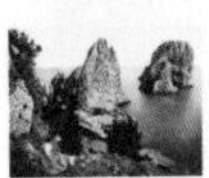

p. 93   Gaetano Esposito, *A woman by the coast with the celebrated Faraglioni in the background*, Isle of Capri, *ca.* 1880.

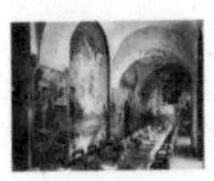

p. 94-95   Giacomo Brogi, *The dining room of Hotel Pagano in Capri*, Isle of Capri, *ca.* 1900.

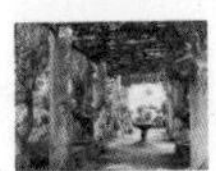

p. 97   *The garden of Axel Munthe's house*, Anacapri, Isle of Capri, *ca.* 1897.

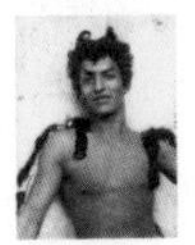

p. 99   Wilhelm von Gloeden, *Portrait of a youth in the guise of a faun* (Carmelo), Sicily, Italy, *ca.* 1900.

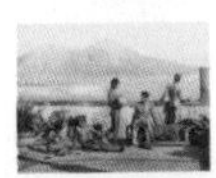

p. 103   Wilhelm von Gloeden, *A classical scene with a view of Vesuvius from Posillipo*, Naples, 1899.

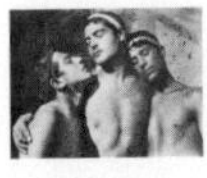

p. 117   Wilhelm von Gloeden, *Study of three male nudes*, Sicily, *ca.* 1900.

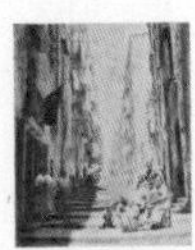

p. 119   Giorgio Sommer, *Santa Lucia, near Wilde's last house in Naples, ca.* 1898. Oscar Wilde lived here at number 31.

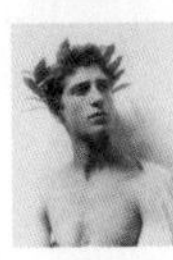

p. 128   Wilhelm von Gloeden, *Study of a youth wearing a wreath*, Sicily, *ca.* 1898.

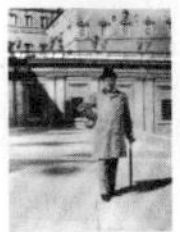

p. 137   *Oscar Wilde, Irish writer and poet in Rome in 1900*, Piazza San Pietro. Probably taken by a friend with Oscar's camera.

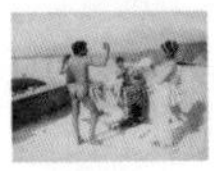

p. 139   Wilhelm von Gloeden, *A group of youths on a terrace with musical instruments*, Sicily, *ca.* 1900.

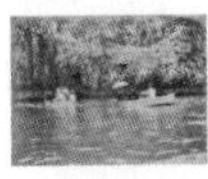

p. 145   *Tourists visiting the Blue Grotto of Capri*, Isle of Capri, *ca.* 1897.

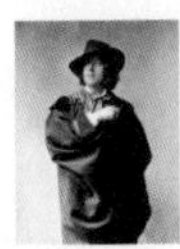

p. 148   Napoleon Sarony, *Oscar Wilde*, New York, 1882.

PICTURE CREDITS

Archivio GBB / Bridgeman Images p. 7; Prismatic Pictures / Bridgeman Images p. 12–13, 34, 103, 117, 122; Historic Images / Alamy Stock Photo p. 14; British Library Board. All Rights Reserved / Bridgeman Images p. 15, 26, 29, 47, 75; Archivi Alinari-archivio Brogi, Firenze p. 18, 87, 89, 90, 94–95; Raccolte Museali Fratelli Alinari (RMFA), Firenze p. 19; J. T. Vintage / Bridgeman Images p. 21; Pictorial Press Ltd / Alamy Stock Photo p. 51, 137; PA Archive/PA Images p. 57; Colonnese and Friends p. 60, 85, 97, 119, 145; The History Collection / Alamy Stock Photo p. 66–67; Bridgeman Images p.71, 148; ARCHIVIO GBB / Archivi Alinari p. 93; Raccolte Museali Fratelli Alinari (RMFA)-archivio von Gloeden, Firenze p. 99, 139.

Acknowledgements

Writing a book, a catalogue, an essay is always an introspective and cognitive adventure. And the nuances of the word "thank you" are as infinite as those of the word "love."

Thank you, above all, to Oscar: I am in complete agreement with Jorge Luis Borges when he asserts: "Reading and rereading Wilde, year after year, I notice a fact that his panegyrists have never even suspected: the elementary and easily verifiable fact that Oscar is almost always right!"

In this voyage, I am grateful to dear friends who are no longer with us; at the top of the list, Gaetano and Maria Colonnese.

I am also indebted to people who unintentionally inspired me: such as the organizers of the wonderful *Oscar Wilde, L'Impertinent Absolu* exhibition, (September 28 2016–January 15 2017), at the Petit Palais, Musée des Beaux-Arts de la Ville de Paris, curated by Robert Badinter, Charles Dantzig and Merlin Holland, Wilde's grandson. Later, the *Queer British Art 1861–1967* exhibition at the Tate Modern (April 5–October 1 2017) curated by Clare Barlow, (which explored the historical reality of homosexual relationships from 1861, the year of the end of the death penalty for sodomy in England), which helped to give me the proper insight into how a new book on Oscar might be reintroduced.

A new vision was also provided to me by the powerful installations created in 2017 by Ai Weiwei, Nan Goldin, Steve McQueen, and Doris Salcedo, inside Reading prison, to celebrate the writer and the man in the place that had changed his life. Because this man today still is a contemporary icon. There is also the "Oscar Wilde Temple", a space created in New York by Peter McGough and David McDermott at the church of Greenwich Village in 2017. All these, multifaceted, wide-ranging interpretations helped me immensely. Thank you! I must also point out that the person who encouraged me from the beginning was Philip Kennicott, a dear friend, who immediately agreed to write the introduction. Thank you also to Dodge Thompson and Colleen Daly who during our morning walks were obsessively asking me where I was with the book. They were constant prodders.

At the Library of Congress, I would like to thank Carla Hayden Librarian, Marie Arana, Lucia Wolf, Giulia Adelfio.

Thanks also to Alfredo and Francesca Mazzei of Colonnese and Friends who wanted to complete a project started long before, and to Catherine Grieco who enthusiastically introduced me to the Damiani publishing house, where Silvia Pesci immediately joined me for the English language co-edition with her collaborators: Eleonora Pasqui, Alex Galán, Luke P. Brown and Enrico Farinazzo. Thank you.

When I held the first draft in my hands, I was a fearful child who needed reassurance: Francesca Pennarola, your observations as a scholar of Italian history and culture, worried me. In retrospect, thank you.

Profound thanks go to Ernesto Beckford with whom I shared not only our daily emotional relationship as a couple but also the cuts, the changes, and my discontent: we often clashed hard. Thank you, you were almost always right! A big thank you goes to Diana Mariotti and Simona Massobrio Howe, precious for their help in some translations, to Riccardo Vecchio and Kikki Ghezzi and to Anna Worthey, who assisted with difficult transcriptions.

A deep thank you to Edmund White, one of my icons ,who accepted to present my book and to Barbara Faedda and Rick Whitaker from Italian Academy at Columbia University.

I want to underline my friendship for and sense of gratitude to Uberto Bowinkel, with whom I reconnected after so many years, and who has enthusiastically opened up his photographic archive to me, a fundamental visual counterpart for this new edition.

Thank you to Elinor and Alan Berg, dear friends and my eternal supporters.

On a more personal note, I am also grateful to my grandson Ludovico, a few months old, and to my granddaughter Eva, who has yet to be born. Knowing that they will read this book has given me an incentive.

I also don't want to forget the many anonymous smiles I met at provincial libraries or in important libraries around the world: a simple gesture can sometimes be fundamental!

Last but not least I would like to dedicate this book to my mom Armida who passed away in the last days of the creation of this work.

Renato Miracco

Oscar Wilde's Italian Dream 1875–1900

The Infamous St. Oscar of Oxford, Poet and Martyr

Undecided between the Cloister and the Café

Renato Miracco

© Text, Renato Miracco

© Introduction, Philip Kennicott

© Damiani 2020

Published by Damiani srl

info@damianieditore.com

www.damianieditore.com

Proofreading: Lucian Comoy, Roberta Pertegato

Design: Enrico Farinazzo

Production Manager: Eleonora Pasqui

Italian edition published by Colonnese and Friends

Printed in January 2020 by Faenza Group SpA, Italy

ISBN 978-88-6208-714-8

Front and back cover:

Wilhelm von Gloeden, *A classical scene with a view of Vesuvius from Posillipo*, Naples, 1899.

© Prismatic Pictures / Bridgeman Images.